# Preside or Lead?

## The Attributes and Actions of Effective Regulators

# Scott Hempling

# Preside or Lead?

## The Attributes and Actions of Effective Regulators

SECOND EDITION

Copyright © 2013 by Scott Hempling

All rights reserved. No part of this publication may be used or reproduced or transmitted in any form or by any means without written permission from the publisher, except in the case of brief quotations embodied in critical articles and reviews. Requests for permission must be obtained by contacting Scott Hempling at shempling@scotthemplinglaw.com or mailing to Scott Hempling, Attorney at Law LLC, 417 St. Lawrence Drive, Silver Spring, MD 20901.

Printed in the United States of America

Second edition

ISBN-13: 978-0-9893277-0-1

ISBN-10: 0-9893-2770-1

# Table of Contents

**Acknowledgements** ..................................................ix

**Preface and Dedication** ..............................................xiii

**Part One—Attributes of Effective Regulators** ........................1

   1. Purposeful ......................................................3

   2. Educated .......................................................7

   3. Decisive .......................................................13

   4. Independent ...................................................17

   5. Disciplined ....................................................21

   6. Synthesizing ..................................................25

   7. Creative ......................................................29

   8. Respectful ....................................................33

   9. Ethical .......................................................37

  10. A Letter to Governors and Legislators: On Appointing Excellent Regulators ...........................41

**Part Two—Actions of Effective Regulators** ..........................45

  11. Commissions Are Not Courts; Regulators Are Not Judges. .........47

  12. The Regulatory Mission: Do We "Balance" Private Interests, or Do We Align Them with the Public Interest? ..................51

  13. Regulatory Brainstorming: When and Where? ...................55

  14. Regulatory Multitasking: Does It Do Long-Term Damage? .........59

  15. Regulatory Literacy: A Self-Assessment ........................63

  16. "Smart Grid" Spending: A Commission's Pitch-Perfect Response to a Utility's Seven Errors. ..................................69

  17. Alfred Kahn, "Prophet of Regulation" ..........................73

## Part Three—Political Pressures ... 77
18. "Politics" I: The Public and Private Versions ... 79
19. "Politics" II: How Can Regulators Respond? ... 83
20. "Regulatory Capture" I: Is It Real? ... 87
21. "Regulatory Capture" II: What Are the Warning Signs? ... 91
22. "Regulatory Capture" III: How Can Commissioners Avoid and Escape It? ... 95
23. The War of Words: Competition vs. Regulation I ... 99
24. The War of Words: Competition vs. Regulation II ... 103
25. Is Learning to Regulate Like Learning to Cook? ... 107

## Part Four—Regulatory Courage ... 111
26. "Affordable" Utility Service: What is Regulation's Role? ... 113
27. Low Rates, High Rates, Wrong Rates, Right Rates ... 117
28. "Protect the Consumer"—From What? ... 121
29. Separating Policy Mandates from Cost Consequences: Will the Public Lose Trust? ... 125
30. Prohibiting Discrimination and Promoting Diversity: Is There a Regulatory Obligation to Society? ... 129
31. "All of the Above" Is Not a National Energy Policy ... 133
32. Supporter-as-Critic: An Expanded Role for Regulatory Professionals ... 137

## Part Five—Jurisdiction: Power Is a Means, Not an End ... 141
33. Legislatures and Commissions: How Well Do They Work Together? ... 143
34. It's April—Do You Know Where Your Legislatures Are? ... 147
35. More on Legislative–Regulatory Relations: Layers, Protections and Cost-Effectiveness ... 151
36. Federal–State Jurisdiction I: Pick Your Metaphor ... 155
37. Federal–State Jurisdiction II: Jurisdictional Wrestling vs. Coordinated Regulation ... 159
38. Federal–State Jurisdiction III: Jurisdictional Peace Requires Joint Purpose ... 163
39. Federal–State Jurisdiction IV: A Plea for Constitutional Literacy ... 167
40. Intra-Regional Relations: Can States' Commonalities Outweigh Their Differences? ... 171

# TABLE OF CONTENTS

**Part Six—Practice and Procedure** .................... **175**
   41. "Framing": Does It Divert Regulatory Attention? ............177
   42. Decisional Defaults: Does Regulation Have Them Backwards? ......181
   43. Utility Performance: Will We Know It When We See It? ...........185
   44. "Prudence": Who's Minding the Store? .....................189
   45. Rate Case Timing: Alertness or Auto-Pilot? ...................193
   46. Interconnection Animus: Do Regulatory Procedures Create
      a "Tragedy of the Commons"? .............................197
   47. Interconnection Animus: The Readers React ..................201
   48. Regulatory "Settlements": When Do Private Agreements
      Serve the Public Interest? ................................207
   49. Competition for the Monopoly: Why So Rare? .................211

**Part Seven—Regulatory Organizations** .................... **215**
   50. Regulatory Resources I: Why Do Differentials Exist? .............217
   51. Regulatory Resources II: Do the Differentials Make a Difference? ....221
   52. The Resource Gap Grows: What Are a Commission's Duties? .......225
   53. Commission Effectiveness: How Can We Measure It? .............229
   54. Commission Budgets: How Do We Know When We're "Worth It"? ..235
   55. Commission Positioning I: Five Actions for Influence..............239
   56. Commission Positioning II: Can "Vision" Avoid "Too Big To Fail"? ..243
   57. Commission "Branding": Can It Improve Utility Performance? ......247
   58. Pharmacies and Regulatory Conferences: Do They Have
      Anything in Common? ..................................251

**Part Eight—Conclusions** .................... **255**
   59. Essential to Effectiveness: Community Acceptance of
      Regulation's Mission ...................................257
   60. A Regulatory Thanksgiving ..............................261

**About the Author** .................... **265**

# Acknowledgements

Among the many influences on these essays, two categories stand out.

There are five people I've known personally—people whose intellectual leadership in utility regulation embodies these essays' themes of public interest purposefulness: George Spiegel, Dan Guttman, Harry Trebing, David Penn and Peter Bradford.

Then there are four people I've known only through their writings—writers and writings whose wisdom and clarity I can only dream of emulating: Peter Drucker (*The Effective Executive*); Edward Tufte (*The Visual Display of Quantitative Information; Envisioning Information; Visual Explanations: Images and Quantities, Evidence and Narrative; Beautiful Evidence*); Garry Wills (*Lincoln at Gettysburg: The Words That Remade America; Certain Trumpets: The Nature of Leadership*); Deborah Tannen (*The Argument Culture*); and Rabbi Marc Rosenstein (*Galilee Diaries*).

... [T]he Commission has claimed to be the representative of the public interest. This role does not permit it to act as an umpire blandly calling balls and strikes for adversaries appearing before it; the right of the public must receive active and affirmative protection at the hands of the Commission.

*Scenic Hudson Preservation Conference v. Federal Power Commission*, 354 F.2d 608, 620 (2d Cir. 1965)


The book is *Mastering the Art of French Cooking*—not "How To" or "Made Easy" or "For Dummies," but "Mastering the Art." In other words, cooking that omelet is part of a demanding, exalted discipline not to be entered into frivolously or casually. But at the same time: You can do it. It is a matter of technique, of skill, of practice.

A.O. Scott, "Two for the Stove," *The New York Times* (Aug. 7, 2009) (referring to Julia Child's classic)


Effectiveness can be learned.

Peter Drucker, *The Effective Executive*

# Preface and Dedication

From local speed limits to federal water quality rules, all regulation has a common purpose: to align private behavior with the public interest.

While the principles in these essays apply to all regulation, I have focused on my professional area: the regulation of our public utilities. These providers of electricity, gas, telecommunications, and water support our local, regional, national, and international economies. Our lives depend on their performance. Defining and demanding that performance is the job of regulators. Regulators set standards, compensate the efficient, and penalize the inefficient. These standards, compensation, and penalties align private behavior with the public interest.

These regulatory actions are taken by real people. For 30 years, I have worked in dozens of proceedings with hundreds of regulators: as an advisor—shaping proceedings, questioning witnesses, drafting opinions, and defending commissions in court; as a litigating lawyer—preparing witnesses, conducting cross-examinations, writing briefs, and challenging decisions in court; and as an expert witness—testifying on the principles of effective regulation.

In this close-up experience, I have been consistently impressed by the power of personal attributes. The public battles feature the parties, their hired experts, and their attorneys. But when the record closes and deliberations begin, the focus shifts to the commissioners. Case outcomes are determined not only by facts, law, and policy, but also by commissioners' attributes—attributes like purposefulness, decisiveness, independence, creativity, ethics, and courage. These attributes, or their absence, influence the actions of regulators—such as whether they "balance" and "preside" or whether they set standards and lead. And even the most purposeful, educated, decisive, and independent regulators—those who make the tough calls and take the right actions—face obstacles: the forces of self-interest and provincialism that can undermine the high purpose of regulation.

To explore the connections among attributes, actions, and obstacles, and to understand the ingredients for effectiveness, I began in 2007 a series of monthly essays. Each is a 1,000-word, five-minute read for the busy decisionmaker or practitioner. The first 32, written while I was Executive Director of the National

Regulatory Research Institute, were published by the Institute in 2010. NRRI has graciously allowed me to purchase the copyright for the pieces I wrote while there, enabling me now to publish this second edition of 60 essays covering 2007–2012. Reorganized under new headings, the essays take into account recent developments in legislative–commission relations, federal–state relations, and market structure. The monthly series continues on my website, www.scotthemplinglaw.com, where readers can leave comments.

While these essays focus on public utility industries, their lessons about attributes, actions, and obstacles apply to all regulation and all government policymaking. I have organized them under eight major headings:

- Part One       Attributes of Effective Regulators
- Part Two       Actions of Effective Regulators
- Part Three     Political Pressures
- Part Four      Regulatory Courage
- Part Five      Jurisdiction: Power Is a Means, Not an End
- Part Six       Practice and Procedure
- Part Seven     Regulatory Organizations
- Part Eight     Conclusions

Inspiring these essays about regulation are the regulators themselves. These multi-billion-dollar decisionmakers are diverse: appointed or elected; ages 25 to 75; some mid-career, moving up the political ranks; others capping their careers after decades of professional contribution in the private sector. At any one time, the supermajority are new to the field—music teachers, physicists, chemists, advertising executives, coal miners, mayors, city managers, Wall Street money dealers, Main Street shopkeepers.

But their diversity pales next to their commonality: a nail-biting realization that their legal obligation—to establish and enforce performance standards in these critical industries—will demand every available ounce of intellect, savvy, humility, grit, and courage. To these individuals, and to their aspirations for effectiveness, I dedicate this book.

Scott Hempling
July 2013

# PART ONE
## Attributes of Effective Regulators

We expect our government decisionmakers to be, at minimum, honest, diligent, judicious, objective, humble, and competent. Regulatory standouts have additional attributes: They are purposeful, educated, decisive, and independent. How they use these attributes is the subject of the first four essays.

The purposeful regulator defines and articulates the public interest, then promotes it by inducing performance—by aligning the utility's private behavior with the public interest. The educated regulator studies regulation's six subject areas, its six legal sources, its five professions, its three processes, and its many local facts. The decisive regulator acts: when and where the public interest requires, regardless of discomfort to herself or the parties. The independent regulator recognizes that in a democracy, there are always forces of which no government official can be independent, but she remains alert to, and resists, those forces that undermine regulation's purpose.

Howard Gardner's *Five Minds for the Future* (2008) offers additional attributes. The disciplined mind recognizes regulation as a profession and strives continuously for mastery. The synthesizing mind integrates regulation's facts with its professions (engineering, economics, accounting, finance and law), then uses this synthesis to make public interest decisions. The creative mind unfastens itself from past practices to discover new solutions. The respectful mind uses open-mindedness, curiosity, and humility as antidotes to divisiveness; it honors knowledge and achievement regardless of source. The ethical mind transcends self-interest, simply doing what is right. It recognizes that "[a] person who is determined to do something constructive with his life needs to come to terms with the fact that not everyone is going to like him."[1]

Summing up these nine attributes, Part One closes with an open letter to governors and legislators, "On Appointing Excellent Regulators."

---
[1] Daniel Barenboim and Edward Said, *Parallels and Paradoxes: Explorations in Music and Society* (2002) at pp. 6, 10, 11 (quoted in Gardner at 122).

# 1

# Purposeful

> The hedgehog is a thinker or leader who "relates everything to a central vision ... a single, universal, organizing principle," ... while the fox "pursue[s] many ends, often unrelated and even contradictory." ... In this sense, Abraham Lincoln can be considered one of the foremost hedgehogs in American history.
>
> James M. McPherson, "The Hedgehog and the Foxes," in *Abraham Lincoln and the Second American Revolution* (1991) at pp. 113–14 (quoting British philosopher Isaiah Berlin's essay on Leo Tolstoy, which, in turn, interprets this sentence from the Greek poet Archilochus: "The fox knows many things, but the hedgehog knows one big thing.")

**The purposeful regulator** articulates her purpose. Regulatory statutes command each commission to pursue the "public interest." They presume that private behavior, unregulated, will diverge from the "public interest." The effective regulator (1) defines the public interest, (2) identifies the private interests that could undermine that public interest, and then (3) shapes regulation to align private behavior with the public interest. These three steps comprise her purpose.

**What is "the public interest"?** The phrase allows flexibility. But flexibility without accountability invites arbitrariness. A regulator is accountable when she defines the public interest and articulates that definition publicly. My definition of "public interest"—one among many—has three components: economic efficiency, sympathetic gradualism, and political accountability.

- *Economic efficiency* means "biggest bang for the buck"—the best, feasible ratio of benefit to cost. We know from elementary economics that if an outcome is inefficient, someone is foregoing some benefit attainable without cost to others. That is not a public interest outcome.

- *Sympathetic gradualism* means smoothing the hard edges of economic efficiency. Strict benefit-cost ratios, calculated for the long term, can downplay citizens' needs in the short term. Sympathetic gradualism means reducing efficiency's short-term pain to preserve the public's commitment to long-term gain, adjusting the angle of change without compromising the direction of change.

- *Political accountability* requires the regulator to win political support for both economic efficiency and sympathetic gradualism. Political accountability does not mean caving in to interest groups. It means educating by explaining.

The public interest is a compromise: not among private interests, but among these three components. Understanding this difference is a prerequisite for purpose.

**Caution:** A public interest purpose does not invite regulators to solve all public interest problems. Their actions are bound by legislative intent. Compare *Gulf States Utilities Company v. Federal Power Commission*, 411 U.S. 747 (1973) (holding that the "public interest," as the phrase is used in the Federal Power Act, requires the Commission to take into account antitrust principles), with *National Association for the Advancement of Colored Peoples v. Federal Power Commission*, 425 U.S. 662 (1976) (holding that the "public interest" phrase does not authorize the Commission to prohibit racial discrimination by regulated utilities).

**How might private interests diverge from the public interest?** Having articulated her definition of public interest, a regulator identifies how each private party's interest could diverge from the public interest. Consider these actors and their aims:

1. Utility corporation (maximize profit, maintain and grow market share, build community reputation)

2. Utility shareholders (increase share price, grow long-term value, maintain dividends)

3. Utility executives (all of the above, plus increase salary, advance career, build personal reputation)

4. Nonutility competitors (enter markets, gain market share, grow through acquisitions)

5. Consumers (keep prices low, keep service reliable, add choices, reduce dependency)

6. Bondholders (maintain utility cash flow and interest coverage, avoid default)

The public interest includes all these private interests in their legitimate form. No consumer legitimately expects power for free; no utility executive legitimately expects compensation exceeding his peers'. But private interests can press for illegitimate ends: e.g., the consumer who wants below-average electricity prices with above-average reliability or "green power" with no land use effects, the investor who wants above-market returns with below-average risks, the utility executive who wants more regulatory deference but less regulatory oversight.

So how does "public interest" relate to regulatory purpose? To align these private interests with the public interest, the purposeful regulator does not seek "compromise" or "balance" among them. She instead establishes a centrifugal force, one that disciplines private expectations and hems in private behavior. That centrifugal force is the public interest.

## Recommendations

The purposeful regulator asks these questions:

1. Do I have a definition of "public interest"? Have I made my definition transparent by articulating it to my fellow commissioners and the parties who appear before my commission? Is my definition consistent with my fellow commissioners' definitions? If not, have I worked out the differences?

2. Have I identified the private interests affected by my decisions? Do I understand how those private interests might diverge from the public interest now and in the future?

3. Has my commission established regulatory rules that cause these private interests to align their behavior with the public interest?

4. Have I ensured that these rules constrain the private interests no more than necessary, since unnecessary regulation can produce unnecessary opposition?

# 2
# Educated

The great aim of education is not knowledge but action.

Herbert Spencer

An educated person is one who has learned that information almost always turns out to be at best incomplete and very often false, misleading, fictitious, mendacious—just dead wrong.

Russell Baker

I was determined to know beans.

Henry David Thoreau (from *Walden*)

I am still learning.

Michelangelo

---

**The purposeful regulator** defines the public interest and then shapes regulation to align private behavior with it. But purpose is ineffective without education. The educated regulator knows regulation's six subject areas, its six legal sources, its five professions, and its three processes.

## Regulation's Six Subject Areas: What Do We Regulate?

Regulation focuses on nouns and verbs: the actors (nouns) whose actions will be regulated and the actions (verbs) requiring regulation. These nouns and verbs interact within six subject areas.

**Market structure:** Markets serve customers well when they are efficient, innovative, and accountable to regulators. For a particular product or service, which type of market structure—competitive or monopoly—will serve customers best? Regulators first selects the market structure and then guides the market's performance. For monopoly markets, regulators establish standards for pricing, quality, infrastructure adequacy, operations, financing, and corporate structure. For competitive markets, regulators license the entrants, open access to bottleneck facilities, review and condition market-concentrating events (like mergers and acquisitions), monitor prices for reasonableness, and prevent market manipulation.

**Pricing:** Effective regulation links pricing with performance. Regulators first ask: Should the regulator set the rates, or is competition among sellers sufficiently strong to discipline the prices? Then comes more complexity. For regulated prices: Should we base them on total cost (so as to recover the "revenue requirement" reliably) or on marginal cost (so as to induce efficient consumption and production)? Should prices be the same for all 8,760 hours of the year, or should they vary by time of day, week, or year to reflect differences in production cost? For market prices: How do we prevent market players from distorting markets by blocking access to bottlenecks, conspiring to withhold supply, and misreporting sales prices? During shortages, how do we distinguish scarcity prices from price gouging?

**Quality of service:** Regulators establish performance standards—the quality of service the customer deserves given the price he pays. These standards are translated into metrics, such as calls dropped, frequency and duration of outages, customer complaints serviced, capital structure maintained, and innovations implemented.

**Physical adequacy:** Infrastructural companies need infrastructural assets. They must plan for the long term. By identifying the physical prerequisites for adequacy—what assets the utility needs now and in the future—regulators can test the utility's readiness to serve.

**Financial structure:** High-quality service and asset adequacy, at reasonable prices, require financial strength. Regulation establishes expectations for financial condition, including the appropriate mix, quality, and cost of debt and equity.

**Corporate structure:** Mergers, acquisitions, divestitures, product mix, territorial expansion, and inter-affiliate transactions—these factors affect everything else: market structure, pricing, quality, and finance. Using structural limits and transactional reviews, regulators align corporate activities with the utility's obligation to serve.

For each of these six subjects, the educated regulator learns the industry-specific and state-specific facts: Which companies are serving the market? What services do they sell and at what prices? What corporate structure do they have? What are their market shares? What are the relevant performance metrics? How do the utilities rate? What infrastructure exists? What is its capability and life expectancy? What are the financial conditions within each company and across each industry? Are they stable? What agencies have jurisdiction over which players and activities?

## Regulation's Six Legal Sources: What Authority Do Regulators Have?

The law of public utility regulation answers three main questions: What are regulators' powers? When exercising these powers, what procedures must they follow? What are the sellers' and buyers' rights and obligations? The answers emanate from six legal sources: state and federal substantive and administrative law (that's four), and state and federal constitutional provisions.

*Substantive law* establishes (1) the regulator's duties and powers; (2) the sellers' and buyers' obligations, rights, and powers; and (3) each player's remedies against the others. *Administrative law* establishes the procedures for decisionmaking and for resolution of grievances.

Five features of *federal constitutional law* protect parties by limiting regulators' powers. The "dormant" Commerce Clause restricts states' powers to regulate and discriminate against interstate commerce. The Contract Clause restricts states' powers to impair existing contracts. The Takings Clause prohibits government regulation that "takes" private property without giving the property owner just compensation. The Supremacy Clause preempts state legislatures and commissions from acting inconsistently with Congressional intent. The Due Process Clause compels procedural fairness.

These sources of law emanate from at least six fora: state legislatures, Congress, state and federal agencies, and state and federal courts. And there are other regulatory agencies: land use, environmental, labor, tax, and financial, all intersecting with utility regulation.

## Regulation's Five Professions: On What Expertise Does Regulation Depend?

*Lawyers* advise on the regulator's substantive jurisdiction, duties, and authorities; on sellers' and buyers' rights and obligations; and on procedures required to make decisions lawfully.

*Accountants* deal with dollars. They track costs and evaluate expenditures. Cost tracking catches cross-subsidies and helps economists assign costs to cost causers. Evaluating expenditures protects against imprudence.

*Finance experts* study the utility's capital requirements, recommend the proper mix of debt and equity, evaluate financial risks, and apply cost–benefit analyses to short- and long-term investments.

*Economists* aim for economic efficiency by making cost causers the cost bearers. They recommend rate designs and evaluate investment prudence. Where regulators use market forces to discipline seller behavior, economists measure and monitor the market's competitiveness.

*Engineers* explain how things work. They evaluate utility performance by identifying the best available technology and by assessing infrastructure adequacy and reliability.

## Regulation's Three Processes: How Do Regulators Make Decisions?

Regulators gather information, make decisions, and enforce those decisions. Each process has variations in formality and finality. Regulators can initiate these actions on their own or in response to prompts from legislators, the regulated utilities, competitors of utilities, consumers, or other citizens.

## Recommendations

"The future belongs to those organizations, as well as those individuals that have made an active, lifelong commitment to continue to learn."[2] The educated regulator asks: Do I know regulation's six substantive subjects, six legal sources, five professions, and three processes? If not, then:

1. Have I created a personal curriculum?

2. How do I first learn the basics and then add the necessary layers of complexity and sophistication?

---

[2] Howard Gardner, *Five Minds for the Future* (2008), at p. xviii.

3. Am I allocating sufficient time to my educational needs?

4. On whom, and on what sources, should I rely for my education? Who out there is objective, and who will take advantage of my inexperience?

5. How do I judge the quality of the education I'm receiving? Is it sophisticated or simplistic? Analogizing it to language-learning tapes: Does it get me only from the airport to my hotel, or does it empower me to participate fully in society?

6. Do my commission and my community take responsibility for educating me on all these topics, or am I on my own? Is this situation satisfactory?

# 3

# Decisive

It has been a stereotype of political wisdom that the bureaucrat is ever ready to exercise authority arbitrarily. But there is the far greater danger that the second-rate, insecure personality who often finds his way into bureaucracy will become uncomfortable at having to exercise authority and will anxiously seek to placate as many interests as possible. This fear to offend, complaisance, and readiness to listen and be "fair" and "reasonable" clog the muscles of the will, and what begins in amiability can end in corruption.

L. Jaffe, "The Scandal in TV Licensing," Copyright 1957, by *Harper's Magazine, Inc.* Quoted in A. Kahn, *The Economics of Regulation*, Vol. II at 88 n.122 (1988 ed.)

---

**The decisive regulator** makes decisions (1) required by the public interest, (2) when the public interest requires it, (3) regardless of discomfort felt, (4) using a logical method and an active approach.

**"Required by the public interest":** Today's regulatory activities are predominantly driven by private interests: rate increases, capital expenditures, mergers, certificates, licenses, and infrastructure siting. The commission that attends only to these private requests puts the public interest on the sidelines. The decisive regulator therefore asks not, "What decisions do these parties want?" but rather, "What decisions does the public interest require?" She identifies the questions no party has asked, converting private pleadings into public interest inquiries. A utility's request for rate increase becomes a commission investigation into the utility's performance; a request for merger approval becomes an inquiry into appropriate market and corporate structure.

**"When the public interest requires it"**: Decision-avoiders disguise their hesitance with the sounds of savvy. Their favorite phrases: "We have to be cautious." "Let's not box ourselves in." "We can't get ahead of the other states." Lacking both facts and reasoning, these statements cede the lead to others. Commissions that have no merger policy give me one of two answers: "We have no merger pending, so we don't care about it," or "We have a merger pending, so we can't talk about it." Three decades and three dozen mergers later, this regulatory "caution"—really a resistance to decisiveness—has produced more consolidation than competition.

Like geological sediments, today's regulatory procedures have layers of historic habit. The decisive regulator questions this status quo. She asks continuously, "Why do we do things the way we do?" and "Why not try another way?" Decisiveness is not impulsiveness. It includes deciding not to decide immediately, just because someone wants a decision. When a utility says, "We need this merger approved by June 30 or the deal disappears," she asks, "Why are the benefits so ephemeral?" Instead of rushing to meet a party's deadline, she revises the proceeding's questions: "It has been 10 years since anyone examined the mix of competition and regulation in our state. Let's begin." (But do complete what you begin. See Mark Twain, *Innocents Abroad*: "I must have a prodigious quantity of mind; it takes me as much as a week sometimes to make it up.")

**"Regardless of discomfort felt"**: In 1999, I was advising a state commission, part of a coalition that sought state legislation to replace a monopoly electricity market structure with retail competition. Due to term limits, one-third of the statehouse was new. The house speaker resisted, complaining, "It's unfair to make new legislators vote on something so complicated." Unfair to whom? Inexperience cannot excuse indecisiveness, because decisiveness attaches to the oath of office.

Discomfort with decisiveness does have honest roots. Most new regulators lack regulatory experience. Even the most experienced face challenges without precedent. For conscientious regulators, inexperience breeds humility, and humility breeds caution. Unguided by purpose, caution becomes indecision. And in a party-driven environment, indecision becomes reaction. Policymaking becomes the sum of approvals and disapprovals of private interest requests. That is not a public interest result.

So what does the inexperienced regulator do? She must decide what she is competent to decide and put the remaining issues on a timeline. Instead of the noncommittal "Now is not the time," try, "We will master this issue and decide by April."

**"Using a logical method and an active approach"**: A decisive regulator decides the right things at the right time. She follows five steps in logical sequence: (1)

determine the industry structure that best aligns private behavior with public interest; (2) establish performance standards for producers and consumers; (3) establish financial consequences for performance that meets, exceeds, or falls below those standards; (4) create processes for evaluating performance and assigning the consequences; and (5) build in reality checks that reexamine the first four steps. The decisive regulator constantly organizes her work life to complete this sequence.

She then couples logic with action. The legendary Peter Bradford had a hierarchy of regulatory decisiveness based on boxing: Rocky, Rope-a-Hope, and Canvasback.[3] Lacking Bradford's metaphorical gifts, I will call these decision-making styles active, reactive, and passive. The *active* decisionmaker directs parties to the commission's questions, organized according to the five sequential steps listed above. This approach converts private interest applications into public interest inquiries. She requires current filings to address future consequences. She critiques present practices (those of producers, consumers, and the regulators), and then realigns them with the public interest.

The *reactive* regulator answers the parties' questions, but fails to ask her own. Reactive regulators can be thoughtful, but their thinking is bounded by the parties' requests. The five steps in the logical method are missing. Consider mergers again. Reactive regulators ask: "Is there any harm?" Active regulators ask: "What industry structure will produce the most benefits for all? Will this merger advance or undermine that market structure?"

The *passive* regulator accepts parties' requests without thinking independently. Passive commissions treat the utility's aspirations as evidence, and reject opponents' objections as speculation. Their opinions have paragraphs copied from utility applications.

Why are regulators so often in "reactive" or "passive" mode rather than "active" mode? State statutes usually entitle private requestors to answers within a specified time. Commissions then allocate scarce resources to these time-sensitive (reactive) proceedings first, leaving insufficient resources for commission-initiated (active) proceedings. These pressures undermine purposefulness. The commissioner coming to work without her own purpose finds her day filled with other people's purposes.

## Recommendations

Active regulators address parties by paraphrasing John F. Kennedy's inaugural speech: Ask not how regulation can advance your private interest; ask how your

---

[3] Peter Bradford, "Gorillas in the Mist: Electric Utility Mergers in Light of State Restructuring Goals," *NRRI Quarterly Bulletin*, Vol. 18, No. 1 (1997).

private behavior can serve the public interest. They require private parties to address public interest questions by establishing expectations for performance. Examples:

1. For rate increase filings, require the utility to demonstrate consistency with optimal practices in all major areas of its business.

2. For rate decrease filings, require the consumer advocate to propose programs by which consumers will use service efficiently.

3. For merger applications, require the utilities to show that (a) they are already achieving all economies of scale and scope available to them as separate entities, (b) the merger's purpose and result are improved efficiency and service quality, and (c) the merger will not reduce competitors' access to "bottleneck facilities."

# 4

# Independent

> Independence ... is loyalty to one's best self and principles, and this is often disloyalty to the general idols and fetishes.
>
> Mark Twain

The **effective regulator's** fourth attribute is independence. But independence from what? And for what purpose? To be casual with the concept is to dilute its power. I will distinguish literal independence (unachievable and undesirable) from effective independence (essential but elusive).

## Literal Independence

Literal independence is unachievable. No regulator is independent of court challenges, legislative overrides, financial markets, or public anger. These pressures constrain action but inject accountability.

**Court challenges:** Regulators must respect substantive and procedural statutes, root their decisions in the record, reason logically and clearly, and explain when they depart from precedent. Otherwise courts will reverse.

**Legislative overrides:** In most states, the commission is created by the legislature and has only those powers delegated by the legislature. (In a few states, the commission is created by the state constitution.) A creature of the legislature is never independent of it. The extent of a commission's discretion depends on the breadth of the legislative delegation. That delegation depends on legislative trust that the commission's expertise, judgment, and speed exceed the legislature's. A commission that loses legislators' trust loses its powers.

**Financial markets:** Utilities are capital-intensive and thus, capital-dependent. Their suppliers of debt and equity—their investors—are volunteers, beyond a commission's command. They do not always act rationally, patiently, farsightedly, or public-spiritedly, but their confidence in the commission is essential to the utility's survival. The commission cannot ignore them.

**Public anger:** Regulatory decisions must embody objectivity: facts, logic, and merits. But those qualities co-exist with an impatient public. The essay on *purposefulness* (Chapter 1) listed the many parts of the public interest—economic efficiency, health, safety, environment, and aesthetics, in the long term and the short term. Regulators must resolve these conflicting components at reasonable cost. Then, they must defend their decisions before a public whose irritability exceeds its expertise. That defense is essential to leadership—creating and keeping followers who share the leader's goals. See Garry Wills, *Certain Trumpets: The Nature of Leadership* (2007). To attract those followers, the regulator must compromise. Regulators are not independent of the public they serve.

The regulator is only one of many actors. Courts overturn commission decisions, legislatures change their statutes, rating agencies lower bond ratings, lenders raise their interest rates, and large customers self-generate. These forces make democracy work and the economy run. Commissions are accountable to them. Literal independence not only is unachievable; it is undesirable.

## Effective Independence

Effective independence means independence from forces that undermine regulation's purposes—forces that block the regulator from aligning private behavior with public interest. The mandatory minimum is freedom from financial influences—stock ownership, bribes, and promises of future employment. But effective independence means more. A regulator must be independent of arguments that are unverifiable (e.g., "An authorized return on equity below 14 percent will cripple us.") or legally irrelevant (e.g., "We need this merger to remain competitive."). Regulators must be independent of phrases aimed at emotions instead of intellect (e.g., "chilling effect," "rate shock," "rate relief"), the parties' habit of substituting "need" for "want," and their persistent use of adjectives and adverbs instead of facts and logic. "God only exhibits his thunder and lightning at intervals, and so they always command attention. These are God's adjectives. You thunder and lightning too much; the reader ceases to get under the bed, by and by." (Mark Twain, Letter to Orion Clemens, 3/23/1878).

Independent regulators are alert to the forces that undermine independence. As the saying goes, "Keep your friends close and your enemies closer." Alertness does not mean selling out; it means monitoring the parties' motivations, exposing their soft spots, and finding ways to align those motivations with regulatory purpose.

Independence does not mean independence from one's own policy preferences, if those preferences are rooted in study and objectivity. A preference is not prejudgment; a hunch is not a bias. A bias is an inability or unwillingness to examine facts and reason objectively. A hunch is a tentative conclusion, based on education, observation, and experience. No one wants a regulatory bench whose mind is a blank. The regulatory mind is full of experiences, prior readings, and stray facts diligently and casually acquired, which together produce hunches. Hunches are unavoidable and useful as long as the regulator establishes a systematic, objective method for testing them, on the record.

**Effective independence is easier to describe than to achieve.** The toughest regulatory decisions implicate at least five traditional tensions: technical (engineering, financial, economic, legal) vs. policy (can the economy stomach higher rates?); short-term vs. long-term (does today's rate freeze weaken tomorrow's infrastructure?); rural vs. urban (uniform rates or distance-sensitive rates?); large customer vs. small customer (industrial development or low-income protection?); and investor vs. consumer (capital market confidence or customer satisfaction?). Regulation, unlike algebra, lacks clear lines between right and wrong. Statutory phrases like "just and reasonable" grant regulators great discretion, allowing for a multitude of sins. That range of discretion invites pressures to give in. The effective regulator studies the pressures but decides independently.

## Questions

1. Have you identified the forces that undermine independence, in the abstract and in your own commission context?

2. Can you tell when a party's presentation crosses the line between advocacy of policy and manipulation of emotions?

3. Are you prepared with verbal signals to move that party away from pecuniary presentation and back to the public interest purpose?

4. Do you know the distinction between compromise and caving—compromise being concessions leaders make to ensure they have followers, caving being giving in to pressures that undermine regulatory purpose?

# 5

# Disciplined

> People unable to engage in disciplined thought may sport trendy dress and use up-to-date argot, [but] they are essentially stranded in the same intellectual place as barbarians.
>
> Howard Gardner, *Five Minds for the Future* (2008) at p. 36

## The Regulator's Role: Thirty Years of Change, More Ahead

Up to the late 1970s, utility regulation had predictable scope: Utilities built and operated infrastructure, served customers, and requested rate increases. Commissions approved projects, sited plants, and set rates. A regulator could describe her role in a single sentence: "We protect customers from monopoly abuse—inefficiency, unnecessary costs and excessive rates." Consumers were passive, at-risk individuals: lacking options, needing protection.

Today, this protect-the-consumer role is but one star in an expanding universe of regulatory responsibilities. Regulators make markets, plan infrastructure, collect and manage funding for new projects, incubate renewable energy, assess mergers, promote broadband, design energy efficiency programs, provide low-income assistance, run power supply auctions. They host interest group gatherings, resolve stakeholder differences, and negotiate regional solutions; even act as political shields for legislators paralyzed by the complexity of it all.

To keep track of these roles, let alone excel in them, will require each of Howard Gardner's five "minds for the future": the disciplined mind, the synthesizing mind, the creative mind, the respectful mind, and the ethical mind. This essay starts with the disciplined mind.

"Those who do not have a discipline, as well as a sense of discipline, either will be without work or will work for someone who does have a discipline."[4] Regulatory success requires both mastering a discipline and being disciplined. What do these concepts mean?

## Mastering the Discipline

"Neither teachers nor students nor policymakers nor ordinary citizens sufficiently appreciate the differences between subject matter and discipline."[5] What is the "discipline" of regulation? What distinguishes it from a series of facts about engineering, economics, accounting, finance, law, and management, and from the subject matters of electricity, gas, telecommunications, and water?

Each of these professional areas and subject areas is its own discipline, giving insights to the regulatory decisionmaker. But the discipline of regulation is more than the sum of these other disciplines. Regulation has a distinct purpose: to induce high-quality performance from entities that, absent regulation, would perform suboptimally. The discipline of regulation requires knowledge not only of facts and subjects; it requires mastery of the forces that cause private performance to diverge from the public interest. These diversions justify regulation but also define its limits, for when private behaviors align with the public good, we need no regulator.

The disciplined regulator therefore focuses on forces that undermine optimality. He masters the tradeoffs. Sales can increase profits but harm the environment. Mergers can increase scale economies but weaken competition. Technology can inspire innovation but distract from the mundane. (Broadband and "smart grid" are exciting, but many Americans still need wireline). Dispersed ownership of infrastructure dilutes monopoly control but can diminish supplier accountability. (If we replace the vertically integrated electric monopoly with independent generators, efficiency suppliers, transmission providers, and "wires" operators, whom do we blame when the lights go out?)

To address these forces and tradeoffs, the disciplined regulator places actors in new roles. Consumers are no longer mere captives needing protection; they are actors to be empowered, but also restrained. They demand quality of service and choice of services. Their actions, unregulated, cause problems for others; their waste is their children's debt. To define regulation as "protecting consumers" both diminishes their status and disregards their damage.

Utilities have new roles, too. They used to control their markets: the supply, the assets, and the customers. Today some customers can choose their own suppliers

---

[4] Howard Gardner, *Five Minds for the Future* at p. xx (2008).

[5] *Id.* at 27.

(choices vary by state and industry), self-generate, cut their usage, or drop off the utility system entirely. And though regulated industries still depend on central "networks," our laws make those networks available to customers and their non-utility suppliers on a nondiscriminatory basis. And as new entrants build their own highways, the networks themselves will have multiple owners. Incumbent control is no longer a given.

Utilities confront this instability in different ways. Some leverage their captive customer base: using ratepayer revenues to acquire new territories or to finance new ventures. Some shed less profitable assets and activities in favor of new products. Some seek market protection through the political process. Some are inert. As novelist John Dos Passos wrote: "Apathy is one of the characteristic responses of any living organism when it is subjected to stimuli too intense or too complicated to cope with. The cure for apathy is comprehension."

That "comprehension" requires more than mere awareness of these facts. Comprehension requires the discipline to pursue regulation's purpose: to produce the performance that serves the public interest. Mastering the discipline of regulation requires asking the right questions. The right questions are not: "Are you for or against 'decoupling'?" or "How do you feel about 'smart grid'?" or "Should we approve this merger?" The right questions are: "What actions must the utility take to fulfill its obligation to serve the public with excellence at reasonable cost?" and "How must consumers change their behavior to avoid waste?" and "What must regulators do to induce those actions?"

## Being Disciplined

"An individual is disciplined to the extent that she has acquired the habits that allow her to make steady and essentially unending progress in the mastery of a skill, craft, or body of knowledge."[6] Having entered the discipline of regulation, what then does the disciplined regulator do? Some suggestions:

1. To avoid overdependence on interest group arguments, *find objective sources*. Know whom to trust for advice on rate design, energy efficiency, return on equity, performance measures, gas hedging options, broadband penetration, water conservation options, and the risks of large construction programs.

2. To avoid intellectual ruts and repeat errors, *identify knowledge gaps*—about technology, legal developments, jurisdictional boundaries, corporate motivations, and customer behavior. The key words here are humility (the state of realizing that one knows less than one should) and curiosity (the state of wanting to know more than one does).

---
[6] *Id.* at 40.

3. To salvage one's ability to think independently, *avoid distractions*, like one more meeting with one more stakeholder, in favor of daily blocks of quiet reading and study time.

4. There cannot be discipline without *self-criticism*; there cannot be self-criticism without humility and confidence. Humility and confidence, seemingly in conflict, mutually reinforce. Confidence comes from the self-improvement produced by self-criticism, which in turn depends on humility.

The most experienced regulators are still humbled by the swirl of statutes, case law, technology trends, financial events, and interest group shifts. The typical regulator has it worse. Most commissioners start their terms with zero regulatory experience, but deal with multi-million dollar decisions in their first month. Humility is helped by knowing history: the billion-dollar cost overruns from nuclear power's first era, the billion dollars in cleanup costs we now face from our use of fossil fuels, the piles of nuclear waste that still have no home. Because the regulators who left us this legacy left their posts long ago, their successors must study their errors to avoid repeating them. Given this history, decisional overconfidence should be in short supply, replaced with skepticism towards those offering easy answers. That skepticism is essential for independence, for those unable to engage in disciplined thinking "are completely dependent on others when they must make decisions about their own health and welfare or vote on issues of importance for their time."[7]

---

[7] *Id.* at 27.

# 6

# Synthesizing

> I have been through this wringer. Synthesizing massive amounts of data, intelligence, slants, opinions, tactics, and trying to maintain a strategic big picture was a challenge. You feel it creeping up into your brain like a numbing cold and you just have to choke it down, sift faster, and stay with it. [It's] challenging,to be sure, but if you practice it, you develop a good tool for the leadership toolbox.
>
> Navy Captain Richard Severs, quoted in Howard Gardner, *Five Minds for the Future* at pp. 46-47

**Daily, weekly, monthly,** and yearly, regulators enter and re-enter their own wringers. Multiple industries (electricity, gas, telecommunications, water, ferries in Hawaii, taxis in Maryland, grain elevators in South Dakota); hundreds of cases (each one dumping a paper pile of pole vault proportions); seven professional disciplines (engineering, law, economics, finance, accounting, management, politics); conflicting policy goals (reliability, cost effectiveness, environmental responsiveness, affordability); multiple pressure points (shareholders, bondholders, consumers, employees, federal and state legislators)—all press for attention. Like Captain Severs, regulators have to "choke it down, sift faster, and stay with it."

## Synthesis Is Survival

"Sources of information are vast and disparate, and individuals crave coherence and integration."[8] Regulators must synthesize not just to satisfy a craving but to

---
[8] *Id.* at 46.

honor their oaths of office. The regulatory universe has everything from atoms to galaxies—from spreadsheets to statutes. The regulator needs both microscope and telescope—and the synthesizing skills to make sense of it all.

Life inside a rate case can feel microscopic—a revenue requirements spreadsheet with a thousand cells. But a rate case is not just numbers; it is hundreds of judgments about prudence, benefit-cost relationships, capital structure, CEO compensation, price signals, fuel mix, short-term economic effects and long-term investment strategies, internal performance, and external influences, all bound together by two central questions: What is the commission's vision for this utility's performance? How can the commission shape its decisions to make its vision the utility's vision?

So the regulator must use both microscope and telescope. Every commission actor, from chairperson to first-year accountant, must synthesize a headful. They must define the agency's mission and establish utility performance standards. They must articulate those standards memorably for regulated utilities and their competitors, and practitioners in their state and colleagues in adjacent states. They must recruit staff and experts, and then marshal these many relationships to achieve the mission.

"Perhaps the most ambitious form of synthesis occurs in multidisciplinary work."[9] In regulation, who has the most influence? Lawyers who can talk capital structure with the economists? Economists who can talk transmission with the engineers? Financial analysts who write with the clarity of Ernest Hemingway? Chairpersons who can design a tariff one day and sway a legislative committee the next? Modeling "multiperspectivalism" (Gardner's admittedly awkward term), these people lead organizations whose success depends on replicating this cross-cultural fluency. The best regulatory orders result not from stapling together each department's recommendations, but from the toothbrush-sharing that occurs when different disciplines live in each other's dormitories.

## Why Is Synthesizing Difficult?

"[A]s a species, we are predisposed to learn skills in certain contexts and to resist—or at least find challenging—their wider generalization and broader application."[10] Synthesizing doesn't come naturally, for the adult mind is inherently conservative. Gardner echoes the thought: "[A]s a species, we evolved to survive in distinctive ecological niches; we did not evolve in order to have correct

---

[9] *Id.* at 47.

[10] *Id.*

theories, to master disciplines, or to transfer lessons encountered in one setting appropriately to others."[11]

Here's the message for regulators: Synthesis requires active thinking. But by whom? The typical case submitted to a regulator reflects the *submitter's* active thinking, rooted in the submitter's self-interest. Synthesis requires the *regulator's* active thinking. She must (1) create and articulate her own vision, (2) articulate principles that align the submitter's interest with that vision, and then (3) craft a strategy that causes the submitter to accept those principles. All this effort takes mental and temporal space, the creation of which requires yet more synthesis—organizing one's day, week, month, and year so that one's own priorities prevail over the stream of others' demands. (On that topic, see the chapter "Know Thy Time" in Peter Drucker's classic, *The Effective Executive*.)

## The Utility's "Obligation to Serve" Imposes on States a Unique Synthesizing Role

State regulators speak warily of an expanding federal footprint, but utility regulation's dominant feature remains the utility's obligation to serve—an exclusively state law construct. Defining, designing, and enforcing that obligation require a special synthesizing effort because federal regulators inject national concerns, often unsynthesized, into state-level contexts.

Congress sees a transmission shortage, so it creates federal regulatory powers to stimulate transmission. Other federal actors see a broadband shortage, so they send money to states to stimulate broadband penetration. The federal Environmental Protection Agency worries about water and air quality, so it sets new standards. Each example produces demands on a regulator's synthesizing mind.

Consider: For transmission construction to be cost-effective and politically acceptable, state commissioners must synthesize state policies on land preservation, environmental effects, aesthetics, and cost-effectiveness (in light of multiple transmission, generation, and demand-side options). Then, they must soften political tensions by consoling (and compensating) the offended. Before spending federal broadband money, the state decisionmaker must identify goals (education or economic development), choose locations (rural or urban), shape market structure (incumbent or new entrants), and then decide which government agencies should make broadband happen. New federal water and air standards will require states to assess the local utility's managerial skill, its structure and rate levels, and its infrastructural readiness.

These examples demonstrate the uniqueness of state-level synthesis. A utility's legal obligation to serve is sourced in state law. To enforce that obligation, state

---
[11] *Id.* at 65.

commissions must satisfy multiple objectives: reasonable cost, environmental compliance, utility financial health, infrastructural adequacy, minute-by-minute physical stability, prompt customer service, and competent outage management. They also must educate customers so that the citizenry's expectations remain realistic. Each of these objectives in turn demands inputs from the multiple professional disciplines that populate regulatory agencies, all synthesized to make decisionmaking possible.

This link between a utility's "obligation to serve" and a state commission's "obligation to synthesize" returns the focus to regulation's purpose: *ensuring utility performance*. State regulators must integrate the disparate federal decisions into a coherent set of expectations about utility performance and a coherent set of regulatory signals that induce that performance. That challenge is what makes state utility regulation unique—and so demanding of the synthesizing mind.

# 7

# Creative

> [C]reativity is never simply the achievement of a lone individual or even a small group. Rather, creativity is the occasional emergent from the interaction of three autonomous elements: (1) The *individual* who has mastered some discipline or *domain* of practice and is steadily issuing variations in that domain ....
> (2) The cultural domain in which an individual is working, with its models, prescriptions, and proscriptions ....
> (3) The social *field*—those individuals and institutions that provide access to relevant educational experiences as well as opportunities to perform.
>
> Howard Gardner, *Five Minds for the Future* at pp. 80-81 (citing the work of psychologist Mihaly Csikszentmihalyi) (emphases in the original)

---

**Today's regulatory challenges** resist on-the-shelf solutions. In energy, we face overconsumption, excess emissions, and the need to mesh new renewable sources with old fossil units while injecting wholesale competition into retail monopoly markets. In telecommunications, we are redefining universal service to accommodate citizens' need for the internet while struggling to preserve competition as the former members of the Bell monopoly re-attach themselves. In water, we search for stable compromises between local management and regional economies of scale, between the need to fix infrastructure while keeping prices affordable.

A century of experience provides plenty of principles, but their application calls for creativity. Let's look at Gardner's three requirements.

"**The *individual* who has mastered some discipline or domain of practice and is steadily issuing variations in that domain ...**": Chapter 5 described the discipline of regulation. Looking within our organizations: Which people are "steadily issuing variations in that discipline"? Who is "perennially dissatisfied with current work, current standards, current questions, [or] current answers"? Who are the ones seeking "to extend knowledge, to ruffle the contours of a genre, to guide a set of practices along new and hitherto unanticipated directions"? Who is "motivated by uncertainty, surprise, continual challenge, and disequilibrium"?[12] Do our regulatory organizations attract, encourage, and recognize these individuals?

In regulatory commissions, inexperience is endemic. Most commissioners are new to the job and new to the field. We can make this fact a weakness or a strength. Many new appointees have the urge to create, but confront staff or parties who stifle that urge, who warn: "We can't do that. We haven't done that before. You don't want to get out in front." These stiflers make newness a weakness. Newness becomes a strength if we (a) welcome the newcomer as someone unhampered by old habits, "disciplined" about missions, and comfortable with gradualism; and then (b) connect that person with those whose experience can guide the newcomer's creativity. By pairing creativity with mastery, a commission can "steadily issue variations" in regulatory practice, producing the improvements that our field needs.

"**The cultural *domain* in which an individual is working, with its models, prescriptions, and proscriptions ...**": Regulation's "cultural domain" has features that both inspire and impede creativity. Among the inspirations are challenges that fall outside regulation's traditional boundaries but demand regulatory action, like disseminating broadband, reducing emissions, making service affordable, and introducing regionalism into a state-based regulatory system. Unlike the traditional issues of rate of return, depreciation and prudence, these challenges have no precedent; they press regulators toward new solutions. Support for creativity can also come from regulatory culture, whose flexible procedures allow commissions to frame questions, gather experts, and seek ideas.

But at least five factors in regulation can impede creativity. (1) If the dominant voices are competing interests rather than objective experts and problem solvers, it is hard to keep the clear-headedness, the unpressured mental balance, necessary for creativity. (2) If the ratio of work to workers and of deadlines to days is unfavorable, creativity becomes luxury instead of necessity. (3) If experience and expertise favor the regulated over the regulator, decisions will reflect deference rather than independence. (4) If civil service rules are inflexible, commission leaders cannot realign staff skill sets with the new regulatory challenges. (5) Finally,

---

[12] *Id.* at 83, 98-99.

creativity requires experiments; experiments often fail before they succeed.[13] Regulators face political pressures that are impatient with experiments and failures.

"The social *field*—those individuals and institutions that provide access to relevant educational experiences as well as opportunities to perform": These access providers, Gardner asserts, should be incubators of creativity, attracting new ideas, spreading them around, shining the spotlight on the risk-takers and their outputs. A commissioner who once asked me to recommend speakers on "the newest, latest technology" was looking to spur creativity.

Here are some thoughts on how to replicate that commissioner's approach:

1. **Look for the most knowledgeable people; they are not always the most prominent people.** The control room operator who watches the power plants ramp up and down as the system's wind generators ramp down and up can explain the challenges of variable power production better than the utility spokesperson.

2. **Look for people unaffiliated with entities having business before commissions.** Among the best speakers I've observed were professors, employees of the DOE-funded national labs, and researchers from consulting firms with client bases so diverse that their independence is unquestionable.

Given limited airtime, these efforts at diversity can cause disgruntlement. While at the National Regulatory Research Institute, I once hosted a teleseminar on the "expanding universe" of commission authority. Within 48 hours of the program, we absorbed two arrows: A Midwest utility official complained that the program focused only on the "public interest and the consumer interest" but had no representative of the "utility interest." A consumer advocate criticized us for having no consumer representative. Had we made two mistakes or no mistake? The program's purpose was not to discuss the latest version of "utilities vs. consumers," but to wonder aloud about how expanding regulatory authority required new agency structures and procedures. The speakers were a law student and his professor who co-authored the paper, a commission chair whose long experience as a legislator and regulator made her an optimal discussant, and a regional transmission organization official responsible for coalescing multiple state commissions toward a regional plan—a task requiring reinterpretations of century-old state statutes. We based speaker selection on relevant experience, not interest group representativeness.

* * *

---

[13] *Id.* at 83.

Gardner describes three prerequisites for creativity—disciplined individuals with the urge to vary, a cultural domain that makes space for those variations, and a social field that invites and rewards these efforts while tolerating failure. In today's regulatory profession, all three are already present. Can we move these three features from presence to prominence?

# 8

# Respectful

> The insights from sociobiology and evolutionary psychology are genuine. No doubt human beings have deeply entrenched inclinations to delineate groups, to identify with and value members of their own group, and to adopt a cautious if not antagonistic tone to other comparable groups, however defined and constituted. But such biologically accented explanations have limitations .... [E]ven if biological bases can be found for dichotomization, stereotypy, or prejudice, human beings in every generation must attempt to deal with these proclivities and, when possible, to mute or overcome them.
>
> Howard Gardner, *Five Minds for the Future* at p. 105

**The effective regulator** establishes a public interest polestar, a centrifugal force that draws private interests toward the common good. The alternatives are divisiveness, provincialism, and zerosumsmanship.

In this effort, what is the role of respect? In this context, respect refers to recognizing and exploiting the value brought by "others." The regulator's challenge is to induce opposing economic interests to show respect for each other and for regulation's purpose. What are the benefits of this respect, what do we lose by its absence, and how can a regulator encourage and sustain it?

## Regulatory Disrespect: Across Industries and Decades

Disrespect is not a pretty sight. Nuclear power opponents in the 1970s and 1980s were labeled "tree huggers," "anti-growth," "anti-jobs." Independent cogenerators in the 1980s and 1990s were derided as "fly-by-nighters" and "PURPA machines," certain to shut down at the first hint of high winds. For several decades prior to FERC's landmark Order No. 888 (the 1996 ruling ordering transmission owners to provide nondiscriminatory transmission access at cost-based prices), proponents of transmission access—mostly small municipal utilities—were caricatured as opportunistic cream-skimmers insensitive to electrical reliability.

How about the hearing rooms, which bring out the adversaries in all of us: the lawyers who shout down their opponents; the witnesses who condescend to commission staff; the CEO who told a commissioner to speed up the questions because "I've got a company to run"; and the lobbyist who got the governor to belittle the commission staff's testimony and threaten their non-civil service jobs?

Then there's Hush-a-Phone. Alfred Kahn recounts the Bell Companies' opposition to this cup-shaped device. Snapped onto the phone, it gave the speaker privacy and reduced room noise. Hush-a-Phone typified what Bell called, in 1955, "foreign attachments marketed by persons who have no responsibility for the quality of telephone service but are primarily interested in exploiting their products."[14]

Disrespect is bidirectional: Opponents criticize incumbent utilities as slothful and lacking in innovation—odd statements to make about the entities that achieved electrification, described by experts as the greatest engineering achievement of the 20th century.[15]

In these situations, disrespect depends on demonizing—oversimplifying, exaggerating, and attaching moral significance to a policy difference. The goal is not merely to win but to vanquish: to pose as the sole source of truth, to assert that the opponent's absence would make the world a better place. This practice hardens differences; it raises the cost of conceding that the other side might have a point.

---

[14] Alfred Kahn, *The Economics of Regulation*, Vol. II at pp. 140-141 (1970, 1988). The FCC granted Bell's request to ban Hush-a-Phone, finding that the device "impair[ed] telephone service" because "the person to whom the Hush-a-Phone user is speaking hears a lower and somewhat distorted sound." The Court of Appeals wasn't buying. It said the caller would achieve the same voice distortion "by cupping his hand between the transmitter and his mouth and speaking in a low voice into this makeshift muffler," a bodily act over which neither Bell nor the FCC had control. "To say that a telephone subscriber may produce the result in question by cupping his hand and speaking into it, but may not do so by using a device which leaves his hand free to write or do whatever else he wishes, is neither just nor reasonable." *Hush-a-Phone Corp. v. FCC*, 238 F.2d 266, 267-69 (D.C. Cir. 1956).

[15] National Academy of Engineering, "Greatest Engineering Achievements of the 20th Century," available at www.greatachievements.org.

## Disrespect's Antidote: Open-Mindedness, Knowledge, Achievement

Experiencing these behaviors can cause one to stereotype the stereotypers. But if one looks past the strategists, demonizers, and opposition-defeaters, one finds a different sort: power supply planners, back-office systems managers, IT experts, control room operators, gas pipeline inspectors, cable layers—the people who make things work. They operate within a hierarchy built not on economic or political power but on performance. This difference helps us understand "respect" as respect for merit.

I once interviewed, in the same week, two different candidates for two different senior positions. Both knew their subjects: nuclear power, transmission access, rate cases, wholesale competition and scarcity pricing in electricity, interconnection comparability, operations support systems, intercarrier compensation in telecommunications. Both were confident, articulate, well-read, good writers. But were they "respectful"? Two pieces of evidence said yes. First, each had worked for and with multiple industry sides—incumbents, new competitors, commission staff, consumers—earning praise from all these stakeholders for being straightforward, thorough, respectful of facts, logic, and the ideas of others. Their former colleagues spoke of a confidence grounded in open-mindedness, objectivity, curiosity, productivity and humility. Second, these candidates, despite their seniority, engaged our non-senior staff in conversations that demonstrated deference to the latter's expertise, a deference reflecting respect for knowledge rather than preoccupation with status.

These are the traits that prevent divisiveness, that define "respect" as honoring knowledge and achievement regardless of source.

## Respect's Results: Better Regulatory Policies

"[A]ccept the differences, learn to live with them, and value those who belong to other cohorts."[16] How might policymakers mirror these values in policies? We are seeing these efforts in real time: The U.S. Department of Energy finding ways to diversify our electric generation base, federal and state telecommunications regulators redefining "universal service" and its funding sources, the Federal Energy Regulatory Commission requiring regional transmission organizations to give "comparable" treatment to demand-side and generation resources, states inducing utilities to purchase renewable energy and fashion energy efficiency programs. These actions form a virtuous circle where respect for merit generates insights that remove barriers to new ideas, allowing new entities to perform and gain respect, leading to more such policies.

---

[16] Gardner at 107.

Psychologists describe "mirroring" as when two people in conversation mimic each other's facial expressions and tone—frowns producing frowns, smiles begetting smiles. The same goes for regulation. Mutual respect attracts diverse participants with the best skills, producing gains; mutual disrespect denies the value of others, pushing us back toward zerosumsmanship. The "respectful regulator" persuades parties that respect raises the gain for all.

# 9
# Ethical

Thus, salute to the career!
When the career is similar
to Shakespeare and Pasteur,
Newton and Tolstoy,

...

Why was mud flung at them?
Talent is talent, brand them as one may.
Those who cursed them are forgotten,
but the accursed we remember well.

All those who strove towards the stratosphere,
the doctors who perished fighting cholera,
they were pursuing a career!
I'll take as an example their careers.

I believe in their sacred belief.
Their belief is my courage.
I pursue my career
by not pursuing it!

Excerpted from the poem "Career," by Yevgeny Yevtushenko (1933–). Translation adopted from Valeria Vlazinskaya. See http://shostakovich.hilwin.nl/op113.html. "Careers" is the fifth of five Yevtushenko poems used in the 13th Symphony of Dmitri Shostakovich.

## Ethics Defined: Narrow and Broad?

**In regulation, we** usually view "ethics" as avoiding wrongdoing—bribes, *ex parte* contacts, favoritism, and conflicts of interest. Gardner defines ethics more broadly: To act ethically is "to think beyond our own self-interest and do what is right under the circumstances."[17] An ethical worker "passes the hypocrisy test: She abides by the principles even when—or especially when—they go against her self-interest."[18] Paradoxically, we can define "broad ethics" in terms of self-interest. Gardner asks: "In what kind of a world would we like to live if we knew neither our standing nor our resources in advance?" His personal answer: "I would like to live in a world characterized by 'good work': work that is excellent, ethical, and engaging."[19]

Can these thoughts help solve regulatory problems? The typical regulatory challenge involves tension between narrow self-interest and broad ethics. Self-interest has multiple versions: my company, my union, my state, my technology, my agency, my customers, my generating units, my profits. Addressing these tensions, we can always behave ethically, in the narrow sense, by avoiding bribes, *ex parte* contacts and conflicts of interest. But what would a broad ethical view require? Two common challenges follow.

## What If "It's Not My Department"?

Eric Filipink's paper, *Serving the "Public Interest": Traditional vs. Expansive Utility Regulation,*[20] explains how a regulator's "public interest" responsibilities are expanding. To the traditional job of policing monopoly power, legislatures are adding new goals, roles, and decisional criteria. The very nature of "utility service" is changing: The public wants service that is not only reliable and affordable, but also environmentally benign, job-producing, and consistent with responsible land use.

What if these new public demands fall outside the regulator's statutory authority? Speaking at a conference hosted by Canadian regulators, I fielded a question from an eloquent advocate for low-income consumers. (The Canadian regulators maintain a fund, supported by utilities, that finances conference attendance by public interest groups.) She urged regulators to address high prices. My inadequate response follows:

> It is painful to say this to someone devoting her career to a cause I care about. But it is not a regulator's job to make service affordable. The

---

[17] Gardner at xiv.

[18] *Id.* at 136.

[19] *Id.* at 127.

[20] National Regulatory Research Institute 10-02 (Jan. 2010).

regulator's job is to get prices right: not low, not high, just right. If that right price hurts the poor, it is a legislative problem. Legislators should not shift their own public interest obligations to regulators.

The questioner thanked me for my "candor," but it was clear I had committed the error of "it's not my department." In my professional role, I do maintain that regulators should focus on utility performance and infrastructure sufficiency, not on wealth redistribution; they should not lower prices below economically efficient levels. But as Gardner points out, "Being recognized as a member of a profession is not the same as acting as a professional."[21] The better answer—the more ethical answer—would have been this:

Regulators are in the best position to know whether price increases are imminent, and whether they will be painful to the poor. Regulators should use that expertise to press the appropriate branches of government for assistance, to argue that the credibility of utility regulation is linked to the credibility of all government action. A government that fails its poor—or picks shortcut solutions like artificially low prices—benefits no one.

The ethical approach is not to hide behind one's professional boundaries to avoid questions, but to use one's professional expertise to cross boundaries and stimulate solutions. A prominent example today: the many state commissioners who, while lacking statutory authority over broadband, are using their knowledge and stature to lead efforts toward broadband accessibility.

## What If Helping Your State Hurts My State?

"We must all hang together, or assuredly we shall all hang separately." (Benjamin Franklin, on signing the Declaration of Independence.) For over two centuries, our 50 states have hung together for the good of the nation, but not without effort. Whether it's allocating transmission cost to you and hydroelectric benefits to me, generating income for my local economy while polluting your lakes, or favoring my state's renewable resources over yours, our states still view each other as both friend and foe. "Human beings have deeply entrenched inclinations to delineate groups, to identify with and value members of their own group, and to adopt a cautious if not antagonistic tone to[ward] other comparable groups, however defined and constituted."[22]

The ethical approach is to find the common denominator, the long-term purpose that benefits all, and then protect that purpose from interference. Doing so aligns self-interest with public interest. Recall Gardner: What world would we choose

---

[21] Gardner at 129.

[22] Gardner at 105.

if we did not know in advance whether our state was hydro-rich, solar-poor, high-income, or low-income? We'd choose a world where long-term national benefit prevailed over short-term provincialism, because then all parties would work to produce benefits accruing to all. This isn't charity. It is still self-interest, and it is ethical. Ethics does not require sacrifice. For some, ethics has roots in religion because ethics spreads goodness. For others, ethics is Darwinian because it ensures our race's survival. Either way, ethics produces the best results for all.

## Downsides and Upsides

"A person who is determined to do something constructive with his life needs to come to terms with the fact that not everyone is going to like him."[23] Ethics-oriented regulators risk caricature as preachers and prigs, as naive non-players moved to the margins—like an orchestra's string bass players who say of themselves, "It's like wetting your tuxedo—you get a warm feeling but nobody notices." Ethics does not disparage legitimate self-interest; it aims to create consciousness of commonalities. That way, the sum of self-interests, ethically oriented, advances everyone's agenda. As Gardner concludes (at p. 129), "ethical orientation" is a "conviction that one's community should possess certain characteristics of which one is proud and a commitment personally to work toward the realization of the virtuous community."

---

[23] Daniel Barenboim and Edward Said, *Parallels and Paradoxes: Explorations in Music and Society* (2002) at pp. 6, 10, and 11 (quoted in Gardner at p. 122). Barenboim is an Israeli pianist and conductor; Said is a Palestinian-American writer. The two created the West-Eastern Divan Workshop, an orchestra of young Israeli and Arab musicians who make music each day, then discuss politics and culture each evening.

# 10

# A Letter to Governors and Legislators: On Appointing Excellent Regulators

> The man of character, sensitive to the meaning of what he is doing, will know how to discover the ethical paths in the maze of possible behavior.
>
> Earl Warren, *The Christian Science Monitor* (May 21, 1964)

Dear Governors and Legislators,

Congratulations on your (re-)election. Your many duties include appointing and confirming public utility commissioners. They are responsible for inducing high-quality performance by providers of electric, gas, water, and telecommunications service. Your appointees' decisions will affect millions of consumers; billions of investor dollars; the local, regional, and national economies; and our air, land and water. Here are eight thoughts on producing top-notch results.

**1. Appointments rooted in principle:** "Regulation" is not a political whipping boy, something to campaign against. Nor is it a one-dimensional spectrum on which "more" is better than "less." Serious regulators do not debate oversimplifications like "command and control" vs. "light-handed" regulation. (The regulatory legend Peter Bradford once noted, "I've heard of light-headed regulation, light-fingered regulation, and red-handed regulation; I know little of light-handed regulation.") Regulation, instead, is about performance: aligning utilities' behavior with the public's needs. Principled regulators ask five questions: (1) What outcomes do we seek to produce? (2) What specific behaviors, engaged in by whom, will produce those outcomes? (3) Which behaviors will occur naturally without regulation because they align with the actor's self-interest? (4) Which behaviors, in contrast, will occur only if regulation intervenes? (5) To produce those behaviors, what specific rewards and penalties must regulation introduce?

**2. Ten jobs in one:** Utility regulation used to be straightforward. Utilities built infrastructure, sold products and services, proposed rate increases. Commissions approved projects and set rates. Their central aim was to protect customers from monopoly abuse—imprudent investments, inefficient operations, and undue discrimination against near-choiceless customers—while setting rates that gave investors a fair shot at a reasonable return. Today's regulators do much more: They make markets, design programs, administer investment funds, incubate renewable energy industries, spread broadband, promote energy efficiency, protect critical infrastructure, and resolve stakeholder differences.

With all these demands, what does it take to excel at regulation? On a personal level, what must regulators be and what must they do to be effective? After some thoughts on attributes, experience, vision, ideological baggage, and political skill, I'll close with an alert about asymmetry.

**3. Personal attributes:** An effective regulator is purposeful, educated decisive, and independent. A purposeful regulator defines the public interest by articulating a vision (see #5 below). A decisive regulator acts to align utilities, and consumers' private behavior with that vision. An independent regulator accepts the pressures of public interest politics (the need to make tradeoffs among meritorious but conflicting goals), but avoids the distortions of private interest politics (the pressures from narrow forces seeking benefits for themselves). She not only presides; she leads. She rejects rhetorical bipolarities like "markets vs. regulation" because she understands, per Dr. Alfred Kahn, that her "central, continuing responsibility" is "finding the best possible mix of inevitably imperfect regulation and inevitably imperfect competition."[24] She prefers facts and logic over adjectives and adverbs.

**4. Professional experience:** Regulation is a bus running 80 miles per hour on a busy road. Someone up front needs to know how it runs and where it should go. Aim for at least one appointee with deep regulatory experience. Promoting a staff person gives a double punch, boosting agency morale while ensuring experience. Add someone who has worked in a regulated industry, not a talker, but a doer—someone who has planned, financed, built, or operated infrastructure, or who connected with customers. You'll take a hit for the "revolving door," but you'll gain someone who knows how it feels to be regulated.

**5. Vision:** A vision is more than a mission statement. It is purpose depicted. The regulator with vision can describe the optimal industry structure (in which motivations, behavior, and performance all align with the public interest), its

---

[24] Alfred Kahn, *The Economics of Regulation: Principles and Institutions* at Vol. I at p. xxxvii, Vol. II at p. 114 (1988 ed.).

microeconomic features (the product array, customers' experience, sellers' profitability); and its macroeconomic features (the industry's overall performance, its contribution to the state and regional economies, its environmental effects). An effective regulator tests that vision against facts, adjusts as necessary, then shapes and sequences the regulatory steps to produce it.

**6. Ideology:** In regulation, the shopworn conflicts are false dichotomies. There is no Republican or Democratic way to regulate. Federal vs. state, markets vs. regulation, urban vs. rural, generation vs. efficiency, incumbent vs. newcomer, publicly owned vs. investor owned, publicly traded vs. closely held—all these "vs.es" lead to zerosumsmanship, usually boiling down to mine vs. yours. The best ideas come not from ideology, hope, rhetoric, or "good faith"; they come from facts, logic, and extrapolation from experience.

**7. Political skill:** Twenty-five years ago, regulatory politics were straightforward. Investors wanted solid returns and customers wanted reasonable rates. Positions were predictable; the parties debated dollars. Today, the interests have multiplied in numbers and diversity. The investment community is no longer just shareholders and bondholders; it has private equity, hedge funds, short sellers, and holding companies from Scotland, England, Australia, Germany, and France. The consumer community is also splintered; the simple threesome of residential, commercial, and industrial has given way to a United Nations of irrigation farmers, computer manufacturers, military bases, casinos, gold mines, and ski resorts. Each technology has its own interest, from wind turbine manufacturers to smart grid installers. There are environmentalists, beachfront property owners, labor unions, privacy advocates, and terrorism consultants. New to regulation's purpose, some of these interests view the commission as just another government agency—a "public resource center" obligated thereby to give out benefits to those who ask.

A regulator has a choice: (a) channel these perspectives toward a long-term vision of industry structure and performance, or (b) organize "compromises" that produce only short-term peace. Dealing with this diversity requires political skill.

**8. Resource asymmetry:** With rare exceptions, utility executives know more than their regulators. This asymmetry invades every relevant knowledge category: costs (including opportunities for cost reductions); operations (e.g., the capability, availability and vulnerability of physical plants); customers (consumption patterns, product preferences, payment histories); market value and financing opportunities; utility staff capabilities; and technological potential.

Addressing this asymmetry is key to regulation's credibility. To induce the utility to provide excellent service at reasonable cost, the regulator must establish standards, then compensate the utility to the extent that it meets those standards.

To do so credibly and effectively, the regulator literally needs to know what he's doing. His expertise must match the utility's. The under-resourced, under-informed commission risks (a) setting performance standards too low or rates too high, causing captive ratepayers to overpay for subpar service; or (b) setting performance standards too high or rates too low, weakening the company and losing investors' trust. Regulation's credibility is undermined by asymmetry.

Governors who want independent regulators must grant them the resources that independence requires: staff whose credentials and pay match the utilities'. Utility customers already pay for the utility's personnel; they won't mind paying for objective staff who can judge utility performance. Allowing commissions to finance their operations through the same rates that pay for utility personnel is the most direct solution to asymmetry.

## Conclusion

It's asking a lot to find women and men with the personal attributes, experience, vision, objectivity and political skill demanded by this ten-dimensional job. But they exist, and they succeed. If you can find them and appoint them, your public will thank you. Good luck.

# PART TWO
## Actions of Effective Regulators

---

Effective regulators use their attributes to act. They recognize that commissions are not courts, and regulators are not judges. They don't "balance" private interests and "preside" over proceedings; they lead, by aligning those private interests with the public interest. Effective regulators join these outward actions with a disciplined inner mental life. They make room for collegial brainstorming, but also know that insights can come from thinking alone. To protect their alone time, they avoid multitasking, a habit that makes people, according to a Stanford professor, "suckers for irrelevancy." And they assess themselves continuously, using measures of regulatory literacy.

Exemplifying these actions, and the attributes described in Part One, is an order of the Maryland Public Service Commission on "smart grid" spending. The utility had sought to impose costs without promising benefits. Unhindered by political pressure, the order first reversed the logic, conditioning cost recovery on the demonstration of benefits.

Part Two closes with a memorial to Alfred Kahn, a "Prophet of Regulation." Dr. Kahn's great treatise, *The Economics of Regulation: Principles and Institutions* (1970, 1988), argued for efficiency and warned against weakness.

# 11

# Commissions Are Not Courts; Regulators Are Not Judges

> [T]he Commission has claimed to be the representative of the public interest. This role does not permit it to act as an umpire blandly calling balls and strikes for adversaries appearing before it; the right of the public must receive active and affirmative protection at the hands of the Commission.
>
> *Scenic Hudson Preservation Conference v. FPC*, 354 F.2d 608, 620 (2d Cir. 1965) (referring to the Federal Power Commission)

**Newcomers to regulation** are not newcomers to government. They understand "executive branch," "legislative branch," "judicial branch." But they are unsure about commissions, asking, "What exactly are we?" Some find comfort in the familiar: Judges sit on benches, await the parties' disputes, use adversarial procedures, find facts, then apply law to those facts. "That seems straightforward," they say; "regulators are like judges."

To view the commission as a court—to "preside" rather than lead—undermines effectiveness. Here's why.

## Commissions Differ from Courts

A commission's purpose derives from its origins. A legislative body receives lawmaking powers from a constitution. The legislature then enacts a statute that creates a commission, delegating to it some substantive slice of those lawmaking powers. The delegation consists of verbs and adjectives, commands coupled with standards: establish just and reasonable rates, ensure reliable service, or approve mergers if consistent with the public interest.[25] Common to these commands and standards is a single legislative purpose: Within a defined substantive space (e.g., activities of electricity, gas, telecommunications and water utilities), make policy for the public actively.

That is not what courts do. Courts and commissions do have commonalities. Both make decisions that bind parties. Both base decisions on facts—evidentiary records created through adversarial truth testing. Both exercise powers bounded by legislative line-drawing. But courts do not seek problems to solve; they wait for parties' complaints. Courts don't promulgate rules for general applicability; they resolve disputes of individual parties. In contrast, a commission's public interest mandate means it literally looks for trouble. Courts are confined to violations of law, but commissions are compelled to advance the public welfare. A court can only eliminate negatives; a commission can also mandate positives.

Even the narrowest of commission decisions—say, approving or disapproving a special contract between a utility and an industrial customer—affects a public interest larger than the parties: Will the low contract price shift costs to other customers or weaken the utility's finances? Will the lucky buyer's competitors seek "me too" treatment? To what effect? Like commission decisions, court orders can make policy affecting non-parties. A class action suit under civil rights or securities laws, an antitrust suit against a Microsoft or an AT&T, can set policy for a generation. But consider this difference: In Court Land, the judge's power to act is defined and confined to the issues stated by a plaintiff's complaint. In Commission Land, a party's filing is stimulation but not limitation. The commission can add issues, combine proceedings, invite the appearance of other parties, or convert a two-party complaint into a multi-party rulemaking, all as the public interest demands.

A commission does "look like" all three branches of government. It looks like a legislature when promulgating rules; like an executive agency when enforcing those rules; like a court when deciding complaints. But utility commissions are not "like" anything. They are what they are: units of government created to exercise powers delegated to the legislature by a constitution, then re-delegated by the legislature to the commission. Commissions, like the legislatures whose powers they exercise, make policy for the public.

## "Acting Like a Judge" Undermines a Regulator's Effectiveness

A judge's substantive power is confined by the plaintiff's complaint. A regulator who acts like a judge confines himself similarly: He assumes that the parties, their interests, their arguments, and their legal citations comprise the full

---

[25] In some states, the commission is created and empowered by the state's constitution. But the legislature still can grant it powers.

intellectual universe warranting his attention. This assumption relies on one or more incorrect premises:

1. that a proceeding's private interest scatterplot will display some pattern from which the commission can determine the public interest;
2. that the private interests appearing in a proceeding are synonymous with the public interest;
3. that those private interests' evidentiary submissions will produce information sufficiently relevant and objective to discern the public interest;
4. that an opportunity for access equals a reality of access (i.e., that all possible private interests have hearing room resources sufficient to get the commission's ear); or
5. that through the *sturm und drang* of private interest opposition, the "truth" will emerge.

A regulator who accepts any of these premises undermines his effectiveness, by:

1. becoming intellectually passive, as the proceeding and the record become party-centric rather than public-centric (i.e., "What are the parties seeking?" instead of "How do I advance the public interest?");
2. imposing the wrong time horizon (the parties' short-term desires rather than the public's long-term needs);
3. reducing the regulator's objectivity because the regulator "learns" the issues from parties' arguments rather than from impartial sources;
4. distorting the regulator's personal time management because as the parties load the record with conversation among themselves—testimony, cross-examination, and briefs exchanged four ways (direct, reply, answering, and cross-answering)—procedural law compels the regulator to read every page, leaving insufficient time and mental space to read and think on her own; or
5. substituting private settlements for public interest solutions (regulation, unlike marital dissolutions and fender benders, requires policymaking, not dispute resolution).

## Why Do Some Regulators Prefer the Judicial Approach?

**Ease of explanation:** In regulatory procedure, adjudication holds center stage. We use it in the "big cases"—rate increases, mergers, complaints about quality. Its formality commands respect. Its familiarity defines the forum: We use judicial techniques, so we are "quasi-judicial." The "quasi" prefix is the tipoff. There is nothing "quasi" about making policy for the public. Adjudication is but one procedural device for discerning and declaring the public interest. Because we use a technique that judges use does not mean we must confine ourselves like judges do. The procedural tail should not wag the purpose dog.

**Inexperience:** Most new regulators are generalists. Faced with regulation's multi-disciplinary complexity, the generalist prefers to focus on the arguments of those with more experience rather than frame the arguments in her own way.

**Overwork:** If one is overrun by paper, it is easier to preside than to lead.

**Aversion to risk:** Acting like a judge carries less risk and involves less responsibility. Politics punishes errors of omission less than errors of commission.

## Recommendations

1. Organize each proceeding by asking, "How do we advance the public interest?" not "What do the parties want us to decide?"

2. Begin each proceeding with neutral tutorials, presented or vetted by an objective entity, rather than depend on the parties' submissions for education.

3. In major policy areas like performance standards, mergers, and rates, create substantive policies before proceedings occur, so that parties' proposals track commission priorities, not the other way around.

4. Approve settlements only if they advance the public interest, not because they buy peace among opponents.[26]

---

[26] For more on settlements, see Chapter 48, "Regulatory 'Settlements': When Do Private Agreements Serve the Public Interest?"

# 12

# The Regulatory Mission: Do We "Balance" Private Interests, or Do We Align Them with the Public Interest?

> In any moment of decision the best thing you can do is the right thing, the next best thing is the wrong thing, and the worst thing you can do is nothing.
>
> Theodore Roosevelt

**A newly appointed assistant** to a newly elected commissioner, both new to utility regulation, asked veteran commission staff, "What is our mission?" The staff answered, "We balance the interests of customers and investors." This notion of regulation-as-private-interest-balancing, so deeply embedded in regulatory practice and psyche, has five main problems. Can we recast the regulatory mission?

## Five Problems

**Ambiguity:** "We balance the interests of consumers and investors." Which *consumers*? Large or small? Today's or tomorrow's? Our state's, our region's, or our nation's? Which consumer *interests*? Short-term or long-term? Low rates or viable supply? Which *investors*? Buy-and-hold shareholders, pension funds, hedge funds, short sellers, current owners, future owners, or bondholders? Which investor *interests*? This year's profits or next decade's viability? What *balance*? "Balance" implies equivalence—the precise midpoint between two interests of equal weight. Are the customer–investor weights exactly equal? At all points in time? Or can they vary from equivalence at any point in time, provided the variations "balance" over some longer period of time?

**Nearsightedness:** If utility service were merely a commercial transaction between supplier and customer, "balancing the interests of customers and investors" would be a logical mission (provided we resolved the dozen ambiguities just discussed). But utility service is not a mere commercial transaction. It is the infrastructure supporting our economy—our schools, hospitals, streetlights, and manufacturing. It sustains life and the quality of life (think water shortages, electricity outages, no dial tones, no streetlights, no movies). That's the positive side. Utility service also has its negatives external to the seller–buyer relationship, the long-term detritus of today's decisions: nuclear waste and carbon emissions from electricity generation, chemical residue from telephone pole treatment, gas pipeline leaks. The regulatory lens must be both wide-angle and long-distance. "Balancing" interests misses this point.

**Presumption of conflict:** A balance presumes opposites—two sides of a scale whose weights compete to dominate. The presumption is wrong. Consumers' and utilities' legitimate aims are consistent and mutually reinforcing. Viable suppliers, satisfied customers, no free lunch, reasonable prices, reasonable returns, high-quality performance, and low-waste consumption—these results benefit everyone—customers, shareholder, bondholder, employees, the environment.

Conflict arises only from illegitimate aims: the cost-causer hoping to shift costs or the shareholder seeking excess returns. If regulation regularly exposed these aims as improper, its assumption of opposites would self-correct. But most regulatory forums do the reverse, by embedding opposition into the core of regulatory procedure. The parties position themselves at the poles, aggrieved and relief seeking, testimonially swearing at their opponents' errors. Then comes the wheeling and dealing in private, producing a "settlement." This settlement contains boilerplate forbidding the commission from changing the terms on pain of undoing the deal, leading to an "approval" stamped by a boxed-in commission.[27] See how the sequence undermines regulation's mission. By assuming a need to "balance," the regulator presumes inter-party conflict, embeds that conflict in regulatory procedure, and finally produces "compromises" among private interests. The public interest remains unserved, because the midpoint between two private interests is still a private interest.

**Passivity:** A commission that balances private interests risks presiding rather than leading. Outcomes are defined by the parties' desires, not the public's needs. The forum ends up serving the parties, rather than the parties serving the forum.

---

[27] For more on regulatory overdependence on settlements, see Chapter 48, "Regulatory 'Settlements': When Do Private Agreements Serve the Public Interest?"

**Legal looseness:** Regulatory proceedings are legal proceedings, bounded by statutes and constitutional law. Those legal sources do not address "interests"; they create rights and obligations. As a matter of law, therefore, the regulatory responsibility is not to balance "interests," but to (1) define the rights and obligations; then (2) honor the rights and enforce the obligations. A mission of "balancing the interests of customers and investors" diverts the commission from its legal obligations. (*Caveat:* The occasional statute does contain a balancing-type phrase in its preamble. In that limited context, my legal argument has less force. But even in those situations, the interests requiring balance are the rights and obligations created by statute (which the commission must define), not the self-interests advanced by the parties.)

## Recasting the Regulatory Mission

A regulator cannot ignore private interests. Administrative law gives everyone a voice. So how can regulators use private interests—rather than the other way around? The answer requires two steps: (1) Determine how the private interests diverge from the public interest, then (2) shape regulatory solutions that convert divergence into alignment.

Start with skepticism. Private interests always claim the mantle of the public interest. A developer of wind farms, a builder of nuclear power plants—both promise "clean" and "green," but their real interest is market share and profit. The industrial customer criticizes a commission's energy efficiency rules as impractical, but its private interest is low rates. Private interest arguments also downplay public interests: Does the wind developer discuss transmission cost? Does the nuclear developer acknowledge the taxpayer-funded research, the federal loan guarantees, the statutory limit on accident liability, and the absence of answers on waste disposal when talking about "competition" and the "free market"?

Exemplifying private interest analysis is Stephen G. Hill's paper, *Private Equity Buyouts of Public Utilities: Preparation for Regulators*.[28] Hill analyzes the motivations of each player (e.g., acquirer's investors; target's shareholders, bondholders, and management; acquisition lenders). He demonstrates their divergence from the public interest, then recommends regulatory actions that preserve the public interest wheat but remove the private interest chaff.

Regulators can move from balance to alignment by modifying traditional practices. Consider the typical "pre-filing" meeting. Usually it begins like this:

> Lobbyist: "I'm here to explain how my proposal advances the public interest."

---

[28] National Regulatory Research Institute Publication No. 07-11.

Try substituting this:

> Regulator: "First let's discuss my vision for the public's needs. Then let's explore how your private interest diverges. Then we'll take a look at your proposal."

Two different meetings, two different outcomes.

Another example: The typical regulatory opinion begins by reciting the parties' positions. One purpose of these pages is to satisfy reviewing courts that intervenors have been "heard." But the optical impression is that the proceeding's purpose is to serve these parties' interests. How different would be the impression if accompanying the required listing of intervener interests was an analysis of how each interest diverges from the public interest?

These two examples of procedural change, applied consistently over time, can produce behavioral change. They can induce parties to educate rather than advocate, while encouraging regulators to probe rather than preside. The focus becomes molding a public interest policy rather than "balancing" a private interest conflict.

# 13

# Regulatory Brainstorming: When and Where?

Building 20 was a fantastic environment. It looked like it was going to fall apart. But it was extremely interactive. You would walk down the corridor and meet people and have a discussion.

Noam Chomsky, Professor of Linguistics, who revolutionized his field by drawing from biology, psychology, and computer science (referring here to a building at M.I.T. to which academic departments were assigned mostly randomly)

What am I supposed to do? Not tell him he's got a bad idea?

Morris Halle, founder of M.I.T.'s Department of Linguistics

These quotes come from Jonah Lehrer, "Groupthink: The Brainstorming Myth," in *The New Yorker* (Jan. 30, 2012). Citing science and anecdotes, this indispensable piece can help utility regulators via two key principles.

**Group brainstorming usually generates fewer new ideas than individuals brainstorming on their own.** Since the 1990s, regulators have introduced "collaboratives," advisory committees, and task forces. Focused more on finding common ground than on breaking new ground, they are more likely to produce consensuses than Nobel Prizes. The internet and email have added listservs, chat rooms, and the wretched "reply to all." This constant conversation—too often among the same people—siphons many fine minds away from the deep thinking needed to solve regulation's challenges.

Here's what Jonah Lehrer discovered: Group work doesn't "unleash the potential of the group, but rather ma[kes] each individual less creative." When group brainstorming does succeed, it follows two rules. First, debate stimulates more than it inhibits, so drop the custom of "no criticism." Second, add outsiders, but not too many: Regular members meeting only with one another lose their edge, while mutual strangers have trouble focusing. A mix of legacy members and new members provides a familiar structure but generates new ideas.

**Thinking-in-isolation also has its limits.** Utility regulation is intensely interdisciplinary. Any decision about rates, finance, market structure, mergers, service quality, product mix or universal service requires input from engineering, economics, finance, accounting, law, management, behavioral psychology and politics. Complex problems demand specialization, but specialization risks isolation. The resource differential between utility companies and their regulators makes it worse.[29] Within utilities, the litigation specialists, legislative strategists, and communications crafters mix with rate experts and financial advisors to shape and package proposals whose effects on customers and competitors can be missed by the more isolated, under-supported regulatory staff.

Here again is what Jonah Lehrer discovered: As intellectual advances become harder to achieve, researchers must become more specialized "because there's only so much information one mind can handle." *But for breakthroughs to occur, specialists need to collaborate* "because the most interesting mysteries lie at the intersections of disciplines."

## Solutions

The problems are insufficient "alone time," groups whose members are overly familiar, and individual isolation. Regulation has in place three structures that, with modest adjustments, can produce solutions.

1. **Regulators' meetings:** Hierarchy, workload, geography, and budget conspire to separate regulatory professionals from one another. The more junior the staff, the greater the separation. By attending thrice-yearly regulators' meetings, commissioners have the most state-to-state interaction, but the benefits are truncated by their short tenures (averaging under 4 years). Senior staff attend the occasional out-of-state conference, but the agendas are so packed with 15-minute surface-scratchers (themselves undermined by deadening, uni-dimensional Powerpoint—see www.edwardtufte.com for a storied professor's critique of "one damn slide after another") that little space, mental or temporal, remains for the multidisciplinary depth needed for breakthroughs.

---

[29] See Chapters 50 and 51, "Regulatory Resources I: Why Do Differentials Exist?" and "Regulatory Resources II: Do the Differentials Make a Difference?"

Making attendance possible for the permanent staff, expanding speaking time to allow for depth, and assigning slots to groundbreakers rather than position-takers, will bring out the community's full value.

2. **Regional transmission organization meetings:** The combination of diverse attendees and frontier challenges could produce breakthroughs. But if the agendas are established by those with funds and the clout—the utilities and the RTOs—the interaction will be less creative than reactive. The solution is to have the priorities set by commissions and consumers, not because they are "stakeholders," but because it is their priorities that the utilities and RTOs are obligated to honor.

3. **"Knowledge Communities":** The National Regulatory Research Institute developed the web-based Knowledge Communities to stimulate relaxed inquiry and interaction across states, disciplines, bureaucracies, and hierarchies, especially by permanent staff at the regulatory commissions. The effort ran into two predictable bumps. Staff professionals' work time was so controlled by the pace, quantity, and complexity of utility filings that they had little time for creative, non-mandatory interaction. And many hesitated to share ideas that might conflict with the positions of their bosses or commissioners.

    Culture change needs leadership—here, leadership commitment to the cause of empowering staff to make external connections. I asked a group of 10 commission leaders—a high-achieving group committed to excellence—if each of them would tell 10 of their staff to spend 15 minutes a week placing short questions or answers on Knowledge Communities. These 100 new interactions weekly would, at negligible cost, attract others to a high-quality oasis of inquiry. The commissioners' response was unanimous and negative. "We don't tell professionals how to do their jobs," one said.

    The error in this response was its assumption that staff members have discretion over their days. They don't. Most of their time goes to following orders, most frequently, statutory directives to process utility filings within a specified number of days. By changing the priorities (in this instance, for 15 minutes a week), commission leaders would not be "telling professionals how to do their jobs"; they would be freeing professionals to practice their professions—to inquire, interact, create and share, unrestrained by someone else's priorities.

**Proceed interdisciplinarily:** Professional disciplines can constrain. A lawyer thinks about avoiding judicial reversal. The engineer aims to avoid outages. The financial analyst wants solvency, the accountant wants the books to balance, the market structure economist measures market concentration and entry barriers, the rate design economist wants price to equal marginal cost. Every professional has her principles. The risk is "academic chauvinism"—an assumption that one's own discipline explains all, that the unfamiliar is unimportant. If "the mysteries lie at the intersections," we can redesign regulatory procedures to make disciplines intersect and interact. The basis for most regulatory decisions is expert evidence. The practice in most regulatory proceedings is one expert at a time, each witness confined to her pre-filed testimony, and that pre-filed testimony confined to the witness's professional credentials. What about requiring each witness to explain how her position takes into account factors from other professional disciplines, thus creating a testimonial obligation to consider the "mysteries [that] lie at the intersections?" Further, how about dispensing with one-witness-at-a-time in favor of panels of opposing witnesses whose expertise and clashing positions can be brought together to help solve the problem?

# 14

# Regulatory Multitasking: Does It Do Long-Term Damage?

> Multitaskers were just lousy at everything.... I was sure they had some secret ability. But it turns out that high multitaskers are suckers for irrelevancy.
>
> Clifford I. Nass, Professor of Communication at Stanford University and coauthor of a study of multitaskers (quoted in "The Mediocre Multitasker," *The New York Times*, Aug. 29, 2009)

**If you're a** commission chair, an advisor to your governor, your agency's chief administrative officer, a contact for your congressional members, and a supplicant before your state legislature, all in the same day, maybe you're excelling. But not if you're "multitasking." Multiple roles are unavoidable, but multitasking is undesirable. Simultaneous attention yields inattention.

## Multitasking Fails Its Practitioners—Currently, and Possibly Long-Term

So says a National Academy of Sciences study published in August 2009. According to the *New York Times* summary,[30] the study "tested 100 college students rated high or low multitaskers. Experimenters monitored the students' focus, memory, and distractibility." The researchers were startled:

**Confusion:** "We kept looking for multitaskers' advantages in this study. But we kept finding only disadvantages. We thought multitaskers were very much in control of information. It turns out they were just getting it all confused."[31]

---

[30] "The Mediocre Multitasker," *The New York Times*, Aug. 29, 2009.

[31] Eyal Ophir, Stanford researcher (quoted in the *New York Times* summary).

**Irrelevancy filter failure:** "'When they're in situations where there are multiple sources of information coming from the external world or emerging out of memory, they're not able to filter out what's not relevant to their current goal,' said [Anthony] Wagner, a [Stanford] associate professor of psychology. 'That failure to filter means they're slowed down by that irrelevant information.'" [32] It gets worse: "'They couldn't help thinking about the task they weren't doing,' adds researcher Ophir. 'The high multitaskers are always drawing from all the information in front of them. They can't keep things separate in their minds.'"[33]

**Long-term damage?** "I worry about the short-term and long-term effects of multitasking," said Stanford researcher Nass. He added: "The researchers are still studying whether chronic media multitaskers are born with an inability to concentrate or are damaging their cognitive control by willingly taking in so much at once. But they're convinced the minds of multitaskers are not working as well as they could."[34]

## Is Regulatory Multitasking Unavoidable? Seventy-Some Sources of Stress

With so many roles, responsibilities, and accountabilities, the regulator falls easily into the multitasking trap. Consider more than 70 sources of stress, in seven categories:

**Four industries:** In one workday, a regulator might confront challenges in four distinct industries—electricity, gas, telecommunications, water, along with taxicabs (Maryland), inter-island ferries (Hawaii), and granaries (North Dakota).

**Six professional disciplines:** A regulator deals with accounting, economics, engineering, finance, law and management.

**Nine sources of political pressure:** Let's call it, politely, "results-oriented advocacy." These efforts emanate from consumers, environmentalists, labor groups, shareholders, utility management, utility competitors, multiple legislators, governors and members of Congress. Few of these forces appreciate the processes and analyses that good regulation must follow. What advocates want are results: plant approvals, rate changes, more renewable energy, concrete poured, wages protected.

**Twelve types of docket entry:** Even the smallest states have dozens of proceedings pending. The caseload diversity encompasses procedure (informal inquiry, formal investigation, enforcement action, rulemaking, contested cases) and substance

---

[32] *Stanford University News*, http://news.stanford.edu/news/2009/august24/multitask-research-study-082409.html.

[33] www.physorg.com/news170349575.html (Aug. 24, 2009).

[34] www.physorg.com/news170349575.html (Aug. 24, 2009).

(rate case, merger, quality of service, interconnection dispute, certificate of need, construction prudence, consumer complaint).

**Eleven sources of accountability:** We call regulators "independent," but they are not independent of democratic, legal, and institutional forces. They must answer to the public, the media, state courts, federal courts, their governor, FERC, the FCC, state statute, federal statute, state legislature, Congress.[35]

**Nine internal activities:** Inside commissions, regulators act as decisionmakers, negotiators, employers, mentors, task force leaders, budget makers, cost cutters, defenders, spokespersons.

**Thirteen types of mental effort:** Issuing any decision requires a regulator to read, meet, listen, think, write, review, debate, analyze, inquire, critique, invent, become curious, ask questions.

**Nine types of external activity:** Want to travel? You can do it weekly: conferences, seminars, congressional appearances, visits to federal commissions, regulator meetings (national and regional, ceremonial and substantive), meetings aimed at multistate problems (e.g., market design, transmission and power planning, telephone company mergers).

## Solutions: Purpose, Focus, Self-Image

So a regulator confronts stress sources daily, by the dozen. Having multiple responsibilities, playing multiple roles, addressing multiple accountabilities—these situations are unavoidable. (It happens in the highest art: in Puccini's *La Bohème*, the same singer plays the landlord Benoit and the lecher Alcindoro.) What is avoidable is a work habit of doing different things at the same time, switching between different roles too quickly, allocating insufficient time per task to appreciate its complexity—disabling one from immersing, absorbing, and gaining sufficient intimacy to produce one's own insights, criticize those insights, and then share the results with colleagues. Here are three ideas:

**Emphasize public purpose over private interest.** We regulate to align private behavior with the public interest. The focus is on performance by regulated utilities and by consumers.[36] Many of the 70-odd stresses are someone's effort to divert the regulator from her public purpose to the advocate's private purpose. By putting the public interest first, we avoid confusing reactivity with productivity or, as my dentist says, "over-brushing and under-cleaning."

---

[35] See Chapter 4.
[36] See Chapter 1.

**Build periods of focus.** As Dr. Ophir stated, "The big take-away for me is to try to build periods of focus, to create times you are really focused on one thing."[37]

**Disconnect multitasking from self-image.** This can be a challenge. The *New York Times* quotes writer Robert Leleux, who describes himself as "'thoroughly cowed by multitaskers.'" He asserts, "'Look at the tortoise and the hare. Even though the tortoise actually ends up winning the race, who would you rather be? A wrinkly, fat old tortoise or a lithe, quick-witted hare? I think the answer is clear.'"

---

[37] Quoted in Bio-Medicine, www.bio-medicine.org/medicine-news-1/Chronic-Media-Multi-Tasking-Makes-It-Harder-to-Focus–55193-2/.

# 15

# Regulatory Literacy: A Self-Assessment

> Surely this instruction which I enjoin upon you is not too baffling for you, nor is it beyond reach. It is not in the heavens, that you should say, "Who among us can go up to the heavens and get it for us and impart it to us, that we may observe it?" Neither is it beyond the sea, that you should say, "Who among us can cross to the other side of the sea and get it for us and impart it to us, that we may observe it?" No, the thing is very close to you, in your mouth and in your heart.
>
> Deuteronomy 30:11–14 (translation from W.G. Plaut, *The Torah: A Modern Commentary*)

**Regardless of their** seniority level, commissioners and professional staff hunger for mastery. They sense that their grasps are soft and slipping, that on the highway of change, traffic is accelerating even as the curves get sharper and the swerves come sooner. They see their decisions affecting not only trillions of consumer and investor dollars, but also non-financial values—privacy, reliability, the environment and health, even citizens' faith in democratic processes.

Here are 30 questions any regulatory professional should be able to answer. It's less important to have the right answer (of which there are few) than to have some answer.

## Regulatory Substance: Purposes and Techniques

1. What is the purpose of regulation?

2. In seeking regulatory outcomes, when is it best to (a) prescribe utility actions? vs. (b) set standards (leave it to the utility to choose the actions)?

3. What are the purposes of rate-setting? What are the main methods? Which methods best achieve which purposes? For example, what are the relative merits of setting rates based on cost vs. based on market value? As to cost, how about embedded cost vs. marginal cost? As to marginal cost, short-run or long-run?

4. What are the alternative ways to cause customers to bear the cost of pollution caused by their consumption?

5. For proposed large capital projects, what are the key sources of uncertainty and risk? What are the ways to allocate those risks?

6. For utility purchase contracts such as purchases of coal, gas or renewable energy: What are the alternative ways to mix short-term, medium-term, and long-term arrangements? What are the advantages and disadvantages of these alternatives?

7. What are the pros and cons of utility self-builds as compared to utility purchases?

## Utility's Responsibilities

8. For each industry, what products and services should make up the utility's obligation to serve?

9. What is the utility's performance obligation—average, above average, state of the art? What are ways to discern the state of the art?

10. What are appropriate ways to assign consequences to a utility whose performance falls below its obligation? What are the specific pros and cons of franchise revocation, fines, and cost disallowance?

## Markets: Their Purposes and Oversight

11. What is a market? (In the 1988 FERC hearing on the PacifiCorp-Utah Power & Light merger, this question by an artful cross-examiner tripped up a Ph.D. economist. In Lexis, search for the words "baffling w/15 annihilating." Unfortunately, that was the day the witness brought his children to see him perform.)

12. How can markets help regulation's mission? How can they undermine that mission?

13. What are the features of a market that is effectively competitive?

14. When should a regulator rely on markets rather than on regulation?

15. For each of the electricity, gas, telecommunications and water industries, what is the optimal market structure for providing each of the essential retail products? What data must we gather to answer the question?

16. Concerning the present services required or desired by utility customers, which are better provided by the incumbent utility and which by non-utility companies? How about future services?

## Regulatory Administration and Procedure

17. What are the alternative ways to organize a hearing to ensure that the focus is on the public interest and that all relevant facts are aired? What are the pros and cons of each method?

18. When is it better for a commission to accept a settlement than to require the parties to litigate?

19. What contributions to regulation are made by each of the major professional disciplines—law, engineering, finance, accounting, economics, management, and politics?

20. What are the skill sets, experiences, and knowledge necessary to have within a commission?

21. What are the relative merits of organizing a commission staff by industry (electricity, gas, telecommunications, water) vs. professional discipline?

22. Should commissions issue press releases or speak only through their orders? What is the role and purpose of a commission's public relations person?

23. When is it useful and appropriate to communicate with utility officials and others with interests before the commission, informally and privately?

## Technology's Role in Utility Service

24. For each of the regulated industries, what are the existing technologies at each stage of production?

25. What technological developments will change the answer to the preceding question?

## Law's Role in Regulation

26. What constraints are imposed on regulators by the U.S. Constitution's five relevant clauses: the Commerce Clause, the Supremacy Clause, the Contract Clause, the Due Process Clause, and the Takings Clause?

27. What duties are imposed on regulators by these common state statutory phrases: "just and reasonable," "non-discriminatory," "public convenience and necessity," "public interest"?

## Commission Relations with Other Government Bodies

28. For each industry—electricity, gas, telecommunications, water—who should be responsible for which elements of policy, taking into account Congress, state legislatures, federal agencies and state agencies?

29. What principles determine the appropriate level of prescriptiveness in legislation? That is, when is it better for a legislature to grant the commission discretion, as opposed to prescribing a result?

30. What are examples of commission–legislative relations that are effective and ineffective?

And those are the easier ones. Up one notch are technical questions like: (a) What are the relative strengths of the three ways to estimate return on equity—discounted cash flow, capital asset pricing model, and risk premium? or (b) What are the components of long-run marginal cost? Then, there are the central questions that resist precise answers, like: (a) When comparing coal, gas and nuclear construction options, what price should we assume for carbon? or (b) What will it cost to bring broadband to every citizen, and is it worth it? Yet the decisive regulator must master these questions also.

While only skimming regulation's surface, these questions are essential to effectiveness. Why are so many of us so readily stumped? Each of regulation's traditional professions—law, economics, engineering, accounting, and finance—has a credentials process (e.g., bar exams, masters theses, Ph.D dissertations, licensing tests). But none of these screens addresses these 30 questions. There is literally no official obligation to know the basics. Imagine: What if your orthopedist could not describe the bones and their purposes, your family lawyer could not draw up a will, your airline pilot could not explain all those dials and switches, your cab driver could not get from the airport to downtown, or your daycare professional did not know CPR? Any of them would lose their licenses and their jobs. Our profession lacks these measures of mastery.

Like Deuteronomy says, it's all within our grasp. With mastery, we maintain regulation's unique attributes: expertise and objectivity. Without it, regulation risks becoming just another government body to be lobbied.

# 16

# "Smart Grid" Spending: A Commission's Pitch-Perfect Response to a Utility's Seven Errors

> The Proposal asks [Baltimore Gas & Electric's] ratepayers to take significant financial and technological risks and adapt to categorical changes in rate design, all in exchange for savings that are largely indirect, highly contingent and a long way off.
>
> *Application of Baltimore Gas & Electric Company for Authorization to Deploy a Smart Grid Initiative and to Establish a Surcharge for the Recovery of Cost*, Case No. 9208, Order No. 83410 (Maryland Pub. Serv. Comm'n June 21, 2010)

**L**ike many two-word phrases (e.g., "competitive markets," "rate relief," "fiscal integrity," "light-handed regulation," "social compact," "adjustment clause," or any word pair containing "reform"), "smart grid" has a simple sound but multiple meanings. Baltimore Gas & Electric's (BGE) 2010 proposal, costing $835 million, had four main components: (1) replace all existing electric and gas meters with "smart" meters, (2) install a two-way communication network linking with customer meters and appliances, (3) establish mandatory residential time-of-use rates for June through September, and (4) recover all associated costs through a surcharge, imposed prior to completion.

In its June 2010 Order, the Maryland Commission rejected the proposal without prejudice. Proceedings aimed at climate change bring out everybody's passions, but the Commission was dispassionate. Its Order (1) aligned risk with reward,

(2) required facts rather than hopes, (3) reframed the issue as one about customer service rather than cost recovery, and (4) prevented politics from impeding objectivity. The Order exemplifies effective regulation. (A subsequent order, dated August 13, 2010, approved a revised proposal, with conditions.)

## The Utility's Seven Strategies

Verbal packaging (who opposes a "smart grid"?) can help sell a product, but in regulation, the product's benefits must justify its costs. BGE's plan failed this test. Its seven errors were both typical and archetypal. Commissions see them all the time.

**Bridge halfway:** Eager to get going, BGE failed to plan—or reveal—the full route. The Commission had to fill out the picture. It detailed the need, if "smart grid" were to succeed, for "an advanced automated distribution control system that utilizes embedded sensors, intelligent electric devices, automated substations, 'smart' transformers, analytical computer modeling tools, high-speed integrated communications, and reconfigured distribution circuits." All these elements were missing from the Company's cost proposal.

**Cost understatement:** The utility claimed a benefit-cost ratio of 3:2. But the Commission found that BGE's cost category omitted items essential to success: (1) "the approximately $100 million in undepreciated value of existing, fully operational meters that would be retired before the end of their useful lives"; (2) "the estimated $60 million [for] … the new billing system necessary to implement" the new time-of-use rates; (3) "the cost of in-home display devices, which easily could exceed another $100 million"; and (4) the cost of new customer appliances that can communicate with the new meters. Why omit costs from a benefit-cost calculation?

**Benefit overstatement:** Smart grid investments can produce two types of benefits: operational savings (e.g., substituting remote for manual meter reading) and power supply savings (e.g., reducing future capacity and energy needs as customers change their behavior). Almost 80 percent of BGE's claimed savings (that is, 80 percent of the "3" in the 3:2 benefit-cost ratio) came from the "power supply savings" category—a category rife with uncertain assumptions about future market prices and customer responses.

**Excess optimism:** Excess optimism is optimism minus risk: "My upside exceeds my downside, I think, but you cover the bet." BGE claimed confidence but avoided risk. Consumers would cover costs-plus-profit but receive no promise. (As the Commission wrote: "Although BG[&]E claims that the assumptions underlying its business case are sound, the Company would have its customers bear all of the risk in the event those assumptions prove incorrect.") Otherwise known as "betting with other people's money," this tactic shares features with Wall Street's 2009 wreckage.

**New customer rate structure without new customer education:** The success of time-of-use rates (which rates vary with the utility's hourly operating costs) depends on behavioral changes by millions who have known only average rates (which the same rate is charged every hour). "Yet the Proposal contains no concrete, detailed customer education plan, includes no orbs or other in-home displays, and provides for grossly inadequate messaging, in our view, to trigger the behavior changes contemplated under the Proposal." (Orbs are balls that glow more intensely as rates rise).

**Payment before performance:** The customers' cost responsibility was clear, but the utility's accountability was not. Absent were metrics: specific commitments to cut demand and usage measurably. BGE forgot what every teenage lawn mower learns: Cut the grass, cut it well, and then get paid. At bottom was an optical error: seeing ratepayers rather than consumers, pocketbooks rather than people. Peter Drucker, the leading scholar of management and leadership, a deep believer in capitalism and author of *The Effective Executive*, had it right: "Business exists to supply goods and services to customers, rather than to supply jobs to workers and managers, or even dividends to stockholders."

**Marbles:** A utility's obligation to serve includes an obligation to adapt technology to its best use, cost-effectively. The obligation is unconditional. But BGE viewed innovation as voluntary, telling the Commission, in effect, that without assured cost recovery it would pull the proposal. (But see footnote 5 in the Commission's order, describing BGE's position as no "line in the sand" concerning cost recovery alternatives). When the game is voluntary, the dissatisfied can take his marbles home. Utility service—excellent service—is not voluntary.

## The Commission's Response

**Cost-effectiveness before cost recovery:** Whereas BGE conditioned its willingness to innovate on cost recovery assurance, the Commission conditioned cost recovery on cost-effectiveness. The purpose of regulation is performance: performance that serves the customer cost-effectively. By pre-approving cost recovery, the Commission would lose its leverage; by conditioning cost recovery on cost-effectiveness, the Commission kept its leverage.

**The dog that didn't bark—"future sunk costs":** The Commission looked beyond BGE's plan, asking, "What's missing here?" It didn't take Sherlock Holmes to find out: hundreds of millions of dollars in future costs, unstated, unexamined, and unplanned for. The risk was this: after spending the first $800 million, BGE could argue that a few more hundred million would be small relative to the benefits—the classic argument to "ignore sunk costs." The Commission got it right: There are no sunk costs before costs are sunk. Place all future costs on the table now, then compare that total to the benefits.

**Not snowed by non-verifiable financial claims:** Like many utilities, BGE cited the "financial community" and "the rating agencies" to support its insistence on a surcharge that guaranteed cost recovery. Referring to these "now predictable" arguments, the Commission's arrow hit its target: "[W]e are not in the business of attempting to predict rating agency reactions, nor of calibrating our decisions to what the utilities say the agencies want or expect."

**Open door, with conditions:** The Commission expressed "hopes, even enthusiasm" for some type of "smart grid" initiative. But it refused to accept uncertainty over facts. It "invited" BGE to return, but only if the company backed its confidence with commitment—commitment to bear the risk that its confidence was misplaced. At the same time, the Commission recognized that (1) future benefits are always less certain than current costs, and (2) insisting on certainty undermines innovation. Ratepayers will share some risk, the Commission said, if we know the risks up front.

**Just and reasonable decisionmaking:** The phrase "just and reasonable" experiences so much repetition it almost loses its meaning. The Maryland Commission gave the phrase content: "just" aligns benefits with cost bearers; "reasonable" requires cost-effectiveness.

## Conclusion

There's a form of regulation known as "If you do that again we'll clobber you—but go ahead this time." (Thanks to regulatory legend Peter Bradford.) The Maryland Commission did the opposite: "The answer is 'no,' until you get it right." Bradford has a boxing-based metaphor for three levels of regulatory willpower: "Rocky," "Rope-a-Hope," and "Canvasback." Maryland chose Rocky.

Mark Twain, in his autobiography, wrote: "The happy phrasing of a compliment is one of the rarest of human gifts, and the happy delivery of it another." I hope this essay qualifies. Congratulations to the Maryland Commission.

# 17

# Alfred Kahn, "Prophet of Regulation"

---

I have never pretended to play the role of a passive receiver of evidence.

Alfred Kahn (rejecting a motion for his recusal as Chair of the New York Commission, filed by intervenors complaining about his active questioning), from Thomas K. McCraw, *Prophets of Regulation: Charles Francis Adams, Louis D. Brandeis, James M. Landis, Alfred E. Kahn*

---

**Alfred Kahn, former** Chairman of the New York Public Service Commission and the U.S. Civil Aeronautics Board, and Professor of Economics at Cornell University, passed away in 2010 at the age of 93. His life and influence, recounted 25 years earlier in Thomas K. McCraw's Pulitzer Prize winner, *Prophets of Regulation: Charles Francis Adams, Louis D. Brandeis, James M. Landis, Alfred E. Kahn*, were legendary.

Kahn's treatise, *The Economics of Regulation: Principles and Institutions*, remains a must-read for everyone in our field. While preparing for my first rate case—Northeast Utilities' 1979 request for a $131.5 million increase in Connecticut retail rates—I lucked into the masterpiece at the local library's used book sale. I used it to struggle through the forest of foreign terms like "test year," "rate base," and "marginal cost pricing." Years later, I finally committed to reading the entire 600 pages: five pages a night for four months. My marked-up, highlighted copy sits near my desk, for whenever I need a pitch-perfect explanation of an economic problem—inevitably solved by Kahn 40 years ago.

**Candor and humor:** As President Carter's inflation fighter, he warned of a "deep, deep depression" if price increases continued. The D-word's pessimism infuriated his boss, so Kahn turned to fruit: "We're in danger of having the worst banana in 45 years."[38] "He later changed that to 'kumquat' after banana companies objected."[39] (The bananaists' balk recalls sausage makers offended by comparisons to lawmaking; unlike lawmaking, they assert, sausage-making has quality standards, allows only one person to be in charge at a time, and forbids the inclusion of unrelated ingredients.)[40]

**Decency and directness:** Kahn was deeply decent but did not suffer fools. During its 1995 inquiry into retail electricity competition, the Connecticut Department of Public Utility Control asked me to examine Dr. Kahn, who was testifying for the utilities. It was not a career high for me. Lawyers test witnesses' reasoning by asking hypotheticals—usually in the form of "If XYZ, then what?" Displeased with one such question—it contained an assumption he thought unrealistic—Kahn responded, "If my grandmother had wheels, she'd be a bus. So what?"

**Theoretical connected to the practical:** In the mid-1960s, airlines invented "youth fares." Access to these discounted deals depended on last-minute seat availability. Kahn's subchapter on price discrimination called the idea excellent idea in theory but problematic in practice: "Several companies found that the marginal costs of the program were well above zero. They encountered a greater demand on the time of the agents in answering questions about the possibilities of finding standby space, greater congestion at ticket counters, and increased annoyance to regular passengers, who were often offended by the sartorial, hirsute and ablutional state, and the comportment of some of their new fellow travelers."[41] And when Irwin Stelzer, a former Kahn student and later prominent economist, wrote a post-flight letter to CAB Chairman Kahn, complaining of "a rather odiferous and bare-footed hippy" seated in his row, Kahn replied: "Many thanks for your letter. I am sure you understand that it would be inappropriate for me to rule in this matter until I have heard from the hippy. Signed: Alfred E. Kahn, Chairman."[42]

## Three Big Ideas

Kahn had membership in that thin stratum of regulators appointed solely for their scholarship, intellect, and independence. (While Chairman of the New York Commission, a sign hung in his office: "I have tenure at Cornell.") In his life's work, three big ideas stand out:

---

[38] See www.time.com/time/magazine/article/0,9171,919922,00.html.
[39] www.bloomberg.com/news/2010-12-28/.
[40] See R. Pear, "If Only Laws Were Like Sausages," *The New York Times* (Dec. 4, 2010).
[41] *The Economics of Regulation*, Vol. I, p. 76 n. 28.
[42] See www.antitrustinstitute.org/node/10267.

**We are regulators first, sector experts second.** Kahn left footprints everywhere: airlines, electricity, ground transport, gas and telecommunications. The economic principles that determine the necessity and value of regulatory action apply regardless of an industry's details. As he said after becoming CAB Chairman: "I really don't know one plane from the other. To me, they're all marginal costs with wings."[43]

**Market structure decisions require facts, not faith; intellect, not ideology; flexibility, not fixed notions.** He declared that the "central, continuing responsibility of legislatures and regulatory commissions" is "finding the best possible mix of inevitably imperfect regulation and inevitably imperfect competition."[44] Some have twisted this quote back on itself, positing that "imperfect competition is better than perfect regulation"—a statement whose certainty and smugness are worlds away from Kahn's humility and fact-fixedness.

**Effective regulators don't preside; they lead.** Kahn would applaud those commissions of today that create their own proceedings, whether on broadband access, energy efficiency, rate design, natural gas contracting, water infrastructure or renewable energy. He worried that

> regulation has been a negative process, with the initiative coming from the companies themselves; ... it proceeds on a case-by-case basis, on issues usually framed and a record made up by contesting parties, rather than on occasions and issues formulated by the government itself in terms of its own, independent judgment of the public concern[; so that the] function of the regulator becomes primarily adjudicatory rather than executive or legislative[,] ... constrained by elaborate rules of evidence designed, principally, to protect the interests of the private litigants rather than for the formulation of general policy by expert bodies[;] ... [with decisions] tend[ing] often to degenerate into pragmatic, timid compromises between the contending private interests.[45]

More darkly, he warned that reacting rather than leading produces a downward spiral:

> It has been a stereotype of political wisdom that the bureaucrat is ever ready to exercise authority arbitrarily. But there is the far greater danger that the second-rate, insecure personality who often finds his way into bureaucracy will become uncomfortable at having to exercise authority and will anxiously seek to placate as many interests as possible. This fear to offend, complaisance, and readiness to listen and be "fair" and

---

[43] www.bloomberg.com/news/2010-12-28/.

[44] *The Economics of Regulation*, Vol. I, p. xxxvii; Vol. II, p. 114.

[45] *Id.*, Vol. II p. 87.

"reasonable" clog the muscles of the will, and what begins in amiability can end in corruption.[46]

Alfred Kahn was a national treasure and an intellectual treasure trove. A teacher, author, regulator, and administrator, Kahn was, above all, a thinker.

---

[46] *Id.* at p. 88 n. 122 (quoting L. Jaffe, "The Scandal in TV Licensing," *Harper's Magazine*, CCXV: 77 (1957)).

# PART THREE
## Political Pressures

---

Even with all the right attributes and all the right actions, regulators face obstacles. Politics, in its positive and negative forms, is a constant. There is risk of regulatory capture—a state of being persuaded by a private interest's identity rather than its merits. Political pressure can be diluted or magnified by language. As illustrated by the decades-long word war between "competition" and "regulation," language can elucidate or obscure, depending on the speaker's motives. Private interests clothe their pecuniary positions in public interest attire, requiring regulators to gain graduate degrees in the art of undressing. Like Julia Child, effective regulators "master the art"—of spotting these obstacles and steering around them.

# 18

# "Politics" I: The Public and Private Versions

POLITICS, n. Strife of interests masquerading as a contest of principles.

Ambrose Bierce, *The Devil's Dictionary*

**In utility regulation,** politics comes in two forms: *public interest politics*—the regulator's obligation to make tradeoffs among meritorious but conflicting goals; and *private interest politics*—the pressures regulators absorb from a growing mix of benefit-seekers. When applied to regulation's public interest mission, one enhances, the other undermines. Understanding the distinction is essential to effective regulation.

This essay categorizes regulation's many political components, distinguishing between commission and legislative decisionmaking. The next essay discusses how effective regulators manage these many pressures.

## Public Interest Politics

**Commissions practice public interest politics when they exercise their statutory discretion:** Regulatory statutes have broad phrases: "just and reasonable," "undue preference or advantage," "public interest." Verbal breadth means policy discretion. Exercising discretion is a political act: using government powers to create rights and obligations, to allocate benefits and costs, to establish expectations and assign consequences. This discretion comes with legal constraints: Decisions lacking facts and logic are "arbitrary and capricious" and thus unlawful. But within those constraints, there are many political choices. For example:

**"Just and reasonable"**: For return on equity, which end of the "zone of reasonableness"—upper or lower? For rate design, which cost basis—average embedded cost, or long-run marginal cost? Scarcity prices to induce new supply and dampen load, or average prices to produce simplicity and reduce volatility?

**"Undue preference or advantage"**: For large commercial and industrial customers, discounted rates below embedded costs (with the difference picked up by residential customers) to keep them on the system? Discounts for low-income customers (paid for by more fortunate customers)? Energy efficiency programs, paid for by all to benefit only some?

**"Public interest"**: Surcharges (a technique for funding public programs through rates without "raising taxes") for environmental improvements, worker retraining necessitated by merger-related job loss, or research investments in experimental technologies?

These choices are all political choices, because they allocate among our citizens rights and responsibilities, burdens and benefits. They reflect the tensions inherent in any policymaking: tensions between the technical and equitable, short-term and long-term, rural and urban, large and small customer, legacy and new customer, investor and consumer, shareholder and lender. Regulation's inherently political nature should cause no surprise, since commissions exercise legislative powers (although they sometimes use court-like procedures).[47]

**Legislatures practice public interest politics when they define a commission's powers and determine its resources.** Regulation's central public interest issue is the performance we should require of regulated utilities: What products and services, at what level of excellence? To answer these questions, the legislature first must decide which decisions to prescribe and which to delegate: Which decisions belong with those who face the voters, and which decisions belong with those whose main tools are expertise, facts, and procedural formality?

When delegating powers to the commission, a legislature then must address three more questions: How much and what type of commission intervention is necessary to induce industry performance? What should be the commission's powers to reward and penalize? What resources, and what flexibility, must the commission have to build the expertise, fact-gathering capability and procedures necessary to serve the public interest?

First, the legislature must decide whether regulation should play any role. It must ask, continuously: What industry structure most effectively will induce accountability in our infrastructural industries? Or, as Alfred Kahn memorably

---

[47] On regulation's legislative character, see Chapter 11, "Commissions Are Not Courts; Regulators Are Not Judges"; and Chapter 33, "Legislatures and Commissions: How Well Do They Work Together?"

wrote in *The Economics of Regulation*, what is "the best possible mix of inevitably imperfect regulation and inevitably imperfect competition"? A principled selection of the "best possible mix"—for example, reducing regulation when competition is effective, or restoring regulation when competition weakens—is "political" because it affects stakeholders. But those stakeholders' interest in the outcome need not divert the legislature's purpose from public interest promotion to private interest protection.

## Private Interest Politics

**The commission's broad discretion attracts private interest pressures.** Statutory breadth is a two-edged sword. While it accommodates legitimate political judgments, it also invites private interests to claim public interest purpose. Examples: (1) A utility insists that only a 14 percent return on equity (a private interest desire) will prevent debilitating bond downgrades (a public interest concern); but then settles at 12.5 percent (exposing the public interest argument as a clothesless emperor). (2) Some generation owners argue that supramarket prices (a private interest desire) are necessary to attract investment (a public interest concern), and that scarcity pricing induces efficient consumption (another public interest concern); but they offer no facts on elasticities of demand (if consumers can't respond to high prices, the public interest argument weakens). Industrial customers often seek discounts below fully allocated cost rates (a private interest desire), asserting that without rate reductions they will leave the system, resulting in fixed costs falling on other ratepayers (a public interest argument); but they offer no facts on their destination (evidence that would reveal the strength or weakness of their argument).

**When responding to private pressures, legislatures can make regulation more effective or less effective.** Legislative prescriptiveness shrinks commission discretion. One state statute actually specifies the types of companies regulators may use as "comparables" when setting the utility's authorized return on equity. Other statutes single out specific costs for accelerated or guaranteed cost recovery. These statutes, produced by private interest pressures, inject constraints and slants unaided by the expertise and fact-gathering techniques normally used by commissions.

By diminishing commission discretion, legislation also can reduce sellers' accountability. Awarding ratepayer-funded "incentives" to sellers without defining their obligations can cause ratepayers to pay extra for performance already inherent in the obligation to serve. Reducing regulation in the name of "competition" without facts on competition's effectiveness makes customers vulnerable to abuse while giving "competition" a bad name. These are not public interest results.

## Conclusion

Private and public interests are Boolean circles: They overlap but do not coincide. Compared to the industries they regulate, commissions and legislatures are overworked and informationally disadvantaged. In this context, effectiveness requires continuous curiosity, alertness, and skepticism.

# 19

# "Politics" II: How Can Regulators Respond?

The hardest part of my job is the politics.

Mid-Atlantic Commissioner

**Chapter 18 described** two forms of regulatory politics: *public interest politics*—the need to make tradeoffs among meritorious but conflicting goals; and *private interest politics*—the pressures from parties seeking benefits only for themselves. One enhances, the other undermines, regulation's public interest mission.

The effective regulator can resolve public interest tensions with traditional tools: facts, logic, statutory language, public explanations and proper procedures. How does she diminish the distortions of private interest politics? Some suggestions follow.

## Explain the Tradeoffs

Outages happen, water pressure drops, even dial tones fail. Perfection is expensive, so regulators make tradeoffs. But when tradeoffs disappoint, private interest pressure rises.

In regulatory disappointment as in human disappointment, understanding assists acceptance, and explanation assists understanding. We can do more with explanation. Consider rate design, which must resolve multiple, competing objectives. Ken Costello has observed that commission tradeoffs are often ad hoc, implicit, and reactive to interest group pressures. "Over time, policy becomes unpredictable, thus diminishing credibility."[48] He recommends that commissions, at the

---

[48] K. Costello, *Decision-Making Strategies for Assessing Ratemaking Methods: The Case of Natural Gas* at 23-25 (National Regulatory Research Institute 07-10), available at http://nrri.org/pubs/gas/07-01.pdf.

outset of a proceeding, identify and weigh objectives systematically and explicitly. Repeating this practice in each proceeding will moderate private interest expectations by putting the parties in the regulator's shoes.

## Channel Private Interests toward Public Interest Goals

No rational consumer wants a weak utility, unable to modernize its infrastructure. No rational investor wants discipline-draining, auto-recovery of a utility's imprudent costs. Even aggressive drivers want red lights to prevent accidents; restaurant check-splitters want pre-dinner guidelines to prevent post-prandial shock. In utility regulation, as in all regulation, unconditional accommodation does no one good.

For no party is purely private. We tend to view the array of regulatory intervenors as a spectrum, each interest occupying a unique segment. This is optical error, magnified in commission hearing rooms by the ethics of advocacy. The industrial customer's lawyer is duty-bound to represent only industrial customers, the utility shareholders' lawyer only the shareholders. But every industrial customer, every shareholder, every individual citizen, is a combination consumer-producer-polluter-environmentalist-investor-worker. Former Vermont Board Chair Michael Dworkin tells of a heated hearing on a proposed power line running through his state, designed to bring hydropower from Quebec to Boston. The farmers' reflexive opposition cooled when one declared, "If those Boston folks can't run their refrigerators, I can't sell my milk."

It becomes the commission's task to hold up a mirror to the parties, display their common interests, and describe the consequences of unconditionally accommodating every private interest. By anchoring every proceeding in the public interest—requiring parties to address the public needs rather than private needs—the regulator can influence private expectations, turn positions into perspectives, and produce better results.

The alternative is not pretty. Analyze major regulatory events—recent and historic, utility and nonutility. The variable that consistently distinguishes failures from successes is the ratio of private interest gratification to public interest insistence.

## Create a Culture of Commitment to the Long Term

Compare two hypothetical statements:

1. One hundred years from now, people need to breathe.

2. Starting in 2011, purchasers of electricity from coal-based plants must pay the cost of pollution.

No one disagrees with the first; plenty of people disagree with the second. Private interest tension is magnified when immediacy is emphasized. The opposite is also true. The longer term the perspective, the less large the differences. Consider the intra-regional disputes over transmission cost allocation. Long-term thinking allows for intergenerational logrolling. Over 20 years, the ups and downs can balance out. Looking only at the next five years, every project has an opponent.

It is not easy for regulators to play the long-term card. The average commissioner term is under four years. The tendency to avoid short-term pain while discounting long-term benefit is understandable. Regulatory legend Charles Stalon (appointed to the Illinois Commission and the Federal Energy Regulatory Commission) described the problem: "There is NIMBY (not in my back yard), and then there is NIMTOO (not in my term of office)."

There are exceptions. The regulatory community is blessed with several dozen commissioners—many in leadership roles—now in their second decade of service. Governors can help: I knew of one who told his commission chairman annually, "You take care of the long term." And in every state, there is an infrastructure of long-term practitioners: commission staff, residential consumer advocates, industrial customer advocates, utility lawyers, all spending more time with each other in hearing rooms than with their families in living rooms. Utilities have the longest term of all—an obligation to serve and a right to provide service exclusively—for as long as performance remains high. The ingredients thus exist for a culture of commitment to the long term. This perspective is neither naive nor unheard of. Readers with relatives who lived through World War II recognize that today's political freedoms and economic opportunities owe much to the generation that bought war bonds, recycled tin cans, rationed food and fuel, and gave lives. Utility regulation, oriented to the long term, is no less important.

Regulators can be political leaders, in the best sense of both words. They can be political by resolving tradeoffs forthrightly. They can be leaders by persuading the populace to make investments today for the public of tomorrow. They can say, "If our generation's usage wore down our infrastructure, our generation's dollars should rebuild it. If our consumption diminished our air quality, our investments should restore it."

## Conclusion

Explaining tradeoffs explicitly, channeling private interests toward public interest goals, and creating a culture of commitment to the long term: These measures are a regulator's best strategy for practicing public interest politics and avoiding private interest pressures. They all call on the commission's strong suits: expertise, objectivity, and legal obligation to serve the public interest.

What about compromises? "Compromise" is a problematic term, ambiguous from overuse. Making tradeoffs among conflicting public interest values is legitimate compromise. Departing from principles is not compromise; it is caving. This distinction translates into several recommendations for regulators.

1. Compromise on techniques, not on purposes.

2. Compromise on pace, not on principle.

3. Compromise on the angle of change, not on the direction of change.

4. Compromise not among private interests that diverge from the public interest, but among conflicting components of the public interest.

# 20

# "Regulatory Capture" I: Is It Real?

> During my eighty-seven years I have witnessed a whole succession of technological revolutions. But none of them has done away with the need for character in the individual or the ability to think.
>
> Bernard Baruch

**Three recent conversations** about "regulatory capture" produced three different perspectives. From these three conversations, we can develop a definition of "regulatory capture," recognize its warning signs, and work to resist it.

## "We'll Lose Our Jobs"

A group of state commissioners and staff felt frustrated by their utility's unresponsiveness. The company opposed their preferences on grounds of "federal preemption." As a result, the commission wasn't the parent setting the rules; it was in family counseling, as a mere intervenor at the Federal Energy Regulatory Commission (FERC).

The commission's strategies were the old and familiar—oppositional meetings with the utility followed by unsuccessful pleadings at FERC. Why put up with this? The legal source of a utility's right to serve the state is the law of the state. Its utility's franchise comes with no lifetime lock. Why not let other, more responsive companies compete for the role? Or a partial role: Hawaii, Maine, Oregon, and Vermont, dissatisfied with their utilities' commitment to energy efficiency, have moved that function to independent, commission-regulated entities, selected competitively. The risk of losing a century of steady income would jolt any incumbent into responsiveness.

"Not while I'm here," said one commissioner. "We'd all lose our jobs."

Finding the best company to would cost the commissioners their jobs? That conceded a lot. And it conflicted with a commission practice now nearly routine: merger approvals. How's that? When the *utility* wants to change the franchisee (like being acquired by an outside holding company), commissions regularly agree, with no commissioner job loss. But if the *commission* wants to change the franchisee, the matter becomes too hot to handle. When the motivation for regulatory action—or inaction—becomes job-saving rather than customer-serving, we are headed toward "regulatory capture."

## "They're Already Captured; There's No Rescue"

In another state, legislators dismayed by the utility's poor outage performance blamed the commission for failing to set standards and punish shortcomings. I suggested they give the commission more support: more staff, more expertise, better salaries, more political cover for its tougher decisions.

A state senator had three responses, two negative and one positive. More resources were not "politically possible"; the legislature won't spend the money. Yet he'd estimated that the summer's outages had cost his constituents hundreds of millions in lost business and freezer spoilage alone. How was it not "politically possible"— with patient, albeit risk-taking, leadership—to spend, say, five percent of that amount to reduce the probability of recurrence by half? Why give ground to the short-term cost-cutters where spending saves long-term money?

Anyway, strengthening the commission was useless, he said next, because the commission was "captured." They weren't "tough enough." This was less than convincing. It's easy for an outsider, unschooled in the law and procedure of regulation, to want a commission that demands more performance, that punishes more assertively. But "tough" is not a statutory term; "tough" turns off investors, and commissions don't control investors. And his reasoning had a hole. He'd voted for a law that raised the maximum per-day penalty for outages. That same law placed the discretion to impose the penalty with the commission that was purportedly "captured." The solution, I suggested, was strengthening the commission, so that it was the utility's professional equal, giving it the credibility that would induce performance. That credibility would be even higher if the commission had the option of replacing a non-performing utility with a new franchisee. (See above.) This brought us back to "it's useless, they're captured." By conceding "capture," this legislator was making himself a captive.

Having dismissed the legislature and the commission, he turned to the citizens. He would create citizens corps that, after an outage, would remove downed wires, cut away fallen trees, and hook things back up. "How hard can it be?"

he said. But (a) dangerous work is best left to the professionally trained; and (b) dispersing these activities to citizen teams would blur the utility's responsibility, when the right answer is to make its responsibility clearer.

## "We'll Prevent Capture through Continuous Commission Improvement"

The third encounter was much more promising. Recognizing that the risk of capture is real, this group of commissioners stared it down. To the entire staff, from the 30-year veterans to the six-month novices, they delivered this message: "We will leverage our statutory authority and our professional ability to create a culture of excellence, within our organization and within the utilities. We will put ourselves on a path to self-improvement so rigorous, so disciplined, so transparent, so determined and so optimistic that we will persuade the utilities, the legislators, and the courts that we deserve not only their respect but their deference."

\* \* \*

## What is Regulatory Capture?

*Regulatory capture* is a ringing phrase, too casually used. But because it is a hyperbolic phrase, it is too readily dismissed. Here's an attempt to define it, so it can be detected, measured, and avoided.

*Capture* is an extreme form of persuasion. To achieve persuasion is to obtain what the persuader wants. To be persuaded is to give the persuader what he wants. To be captured is to be in a constant state of "being persuaded" by a particular persuader—based on the persuader's identity rather than an argument's merits.

Regulatory capture is not persuasion through illegal acts—financial bribery, threats to deny reappointment, promises of future employment. These things all have occurred, but they are forms of corruption, not capture. Nor is regulatory capture a state of being controlled, where regulators are robots executing commands issued by interest groups. Regulatory capture is neither corruption nor control. Regulatory capture is a surplus of passivity and reactivity, and a deficit of curiosity and creativity. It is a body of commission decisions or non-decisions—about resources, procedures, priorities and policies—where what the utility wants has more influence than what the public interest requires.

Regulatory capture is defined by the regulator's attitude, not by the utility's actions. The active verb "capture" signals an affirmative effort, "to take someone captive." But the passive phrase "to be captured" signals a state of being. One can enter that state through one's own actions or inactions. One can allow oneself to be captured. One can assist, and sustain, one's own captivity.

If regulatory capture is a state of being, assisted and sustained by the captive, what roles are played by others? Plenty. Regulatory capture is enabled by those who ignore it, tolerate it, accept it or encourage it: legislators who underfund the commission or restrict its authority, governors who appoint commissioners unprepared for the job, human resource officials who classify staff jobs and salaries based on decades-old criteria unrelated to current needs, intervenors who treat proceedings like win–loss contests rather than building blocks in a policy edifice. These actions and inactions feed a forest where private interest trees grow tall, while the public's needs stay small.

\* \* \*

Regulatory capture is real. This essay described three conversations, each dealing with the challenge differently. These conversations helped to define regulatory capture in a way that allows us to detect its presence and its sources. The next essay asks two questions about regulatory capture: What are the warning signs? What can we do about it?

# 21

# "Regulatory Capture" II: What Are the Warning Signs?

> Professional skepticism is an attitude that includes a questioning mind and a critical assessment of evidence. Professional skepticism includes a mindset in which auditors assume neither that management is dishonest nor of unquestioned honesty.
>
> U.S. Government Accountability Office, *Government Auditing Standards*, Section 3.61

**The previous essay** defined "regulatory capture." To be captured is to be in a constant state of "being persuaded," where the persuasive force is persuader identity rather than facts and merits. What are capture's warning signs? Within each of five categories are 18 conditions or practices that contribute to, reflect or perpetuate the problem.

## Vision and Priorities

1. The commission's leaders don't ask the big questions: What products best serve the public? What performance standards must utilities meet to deliver those products? What price levels are necessary, and sufficient, to support those standards? What market structures will yield these products, performance, and prices? Within those market structures, what corporate structures will induce the utility's executives, managers and professionals to produce those results?

2. The commission devotes more resources to processing parties' petitions than to pursuing its own priorities. (This is not necessarily the commission's fault. When a legislature sets deadlines for commission

responses to parties' growing requests while denying commission resources, it is inevitable that the commission's workload reflects what well-resourced parties want rather than what the public needs.)

3. Statutory deadlines are asymmetrical: On deadline day, no action on a utility's request means auto-approval; no action on a customer's complaint means auto-rejection.

4. The commission lacks a program of continuous self-improvement: a program that has for each department, department head, and employee a specific plan for professional advancement; a program whose resources and momentum are not compromised by the commission's other pressures.

5. The commission does not regularly recommend legislative changes to strengthen its ability to improve industry performance.

## Hearings and Procedures

6. In commission proceedings, the parties emphasize positions over perspectives. They assert their interests rather than offer their expertise.

7. The commission invites and rewards this practice by structuring proceedings around parties' requests. Hearing orders (the initial orders stating the issues to be decided) merely restate the parties' requests, rather than articulate a public interest purpose. The commission becomes a commercial interest arbitrator rather than a policy leader.

8. In the hearing room, the parties ask each other hours of questions aimed at their own interests. The commissioners mostly observe, on the premise that oppositional sparks reveal a public interest path.

9. The parties treat the commission staff as a mediator for short-term settlements rather than as a transmitter of the commission's vision. (A real likelihood if there is no vision; see #1 above). The commission accepts these settlements instead of directing its staff to pursue its vision.

## Professionals and Professionalism

10. The "revolving door" is a one-way door: More commission staff take utility jobs than utility staff take commission jobs. This tendency signals neither corruption nor conflict of interest; it is rather the natural economic result of government failing to pay good people what they're worth.

11. Similarly: Top professional school graduates prefer the regulated over the regulator, even though a career in the public sector has no match in intellectual engagement and public service opportunity.

12. Regulatory leaders cement the salary differential by discounting the need for credentials. We require licenses for pedicurists but not for rate case witnesses; we award "certificates" for conference attendance but not for subject matter mastery. Utilities, in contrast, require advanced credentials for plant operators, fiscal officials, executive officers—anyone whose hand or pen touches operations, finance, or management.

13. The difference in credentialing reinforces, unremarkably, the difference in salaries; leading, unremarkably, to a difference in motivation and morale; leading, unremarkably, to a difference in tenure for the talented. They spend their formative years learning on the taxpayer dime, then move to the regulated sector. No one with the power to fix the problem notices or reacts.

## Politicians: Support or Undermine?

14. The governor influences the commission non-transparently, "requesting" outcomes on behalf of interest groups. The commission consents, rather than reminding the governor, transparently, that her influence over sitting commissioners is no greater than any other citizen.

15. When the commission makes the tough calls (e.g., utility service cannot be below-cost-but-high-quality, shareholder investment cannot be low-risk-but-high-profit), politicians join the protests rather than signal support.

16. The legislature diminishes the commission's stature by passing laws urged by interest groups without clearing them with the commission.

## "Bigger is Better"

17. To support its proposals for mergers and corporate restructuring, the utility asserts its "need to position itself competitively." The commission adopts the argument, viewing its regulatory duty as supporting the utility's competitive interests. The irony of using government orders to serve a private competitive interest, and the resulting market distortion, goes unnoticed. (There is a difference between (a) keeping a well-performing utility monopoly financially capable of providing its obligatory service, and (b) becoming a volunteer in the utility's competitive campaigns. When that difference disappears, when "bigger

is better" becomes the guide for decisions, the utility's goals become the commission's. That's capture.)

18. Along with supporting the utility's expansion, the commission protects the utility from contraction. Some commissions cite "competition" as a basis for approving utility proposals, but then undermine competition by resisting competitors' proposals—proposals to perform functions currently assigned to the utility. These commissions' reason for resisting—a reason offered by the utility and adopted by the commission—is that reducing the utility's role will weaken its ability to perform. (This approach confuses total profit with rate of profit. A utility whose obligatory, exclusive role shrinks will see lower total profits; but its return on equity, its coverage ratios and its other financial metrics can remain strong.)

\* \* \*

The warning signs of capture are not the actions of utilities, but the actions and inactions of regulators. This makes the term "regulatory capture" both imprecise and inaccurate. The "captured" commission's cage is not locked and guarded by its enemies; its door is opened and closed by the commission itself. The next essay will discuss ways to escape—and how to avoid capture to begin with.

# 22

# "Regulatory Capture" III: How Can Commissioners Avoid and Escape It?

> Courage and perseverance have a magical talisman, before which difficulties disappear, and obstacles vanish into air.
>
> John Quincy Adams

The two preceding essays defined regulatory capture and described the warning signs. A commission is "captured" if it persists in "being persuaded," based on the persuader's identity rather than an argument's merits. Capture's warning signs include (a) a void where vision should lie, (b) priorities and procedures that reflect parties' requests rather than public interest priorities, (c) a chronic resource differential between the regulator and regulated, and (d) fair-weather politicians whose support for regulation sags under pressure from those who would weaken it.

The bad news is that regulatory capture is always a risk. The good news is that many in our community embody capture-resistance. Their common characteristics include long tenure, expertise (if not in utilities, then in government operations), confidence in their future employability regardless of whom they irritate, and the ear and respect of the governor and legislature. Among the many I've worked with, for, or before are Susan Ackerman, Bob Anthony, Peter Bradford, Sam Bratton, Ashley Brown, Carl Caliboso, Paul Centolella, Rich Cowart, Michael Dworkin, Mike Florio, Jeanne Fox, Dave Hadley, Bill Massey, Brandon Presley, Paul Roberti, Cheryl Roberto, Judy Sheldrew, Charles Stalon, Jon Wellinghoff and the late Brian Moline. How can we replicate their characteristics in our commissions?

First, a word on where to aim the effort: at helping commissions avoid or escape capture, not at preventing parties from attempting it. Attempts are inevitable. As Cole Porter sang, everyone does it: "Birds do it, bees do it, even educated fleas do it …. Some Argentines without means do it; I hear even Boston beans do it."[49] Utilities, consumers, environmentalists, workers: Everyone tries to capture the commission. These attempts are both unavoidable and non-preventable. Once we prohibit actual crimes, like dollar-filled shoeboxes and jobs-for-votes trading, the First Amendment kicks in; persuasion is constitutionally protected. But capture—the "state of being persuaded"—is not. The aim is to shrink the susceptibility to capture. That is what we can do something about.

"Captured" can describe both a person and an institution, so the solutions are both personal and institutional. The personal protection is the armor of attributes described in the first four essays: purposefulness, education, decisiveness, and independence. Here are five institutional elements.

**Go back to the big questions:** "Ask and you shall receive" (Luke 11:9–12) works as biblical reassurance, but it is a recipe for regulatory somnambulance. The utility's legal right to seek a benefit is not a right to frame the case.[50] The alert commission will reframe the utility's request as a public interest question; specifically, "Products, prices, performance: What do customers deserve?" "Market structures and corporate structures: Which ones produce the best performance?" Reframing means the public interest dog wags the utility's tail, not the other way around.

**Connect commission performance to industry performance:** Regulation works when we link inputs to outputs, when we design commission actions to produce industry performance. This chain has four links: (a) describe a public interest vision, measured in results (investment, innovation, prices, service quality, safety); (b) shape internal commission actions (budgeting, staffing, education) to prepare for external actions (orders aimed at performance); (c) take external actions to induce utilities and consumers to produce that performance; and (d) evaluate and revise. As Peter Drucker wrote, "What is measured, improves."[51]

**To professionals, offer indispensable roles and advancement opportunities:** Once the wages are sufficient, professionals crave achievement. Connect professional achievement to industry performance, and you have a commission culture that perpetuates improvement within and without. Each department should have, for each department head and employee, a work plan that recognizes their indispensable roles, propels them to achieve, and expects them to advance. That work plan must be backed by an education plan. Instead of budgeting for undefined

---

[49] *Let's Do It, Let's Fall in Love.*
[50] See Chapter 41, "'Framing': Does It Divert Regulatory Attention?"
[51] Peter Drucker, *The Effective Executive.*

"training," design individual education plans that, according to accountable schedules, grow juniors into seniors—leaders in the regulatory profession. And pay them their utility equivalent in salaries. Professional staff being the commission's core, these education plans deserve resources and momentum uncompromised by arbitrary budget caps, or by overwork caused by staff shortages. Recruiting and nurturing professionals, and paying them their worth, is more cost-effective than wishing and watching: wishing utilities would perform better, and watching the best commission employees migrate to private sector jobs.

**Insist on resources:** As the preceding essay explained, a captured commission "devotes more resources to processing parties' petitions than to pursuing its own priorities." This sad state occurs when legislatures impose deadlines without providing enough funding. The habit is to cap the commission's resources arbitrarily, basing next year's budget on last year's, regardless of new demands. Instead, allow the commission to set and fund its own budget. The funding source can vary with the activity. Charging fees for utility requests, the fee levels varying with the case's complexity, ensures sufficient resources while assigning costs to the cost-causer. When a utility proposes a conglomerate merger lacking a public interest purpose, the cost of regulatory review belongs with the merging parties, not the taxpayers or ratepayers. For commission-initiated work, the revenue source can be general fees charged to the utilities based on some combination of revenues, profits and assets, with these fees recoverable through ratepayer charges, since ratepayers are the beneficiaries. This approach produces symmetry: Utilities recover their legitimate regulatory costs through rates; so should the regulator.

Yes, the commission could overfund itself, and there are agencies that act inefficiently. But until we hear of commissions with surplus, we can assume that the risk of overfunding is lower than the risk of under-regulating. For commissions that spend inefficiently (which is different from over-regulating), the solution is not to cut their staff but to help them spend wisely. A regular assist from independent experts in commission management, coupled with supportive legislative and executive oversight, should be par for all state agencies inside and outside regulation.

**Make hearings issue-centric and commission-centric, not party-centric and lawyer-centric:** Most regulatory hearings are a cross between boxing and ping pong. Questions and answers fly between lawyer and witness, each trying to out-hit, out-fake, out-spin and out-smart the other. Based on parties' positions rather than the public's needs, the verbal friction produces more heat than light; the ratio of useful information to hours consumed is always low. Through most of this counterpunching, the commissioners are spectators, occasionally interrupting to separate the combatants from their clinches or to ask a few "follow-ups." Try reversing the order and the priority: The main questioners should be the commissioners, and their questions should come first. Further, organize the hearings by issue, not parties. For each issue, put all opposing witnesses on a panel. Then, cause them to compete for the commission's favor by helping solve the commission's problems rather than defending their clients' interests. Once the commission has extracted the value it wants, the parties' lawyers can cross-examine—if any need remains. This approach emphasizes commission goals over private party strategies, and it reverses the ratio of commissioner questions to cross-examiner questions from 5:95 to 95:5. Most importantly, it causes the commission to enter the room with a goal and a plan—to lead rather than to preside. Everyone still gets his or her say, but everyone learns more.

* * *

"Regulatory capture" is too frequently attempted, too readily accepted. The attempts are not preventable, but acceptance is not inevitable. To avoid and escape capture, focus on the big questions, on planning for performance. Acquire the resources and shape the procedures that make the commission central rather than marginal.

# 23

# The War of Words: Competition vs. Regulation I

> [The] "central, continuing responsibility of legislatures and regulatory commissions [is] finding the best possible mix of inevitably imperfect regulation and inevitably imperfect competition."
>
> Alfred Kahn, *The Economics of Regulation: Principles and Institutions*, Vol. I, at p.xxxvii; Volume II at p.114 (1988 ed.)

Alfred Kahn said it all. Resist either/or, expect imperfection, show curiosity continuously. Skip the ideology; use facts, intellect, integrity, and humility. These are the paths toward "the best possible mix of inevitably imperfect regulation and inevitably imperfect competition."

To what end? Competition and regulation share a common purpose—to align private behavior with the public interest. Effective competition induces competitors toward efficiency, customer service and reliability. Effective regulation does the same. Together, they cause accountability—to the consumers, investors, and the public.

Do our debates over market structure serve this purpose? Do we emulate Kahn's insistence on facts, intellect, integrity, humility, and the absence of ideology? How well do our words assist our aims?

## The Stakes

At stake are trillions of investor and consumer dollars, the reliability of our infrastructure, and the health of our economy. In the electric industry, FERC and the states struggle to determine the mix of competition and regulation, at both wholesale and retail. Their efforts intertwine. Wholesale markets need wholesale buyers. But there will be no wholesale buyers if states, distrusting wholesale markets, order their utilities to build rather than buy. Effective wholesale competition requires efficient price signals to retail customers. But those signals remain blurred when retail prices reflect average embedded cost rather than hour-by-hour production cost. Effective retail competition requires a host of factors: multiple, viable sellers; economic access to bottleneck facilities; active, educated shoppers; and the absence of unearned incumbent advantages. But the politics of retail competition often demand deviations from these principles: The incumbent utilities insist on competing in the immature markets, using their century-long advantage against the newcomers; while customers insist on "protection from competition" in the form of artificial rate caps.

The telecommunications industry has struggled with similar questions. In the many markets for telecommunications services, when are competitive forces sufficiently vigorous, sustained and customer-responsive so that traditional policies like "carrier of last resort," "universal service," quality of service, and intercarrier cooperation no longer require regulatory mandates?

## Semantic Suboptimality: Three Examples

Conversation about regulation is challenging, because it is difficult to distill its complexity. But our efforts to abbreviate have produced phrases that are oversimplified to the point of meaninglessness. Consider three examples.

"Deregulation": To the experienced practitioner, this term means "The statute authorizes entry by multiple competitors." But the term is hopelessly ambiguous because (a) "authorized" competition is not "effective" competition; (b) authorized competition, after a century of monopoly, still requires "regulation" for licensing, fraud prevention, access to bottleneck facilities, prevention of affiliate abuse, and assurance of last-resort service; (c) the term literally could mean either "elimination" or "reduction" of regulation (e.g., the term "decelerate" means reduce speed, not eliminate all motion); and (d) if implemented incorrectly, the result of "deregulation" is still "regulation," except that it is regulation of the market by the incumbent to protect its position, rather than regulation of the incumbent by the commission to protect consumers.

Proponents of "deregulation" intend the prefix "de-" to replace a negative (regulation) with a positive (elimination of regulation). But the phrase cannily avoids accountability; for if they labeled their goal "effective competition" rather than "deregulation" they'd have to show evidence in place of rhetoric. The converse applies as well: Critics of "deregulation" imply that "regulation" creates benefits, but they do not always identify (and guarantee) those benefits. In short, the bipolarity implicit in "deregulation" makes discussions more stick-figured than sophisticated.

**"Competition works":** I once shared a panel with someone who said, platitudinously, "Competition works." How much ambiguity can two words hold? "*Competition*" in which geographic markets? Which product markets? For which consumer segments? During which time periods? "*Works*" when? Overnight? After years of investment by newcomers, during which time period incumbents enjoy "first mover advantage" without facing competitive pressure? "Works" how well? For whom? For the incumbent? For the newcomer? For some customers? For all customers? How does someone say "Competition works," without being "hooked" off the stage, vaudeville-style? Why does our community tolerate such mental muddiness?

**"Market share":** In the electric industry, we often say that "generation is competitive." Competitiveness refers to a market. A market has a geographic component and a product component, and sometimes a temporal component. "Generation" is not a market. "Generating capacity serving Maryland's Eastern Shore on August afternoons" is a market. A company can own a generating unit constituting one percent of the generating capacity in the PJM region (Ohio to Virginia), suggesting, to a layperson, no market power. But due to locational luck, those same generating units could constitute 90 percent of the capacity available to a transmission-constrained subregion on a hot afternoon. "Generation" is not a market.

Further, low "market share" does not readily translate into low "market influence." The reason lies in the distinction between "market share" and "pivotality." Both are necessary to measure competitiveness. A company can have a small market share (say, 1 percent), yet in certain time periods be "pivotal." A pivotal supplier is an indispensable supplier—its supply is essential to meet demand at the specific time. If the total capacity in a market is 100 MW, and demand is 95 MW, then any supplier with more than 5 MW of capacity (a mere 5 percent of the total) is indispensable, because if that supplier withdraws its supply a blackout occurs. At the other end of the market share spectrum, a company can have a high market share (say, 75 percent), but if there are potential entrants poised at the perimeter, their entry threat can discipline even a monopolist. Facts matter.

## A Sequence of Questions

In these three examples, efforts at semantic simplicity yield words with multiple meanings. Confusion replaces comprehension. Finding the "best possible mix" of competition and regulation is complicated. Our language should expose that complexity, not hide it. Dinner guests will wish they'd never asked (it happens to me all the time), but at least they'll understand why. Instead of opining on "competition vs. regulation," consider framing a sequence of questions:

1. Which geographic and product markets do we wish to discuss?

2. Is competition economically desirable (i.e., are economies of scale and scope sufficiently low that competition will not damage "static efficiency")? (See the work of Dr. John Kwoka of Northeastern University.) And if there is potential loss of "static efficiency," will this loss be offset by gains in "dynamic efficiency" as the rivals pressure each other? (Thanks to Dr. Kenneth Rose for his explanation of the difference between "static" and "dynamic" efficiency.)

3. Is competition technically feasible? Can the physical and communications networks accommodate the new traffic stimulated by competition?

4. Are consumers ready and willing to shop? Theories must confront practice. If consumers are too busy going to work, attending soccer games, and cooking meals to compare prices and offerings, competition will not work.

# 24

# The War of Words: Competition vs. Regulation II

Words strain,
Crack and sometimes, break, under the burden,
Under the tension, slip, slide, perish,
Decay with imprecision, will not stay in place,
Will not stay still.

T.S. Eliot, "Burnt Norton," *Four Quartets* (1943), quoted in Edward Tufte, *Beautiful Evidence* at p. 139 (2006)

---

**The preceding essay** addressed ambiguities and imprecisions in our conversations about "competition" and "regulation." Some commenters said the essay aimed arrows disproportionately at competition-speak. I acknowledge the imbalance but intended no bias. To compensate, this next essay addresses regulation-speak. These two essays intend no critique of "competition" or "regulation." Their aim is conversational clarity.

In utility regulation, three of the most commonly used phrases are "revenue requirement," "cost-based pricing," and "subsidy." Let's consider their multiple meanings.

### "Revenue Requirement"

This phrase dominates ratemaking. It forces attention to the utility's need for revenues sufficient to cover the expenses and capital costs (including reasonable profit) associated with serving the public.

Ambiguity arises because the term "requirement" carries two distinct meanings. First is the *utility's* requirement: the dollars the utility needs to cover its costs, including building, operating, maintaining and replacing the infrastructure;

paying its taxes; compensating its employees and vendors; paying interest on its debt; and paying shareholders sufficient returns to attract and retain their dollars.

Second is the *legal* requirement. Regulatory law, in the form of statutes and the Constitution (specifically, the Takings Clause of the Fifth Amendment), nowhere *guarantees* revenues sufficient to meet the utility's needs. The law requires only a "fair opportunity" to earn a reasonable return. Legally required revenues (what the utility is entitled to receive) can differ from utility-required revenues (what the utility needs to receive) for at least two reasons. First, commissions need not authorize recovery of imprudent costs, even if their non-recovery drives a utility's actual return on equity below the level normally "required" to attract capital. Second, if actual cost levels exceed, and/or sales levels fall below, the estimates used to compute the revenue requirement, there is no legal requirement to "true up" the revenues by allowing retroactive rate increases (except where statutes specify recovery, such as with fuel adjustment clauses or extraordinary storm costs).

So the phrase "revenue *requirement*" sends a linguistic signal that is misleading, implying a regulator's obligation to ensure cost recovery. The law leaves the regulator more running room.

## "Cost-Based Pricing"

Experienced utterers of this phrase usually mean "a price set by regulators rather than the market." But what type of "cost" do we mean? Historic cost or future cost? Embedded cost, marginal cost or variable cost? If marginal cost, long-term or short-term? If variable cost, average variable cost or variable cost at the margin? Replacement cost or reproduction cost? Practitioners have seen "cost-based" prices based on each of these factors. And since when are "market-based prices" not "cost-based"? Economists tell us that if the market is effectively competitive, price will tend toward a cost basis—specifically, marginal cost.

Further, in the phrase "cost-based pricing," what does "based" mean? Is "cost" a starting point or an ending point? For example, commenters usually distinguish "performance-based ratemaking" (PBR) from "cost-based ratemaking." But designers of PBR typically start with a baseline of historic cost, then inject "X" factors for productivity gains or losses, passthroughs for various unavoidable costs, and "sharing mechanisms" that allocate excess returns between shareholders and ratepayers. For each, there is a cost basis.

While more clarity would assist policymaking, there is a deeper problem here. The phrases "revenue requirement" and "cost-based pricing" enjoy an iconic status that distracts from a disturbing fact: They produce prices remote from economic efficiency. Economic efficiency is not regulation's only goal, but it's a good starting point, since inefficiency means we can make someone better off without making anyone worse off. Who's against that?

There is legitimate debate over what price-types produce economic efficiency, but embedded cost pricing is not in the running. Embedded cost pricing persists because our focus is on "revenue requirement." Embedded cost pricing is the way we allocate the revenue requirement (the revenues a utility needs to recover its costs and earn a reasonable profit) among all customers based on their likely demand and consumption, so as to make full cost recovery likely. Embedded cost pricing does have some elements that aim at economic efficiency, such as allocating some portion of load-related costs in proportion to load, and striving to place some fixed costs in fixed charges and all variable costs in variable charges. But the central purpose of embedded cost pricing is recovery of the revenue requirement, not economic efficiency. For a century, our profession has placed two compatible goals (sufficient compensation and economic efficiency) in conflict. Had we relabeled "cost-based rates" as "rates that deprive society of savings," we might have fixed them faster.

## "Subsidy"

There is no denying this word's political content. Russell Long, the former Chairman of the U.S. Senate's Finance Committee, used to say, "A tax loophole is something that benefits the other guy. If it benefits you, it is tax reform." And, on one's responsibility for government's costs, he said: "Don't tax you, don't tax me, tax that fellow behind the tree." It's the same with "subsidy." If the allocation benefits you, it's a "subsidy"; if it benefits me, it's "investment."

Even at the technical, nonpolitical level, there are multiple definitions of "subsidy." I was taught that a subsidy occurs when the regulator sets a customer's price below incremental cost, because then the customer's act of consumption causes costs that others (either shareholders or other customers) must bear. This consumption also reduces society's wealth, because when price is below the cost caused by the consumption, the consumer over-consumes, wastefully.

Would that that were the only definition. Many people use "subsidy" to describe any situation in which one person bears *any* costs (not just incremental cost) attributable to someone else. This definition differs from my prior one, because in the former case the subsidy occurs only when the subsidisee causes *new* costs, whereas in the generic definition the subsidisee avoids an appropriate share of *existing or* new costs. Allocating sunk costs on a basis other than load share is not necessarily a subsidy. It can cause inefficiency, especially if the sunk costs are recovered through a variable charge, but that is not a subsidy. This definition appears in multiple other situations, such as when (a) the customer's contribution to fixed costs deviates from his contribution to the utility's load; (b) different customer classes pay rates that produce different returns on utility investment incurred for those classes; (c) an allocation of costs between fixed and variable charges results in some high-consumption consumers paying, through their consumption, for fixed costs incurred initially to serve low-consumption consumers; and (d) average cost pricing, when there is variation in the cost to serve different locations—as, for example, when urban customers complain that they "subsidize" rural customers because the urban service costs are below average while rural service costs are above average.

A common, clearer definition of the term would decrease its political content and increase its usefulness.

## Recommendations

When terms carry political or propagandist content, they make dialogue and decisionmaking difficult. The recommendation is simple: When we speak, take care to define; when we listen, ask for the definitions. The clearer the conversation, the better the decisions. See especially Georgetown linguistics Professor Deborah Tannen's book, *The Argument Culture: Stopping America's War of Words* (1998).

# 25

# Is Learning to Regulate Like Learning to Cook?

The book is "Mastering the Art of French Cooking"—
not "How To" or "Made Easy" or "For Dummies," but
"Mastering the Art." In other words, cooking that omelet is
part of a demanding, exalted discipline not to be entered
into frivolously or casually. But at the same time: You can
do it. It is a matter of technique, of skill, of practice.

A.O. Scott, "Two for the Stove," *New York Times* (Aug. 7, 2009)

The secret is to pat dry your beef before you brown it.

Michael Pollan, "Out of the Kitchen, Onto the Couch," *New York Times Magazine* (Aug. 2, 2009) (referring to success at cooking *boeuf bourguignon*)

---

**Don't miss the** movie *Julie & Julia*, in which one icon of integrity (Meryl Streep) plays another (Julia Child). We learn how one tall student-chef-writer-teacher displaced mystery with mastery. Meanwhile, science journalist Michael Pollan (author of *The Omnivore's Dilemma*) wants us to cook for ourselves more, consume what others sell less. Are there analogs here to inspire our regulators? Consider ten quotes from Pollan's piece, divided into two main themes.

## Pre-Fabbed Food: Consumption without Quality

1. Pollan bemoans "the rise of fast food, home-meal replacements and the decline and fall of everyday home cooking." Regulators get executive

summaries, 15-minute panelists, and PowerPoint—more pitch than empowerment, the bullets blaring the obvious while concealing complexities. (See Professor Edward Tufte's monograph, *The Cognitive Style of PowerPoint: Pitching Out Corrupts Within*). The focus is on audience consumption, not audience engagement.

2. "[A] great many Americans are spending considerably more time watching images of cooking on television than they are cooking themselves—an increasingly archaic activity they will tell you they no longer have the time for." Do commissioners spend more time watching advocates argue for their interests, rather than studying objective materials? And what about the performers—how many are real cooks? Are regulatory witnesses the real cooks—people who actually run things, make things work—or are they spokespeople, stand-ins for the real thing, performers with a script, who make hard decisions look easy? Can we really learn cooking from such performances? Can we really learn regulation from actors?

3. "Many of today's cooking programs rely unapologetically on ingredients that themselves contain lots of ingredients: canned soups, jarred mayonnaise, frozen vegetables, powdered sauces, vanilla wafers, limeade concentrate, Marshmallow Fluff." How many of the presentations we hear offer canned arguments, frozen positions, assertions more powdery than persuasive, rhetorical fluff substituting for researched facts?

4. "[P]rocessed foods have so thoroughly colonized the American kitchen and diet that they have redefined what passes today for cooking, not to mention food." Does advocacy argument now so dominate regulatory conversation—at informal conferences and in formal proceedings—that regulators have no space in which to use their own instincts, develop their own records, do their own thinking?

5. "Over the years, the food scientists have gotten better and better at simulating real food, keeping it looking attractive and seemingly fresh...." Did you know that "food psychologists" have discovered a magic ratio of surface tension to internal "give," so that designers of candy bars and tortilla chips can induce in humans the repeated act of moving the product from bag to hand to mouth, almost mindlessly? Do regulatory lobbyists employ their own magic—phrases that induce reflexive agreement rather than stimulate independent thought?

6. Pre-fabricated food is "bound to go heavy on sugar, fat, and salt; these are three tastes we're hardwired to like, which happen to be dirt cheap to add and do a good job masking the shortcomings of processed food." With what ingredients do advocates appeal to our hard wiring, sacrificing future health to current

consumption? Do they emphasize short-term benefits to distract us from long-term costs? Do their opponents emphasize short-term costs to distract us from long-term benefits? Are we hardwired to accept statements like "Everyone else is doing it," "The situation is urgent," and "This is not a precedent"?

7. "... [A]s the 'time cost' of [commercial] food preparation has fallen, calorie consumption has gone up, particularly consumption of the sort of snack and convenience foods that are typically cooked outside the home.... [W]hen we don't have to cook meals, we eat more of them...." Pollan cites a decline in the percentage of the family dollar used by a human being actually making food. By eating out rather than cooking in, we overconsume what others want to feed us. What percentage of a regulator's time goes to listening to the persuaders, rather than the people who actually make a utility run well? A northwestern regulator told me his governor had urged him to get outside the hearing room and inside the control room—to see what utility employees actually do. Do we make time to do it?

## Culinary Competitions: Converting a Nation of Cooks into an Audience of Consumers

8. Television's Food Network has "shifted [its] target audience from people who love to cook to people who love to eat." Do we consume the arguments of others more than we create thoughts of our own?

9. Consider "'Iron Chef,' where famous restaurant chefs wage gladiatorial combat." These culinary contests focus more on competition than communication. The contestants make miracles that home cooks could never replicate. Do our hearing rooms host battles for position, or opportunities for education?

10. "If you ask me, the key to victory on any of these shows comes down to one factor: bacon." Is there, in every advocacy argument, some special ingredient, some theme, phrase, or flourish that, being both soothing and filling, seems so inarguable as to sway the psyche? Do phrases like customer "harm," financial "integrity," "reliability," "global competition," "light-handed regulation," and "green" induce us to swallow dishes that, exposed, we might send back?

Julia Child "filled the air with common sense and uncommon scent" (Harvard University citation accompanying her honorary doctorate). She succeeded the hard way: through technique, analysis, and practice. As can regulators. So what will be our goal—finding "The Next Food Network Star" or "Mastering the Art"?

# PART FOUR
## Regulatory Courage

---

Courageous regulators deal with dissatisfaction by recasting the conversation. Rates are not "high" or "low"; they are right or wrong. Courageous regulators choose between "regulation" and "competition" based on facts, not philosophy. They understand that while affordable service is a societal goal, regulation's role is to price properly, then press legislators to help the poor. Consumer protection, an oft-cited purpose of regulation, is protection from abuse by monopolies, not from costs caused by the consumer. Consumers must carry their own weight.

Courageous regulators also are critics. They call out those who impose new mandates without considering the costs, and those who confuse "all of the above" with coherent policy.

# 26
# "Affordable" Utility Service: What is Regulation's Role?

> There are those who look at things the way they are, and ask why. I dream of things that never were, and ask why not.
>
> Robert F. Kennedy

When the nation's economy is stressed, politicians pressure regulators to make utility service "affordable." This picture has three problems.

## Wealth Redistribution Is Not Regulation's Department

Under embedded cost ratemaking, the regulator identifies prudent costs, computes a revenue requirement to cover those costs, predicts consumer consumption, then designs rates that are likely to produce the required revenue. Each customer category bears the costs it causes. None of these steps involves affordability. Affordability becomes a factor only if we jigger the numbers—if we lower rates for the unfortunate by raising rates for others. Achieving affordability through rate design means compromising cost causation to redistribute wealth. It resembles taxation of one class to benefit another, with this exception: With taxation, citizens can retire representatives whose votes offend; but with utility service, captive customers are stuck with the rates regulators set.

Instead of shifting costs between customer classes, regulators might redistribute wealth in a different way: by "taxing" shareholders, i.e., lowering utility rates by reducing shareholder returns below the appropriate level. But tapping shareholders to help the unlucky is no more the regulator's domain than is tapping other customers. And in the context of regulation, it's unlawful. Having invested to serve the public, shareholders legitimately expect to earn the constitutionally mandated "just compensation," undiminished by a forced contribution for affordability.

Moving money among citizens is essential to a fair society. Poverty is intolerable, private charity never suffices, so government steps in. But helping the luckless should be done by political leaders, who must justify their actions to the electorate, not by professional regulators whose focus must be industry performance.

Affordability of any given product—groceries, mansions, or utility service—depends on one's wealth and income and on the cost of other products. The poor could better afford utility service if we raised their income and increased their wealth. Or if we lowered their costs of housing, healthcare, transportation or education. But these initiatives are outside regulators' authority. To make regulators responsible for affordability is illogical.

## Cheap Energy Is Cheap Politics

Politicians who argue for affordability take the easy road. They like to legislate economic development, "greenness," reliability, energy independence, and technology leadership—all efforts that *increase* costs, at least in the short term. To legislate these improvements, while simultaneously calling on regulators to make service "affordable," is low-risk politics, responsibility-avoidance politics, cheap politics.

When politicians call for "lower rates," the electorate feels entitled to receive rather than urged to contribute. But no family, no congregation, no civil society thrives if its key verb is "take" rather than "give." And when artificially low rates now lead to higher costs later, citizens become cynical. And self-doubting, as they question their ability to distinguish pander from policy. These are the results when politicians avoid their responsibility for affordability.

## "Affordability" Undermines Regulation's Responsibility

Mathematician Carson Chow says he's found the cause of our obesity epidemic: low food prices. Studying 40 years of data, he spotted both correlation and causation between girth growth and cost declines. He traced these trends to government farm policy shifts (from paying for non-production to stimulating full production) and technology boosts (which lowered production costs). The lower the cost, the more production; the more production, the more (fast) food; the more food, the more calories available; the more calories available, the more calories consumed.[52]

---

[52] See C. Dreifus, "A Mathematical Challenge to Obesity," *The New York Times* (May 14, 2012).

We are both over-consuming and under-appreciating: Dr. Chow found that "Americans are wasting food at a progressively increasing rate."[53]

What does food have to do with "affordable" utility service? A regulator's job is to regulate—to establish performance standards, then align compensation with compliance. In this equation, affordability is not a variable. To make service affordable to the unlucky, the commission would have to lower the price below cost. That leads to overconsumption, to Dr. Chow's "waste." This inefficiency hurts everyone.

Economic efficiency exists when no further action can create benefits without increasing costs by more than the benefits. Conversely, economic inefficiency exists when we forego some action that, if taken, can make someone better off without making anyone worse off. To over-consume, to waste, to act inefficiently, to leave a benefit on the table, makes everyone worse off. Underpricing in the name of affordability makes someone worse off unnecessarily. How sensible is that?

## Actions for Affordability: The Right Roles for Regulators

Unless essential services are affordable, government will not be credible. Regulators, being part of government, have to help. (A commission staff chief once told me, "Sometimes you have to put aside your principles and do what's right.") And some regulatory statutes explicitly require the regulator to make service "affordable." (As is the case, I am told, in Vanuatu, an 83-island nation in the South Pacific.) Here are three ways, consistent with economic efficiency, for regulators to address affordability.

**Help the unlucky reduce usage.** Regulators can advocate for affordability by pressing for policies that make consumption less costly, like improved housing stock, "orbs" that signal high prices, and efficient lighting and appliances. Analogy: Doctors save lives not just by treating gunshot wounds, but by advocating for gun safety. (American Academy of Pediatrics: "The absence of guns from children's homes and communities is the most reliable and effective measure to prevent firearm-related injuries ....")

**Interpret "affordability" as long-term affordability.** Getting prices right and preventing overconsumption, even if it raises prices in the short run, reduces total costs in the long run.

**Expose the dark side of underpricing.** Rather than follow politicians down the low-price, low-risk, cheap politics path, regulators can emulate Dr. Chow by talking facts: about the real costs of utility service, the problem of

---

[53] Fairness point: Chow has his doubters. See Michael Moyer, "The Mathematician's Obesity Fallacy," *Scientific American* (May 15, 2012).

overconsumption, the error of underpricing. With their credibility rooted in expertise, regulators can pressure legislators to act on affordability directly by enacting income-raising policies. Better education, housing, health care, access to fresh food—all these lead to higher incomes, so that citizens can afford utility service priced properly.

# 27

# Low Rates, High Rates, Wrong Rates, Right Rates

One fish, Two fish, Red fish, Blue fish.
Black fish, Blue fish, Old fish, New fish.

Dr. Seuss (1960)

### Utility Cost Increases—Big Ones—Are Unavoidable

In the U.S. utility industries, the long-deferred capital needs are heading north of hundreds of billions of dollars. Electricity faces shrinking capacity margins, transmission construction for new renewables, the possible return of nuclear power, and the likelihood of climate change legislation. Natural gas needs billions for new main and service pipes and compliance with new federal safety regulations. Water, too: The EPA says that over the next two decades, we need $500 billion to $1 trillion for water and wastewater infrastructure improvement and replacement. Telecommunications decisionmakers are considering universal access to broadband. Utility employees' pensions are now underfunded due to stock value declines.

Are we ready to raise rates? What are the obstacles? What are the solutions? Getting rates right is integral to effective regulation. The purpose of regulation is performance: setting standards for excellence, then enforcing compliance. The traditional focus is on the performance of the sellers: How well are they operating today's infrastructure while planning and creating tomorrow's? What about the performance of the buyers? Regulators serve the public interest, the public interest includes economic efficiency (biggest bang for buck, maximizing benefits for all), and economic efficiency requires getting rates right so consumers do not waste scarce resources. So regulators do address customer performance. Where economical customer performance requires higher rates, are regulators ready to do the job?

## Four Obstacles to Getting Rates Right

**Blurred mission:** Utility regulation has a "consumer protection" component. But protection from what? In traditional markets, consumers depend on a single seller, so "protection" means protection from excessive prices and inadequate quality. Have we allowed this "consumer protection" purpose to transmogrify from protection against monopoly inefficiency to protection against high costs in general? Some regulators define their effectiveness by how their rates rank. Some lobby against climate change legislation because it will "raise rates." Rates are not right or wrong based on whether they are low or high but based on whether they make customers pay for the costs they cause.

**Lulled customers:** Years-long rate freezes lull the public into viewing rate stability as an entitlement. Then when the commission realigns rates with cost, we know what happens: (1) Voters don't offer thanks for the prior windfall; they protest the new levels, loudly. (2) Politicians fan these flames, making rational policy-making difficult. (3) Some compromise arrives, usually deferring pain rather than sharing pain. What often works in politics—mediating between positions—rarely works in regulation, where the midpoint between two wrong answers is a third wrong answer.

**Skeptical public:** When a utility seeks a rate increase, the public usually blames the utility because the public is reflexively skeptical of bigness. This public reaction is asymmetrical: Citizens take for granted the technical achievements that give us electricity production, water flows, gas transportation and instant telecommunications, all delivered nearly flawlessly. It's easy to view costs as concocted. This skepticism has its bases: the utility that swears that the $100 million increase is necessary for "viability," only to settle, satisfied, at $65 million; the merger proposal that cites "synergies" that no one can prove or disprove; the persistent asymmetry in persuasive resources that allows utilities to occupy the most space in the evidentiary record.[54] In regulation, trust requires verification; verification requires resources. If the public remains uninformed and thinks all rates are rip-offs, efforts to explain will have no traction.

**Utility hesitance:** A utility has reputational risk. Rate increases produce headlines, commission audits, politicians' denouncements. There also is financial risk. Some utilities hesitate to make infrastructural investments without advance regulatory commitments of ratepayer dollars. (This hesitation is not necessarily lawful. A utility may not delay necessary investment because it worries whether regulators

---

[54] See Chapters 50 and 51, "Regulatory Resources: Do the Differentials Make a Difference?" (Parts I and II).

will set rates right. It must act when action is necessary and if rates are insufficient, take the commission to court.)

In sum: This combination of regulatory hesitance, lulled customers, customer skepticism and utility hesitance produces headwind in our efforts to make rates right.

## Five Responses

How can regulators help the public accept necessary rate increases? Here are five thoughts.

**Accountable planning:** Commissions should direct their utilities to produce an inventory of all capital needs, their cost, and a proposed schedule, all continuously updated. Inside utilities, there should be task forces containing the relevant engineering, finance, quality control and regulatory affairs experts to create and manage the projects. The public should see a full improvement plan before it hears of rate increases. The purpose of rates is not to cover costs but to compensate for performance.

**Regulatory resources:** Regulatory staff must be sufficient in size, compensation, and expertise to evaluate billion-dollar proposals and multi-year performance. Insufficient staff means passive oversight—an oxymoron.

**Cost recovery commitment:** When should regulators commit ratepayer dollars: at project commencement, project completion, or project milestones? Each choice has tradeoffs.[55] If utilities are to commit to a project, commissions must commit to cost recovery.

**Rate design:** Until the late 1980s, ratemaking focused on making the utility whole: We calculated the revenue requirement, then allocated fixed costs among customer categories. From there, we set rates based on some combination of customer demand, customer usage and political sensitivity (i.e., when regulators allocate to some customer classes a share of fixed costs that varies from their share of demand). Economic efficiency made an occasional appearance (remember the studies on "marginal cost pricing" in the 1980s?), but it was hardly center stage. Decades of declining costs gave no hint of today's infrastructural needs. We know better now. Rate design is key to consumer protection. To moderate cost increases, we must moderate the demands that cause costs. Rate design offers the double anti-oxymoron: Price increases are consumer protection because price increases yield lower total costs. Prices must track costs when those costs are caused: seasonally, daily, even hourly.

---

[55] See Scott Hempling and Scott Strauss, *Pre-Approval Commitments: When And Under What Conditions Should Regulators Commit Ratepayer Dollars to Utility-Proposed Capital Projects?* (National Regulatory Research Institute 08-12 Nov. 2008).

**Political leadership:** Leadership requires followers committed to the leader's mission.[56] Commissions must have understandings with legislatures about the capital program, the utilities' obligations, the commission's role, and the commission's resource needs. Those understandings will reduce surprises while discouraging forum shopping—those episodic, opportunistic efforts to have legislatures anoint some technologies or capital programs over others, without basis in careful cost comparisons. And when legislators appreciate the regulator's job, legislators will be more likely to do their job. That job includes helping the unlucky with their incomes, so that regulators can expose customers to the real costs of their consumption.[57]

All involved—commissioners, staff, utilities, legislators, practitioners, and the public—must share clear expectations: Infrastructure upgrade and modernization is essential, it must happen, and it will cost.

---

[56] See Garry Wills, *Uncertain Trumpets: The Nature of Leadership* (2007).

[57] See Chapter 26, "'Affordable' Utility Service: What is Regulation's Role?"

# 28
# "Protect the Consumer"— From What?

We have too many high sounding words, and too few actions that correspond with them.

Abigail Adams

## Today's Consumers: Victims or Actors?

**In statutes, orders,** and conversations, "regulating utilities" and "protecting consumers" are phrases joined at the hip, often offered as synonyms. They are not synonyms. "Regulating utilities" means "inducing performance." Regulators define the required performance, then condition utilities' compensation and other approvals on that performance. Performance becomes embedded in a commission's processes when it frames regulatory proceedings as performance inquiries and regulatory opinions as performance assessments.[58]

If "regulating utilities" means "inducing performance," what do we mean by "protecting consumers"? Protect them from what? If the real purpose of regulation is performance, then regulation protects consumers from poor performance—price gouging, false advertising, suboptimal service, and voicemail hell. Regulation protects consumers when markets fail consumers—when seller misbehavior draws no consequences because customers are captive.

This view of consumer protection is incomplete. It leaves customers exposed to the costs arising from their own inefficient behaviors, like overconsumption, and those of their neighbors (in my county, a resident can forbid the utility from cutting down trees on his property, even if that tree's collapse could cause outages elsewhere). Customers are not just captives to be protected; they are actors to be

[58] See Chapter 43, "Utility Performance: Will We Know It When We See It?"

empowered and influenced—empowered to avoid becoming captive and influenced to own their actions. By creating choices, by educating consumers on those choices, and by assigning consumers the consequences of their choices, regulators can improve the performance of consumers and utilities alike.

## Today's Consumer Education: Empowerment and Responsibility

Traditional consumer protection produced traditional consumer education: how to read a meter, interpret a bill, light a pilot light, report an outage. This approach was rooted in an industry structure where the seller was a monopoly and the customer a captive, where energy consumption was an unconditional right (provided the customer paid his utility bills). The customer was a ward to be protected, consumption an act to be encouraged.

Things are different now. With retail competition (telephone in all states, gas and electricity in some), the customer has choices. My consumption dirties your air and water. Price increases prompt protests, but not every increase stems from utility abuse. There is no avoiding the price increases necessary to wean us from fossil fuels, to spread broadband, and to modernize our water and gas pipelines. The educated consumer knows not only his rights but his responsibilities. Consumer education must reflect these facts. To transmit these multiple messages, and cause consumers to absorb them, will require education on six themes:

**It's our turn to help:** Yesterday's consumers helped pay for today's infrastructure. Now it's our turn to contribute for tomorrow's consumers. Responsibility does not skip generations.

**We are all cost causers:** Consumers' decisions about house size, commuting distance, appliance use, and room temperature settings cause costs—pollution today, new capacity costs tomorrow. We can shift these costs to our successors or we can bear them now.

**Cost increases are unavoidable:** Infrastructure obsolescence, equipment breakdowns, new grids and grid services, clean power sources, communications technology—these costs do not respond to protests. Cost increases and rate increases are inevitable.

**"Protection" will depend more on discipline than on protest:** The more we educate consumers about their alternatives (in terms of consumption patterns, equipment, sellers, and rate designs), the more they can adjust their behavior to reduce everyone's costs. The best consumer protection is self-protection.

**The reliability–cost tradeoff deserves a second look:** In the developed world we expect and demand near-perfect availability. That standard comes at a cost. It is not the only possible standard. Educating customers on perfection's cost opens doors to discussions of tradeoffs at lower cost.

**Customer education must line up with industry facts:** Here's what the Maryland Commission said in its order conditioning its approval of BGE's "smart grid" proposal:

> [W]e cannot emphasize this strongly enough: the success of this [smart grid] [I]nitiative, and the likelihood that customers will actually see the benefits this project promises, depend centrally on the success of the Company's customer education and communication effort .... Timing is crucial—customers must get the information they need before BGE installs meters in houses, before Peak Time Rebates begin, and before any other programmatic changes would take effect.[59]

## Consumer Education's Challenges: Politics and Metrics

Consumer education succeeds if it converts consumers from victims to actors, if it shifts their attitudes from "Shield me!" to "How can I help?" Success will require politicians and regulators to play their distinct roles. We need political leaders to lead—to inspire citizens to choose well and bear the costs of their choices. Then regulators can succeed in their jobs—planning infrastructure, designing rates, and setting performance standards.

Easier said than done. Our electoral reality is that candidates who tout "green power," "smart grid," "energy independence," and "universal broadband"—leaving costs unmentioned—beat those who predict tough choices, rate increases, and the need for sacrifice. These political "winners" leave the problem to regulators, who then must persuade citizens accustomed to prices below cost to start paying prices reflecting all costs.

Accompanying the realities of politics is the challenge of metrics: How do we test education's effects? Traditional metrics measured inputs (meters installed, customers contacted, flyers distributed, advertising dollars spent, coupons redeemed, customer calls answered). Today's metrics must also address outcomes: Has consumption dropped? Demand shifted? Broadband been disseminated? Is there a rise in public-spiritedness?

## Conclusion: Bases for Optimism

Regulation's mission of cost effectiveness requires us to treat consumers not as interests to placate but as actors to inspire. We can inspire best if we assume a

---

[59] *Application of Baltimore Gas & Electric Company for Authorization to Deploy a Smart Grid Initiative and to Establish a Surcharge for the Recovery of Cost,* Order No. 83531 (Aug. 13, 2010).

consumer mindset of "How can I contribute?" rather than "What's in it for me?" Consumer education that stretches perspectives, that demands active choosing, that explains how the community's welfare depends on each customer's actions, is better than education that merely instructs customers in how to cut their bills. Which do you think reduced littering more: highway signs warning "Littering Prohibited—$500 fine" or the ad slogan "Don't Mess with Texas"?

# 29
# Separating Policy Mandates from Cost Consequences: Will the Public Lose Trust?

> Public services are never better performed than when their reward comes in consequence of their being performed, and is proportioned to the diligence employed in performing them.
>
> Adam Smith, *The Wealth Of Nations*

A **law student asked** me to explain "what utility regulators do" in one sentence. Here was my response:

Regulators establish standards for performance, tie compensation to performance, then design market structures (and rates, for monopoly structures) that both produce the compensation and cause consumers to consume efficiently.

Three tasks, knotted together in tight interdependency. For newcomers to regulation, whether legislators, governors, their cabinet members, or average citizens, it is easy to miss these interdependencies.

## Three Regulatory Tasks

**Establish expectations for performance.** A regulated utility has an obligation to serve. But at what quality level must it serve—average, above average, top-flight, or just scraping by? What range of services must it offer—mere dial tone, electricity current, gas flow, or also broadband, time-of-use meters, energy audits, and storage? Is the obligation merely to keep today's lights on, or does it include saving resources for our successors?

**Tie compensation to performance.** The Constitution commands commissions to grant the utility "just compensation." (Fifth Amendment: "[N]or shall private property be taken for public use, without just compensation.") Utilities commonly argue that "just compensation" means "recovery of costs." That pecuniary plea misses regulation's purpose. The purpose is not to align rates with cost, but to align compensation with performance. Cost is input; performance is output. The proof of performance is not dollars spent, but innovations implemented, customers empowered, accountability displayed.

**Cause consumers to consume efficiently.** The arithmetic of ratemaking is straightforward: Divide the annual revenue requirement (the amount the utility needs to cover its expenses and earn a fair return for its investors) by the expected sales to get a dollar-per-unit rate. But that average rate has no relation to reality. Reality is the costs consumers cause, and in each hour actual costs diverge from the average. Economic efficiency and societal fairness require that cost causers be the cost bearers; an average rate fails both tests. But insisting on true cost causation triggers other concerns—metering and measurement costs, burdens on low-income users, revenue stability, public acceptance. So some adjustments are necessary.

## Interdependence and Inseparability

Regulatory practice often places performance, compensation and ratemaking into separate proceedings, even assigns regulatory responsibility to different agencies. But these three activities are interdependent and inseparable.

**Performance costs money.** No one chooses a Lexus over a Volkswagen without considering cost. Perfect reliability costs more than one-outage-per-year reliability. So standard-setters consider customer impact. Performance also faces technical limits. High schools don't require students to run four-minute miles. Renewable energy requirements and broadband expectations must jibe with transmission constraints, access to raw materials, land and labor availability—all of which involve costs.

**Performance quality varies.** Electricity, gas, and water are commodities. Performance is not. The pace of innovation and improvement, the quality of construction and repairs, the responsiveness to customers—all these vary among utilities. In most industries, pay reflects performance; we pay less for the high school play than the Broadway musical. Utility regulation should have the same gradations: compensation for quality not cost. But to treat investors fairly, the signals must be clear and consistent. Those who determine performance standards and set rates must have common metrics for compensation.

**Efficient consumption depends on planning.** As rate-setting moves from average cost to actual cost, regulators need to decide what "costs" to reflect in rates. They can be actual costs caused, future costs avoided, or a combination. Integrated resource planning identifies the resource mix (including resource-avoidance measures like demand management) that consumers will need under stated assumptions of population and load. Because prices affect demand and demand affects prices, plans and prices must emerge from a common process.

## Bureaucratic Separateness Undermines Benefit-Cost Accountability

The inseparability of standards, compensation and rates argues against bureaucratic separation. In traditional utility regulation, these three functions remained largely within the utility commissions. Armed with two statutory phrases—"just and reasonable rates" and "no undue discrimination"—the commissions would set service quality standards, establish each utility's annual revenue requirement, then allocate that revenue requirement among customer categories and set rates based on predicted sales. "Performance" assessment was confined to outages and cost overruns.

In the past decade, the public and its representatives—legislators, governors, and cabinet appointees—have recognized that utility service does more than deliver electricity, gas, water and phone calls. It does damage to the air, water and delicate computer equipment. Properly guided, utility service also does good by boosting economic development, diversifying fuel sources, building broadband and weatherizing homes. So policymakers outside commissions are injecting new policy goals into the regulatory process, supplementing—sometimes supplanting—the traditional regulatory role. They are establishing outage standards, renewable purchase obligations, broadband investment requirements, water quality metrics and energy efficiency quotas.[60]

Some legislatures are placing responsibility for designing and even implementing these policies with state agencies other than the traditional utility commission. If policies are set by agencies that perform no rate analysis, while compensation and rates are set by agencies that perform no policy analysis, we risk separating policies from their cost consequences. Sellers can lobby for policies that favor their products, free of the benefit-cost discipline normally imposed by utility regulators who examine witnesses under oath. Separating policymaking from rate-setting reduces accountability, like candidates who promise a police cruiser in every neighborhood without committing to the necessary tax increase.

---

[60] For a comprehensive study of this trend, including its fate in the courts, see Eric Filipink, *Serving the "Public Interest": Traditional vs. Expansive Utility Regulation.* (National Regulatory Research Institute 10-02 Jan. 2010).

## Conclusion

Utility regulation is political. Regulatory decisions make value judgments, assign rights and responsibilities, and establish rewards and penalties, all of which affect every citizen's lifestyle and wallet. Political bodies must be and should be involved. The challenge is to mesh that involvement with benefit-cost accountability and performance standards. Anyone with a 30-year memory (nuclear power), 20-year memory (savings and loan), 10-year memory (Enron), or one-year memory (investment banking) knows that when we separate policy excitement from cost accountability, and add captive customers, we risk cost overruns, public distrust, and rollback of the very policies we intended to advance.

# 30

# Prohibiting Discrimination and Promoting Diversity: Is There a Regulatory Obligation to Society?

We may have all come on different ships, but we're in the same boat now.

Rev. Dr. Martin Luther King, Jr. (1929–1968)

**When utility regulators** talk about "diversity" and "discrimination," they usually are referring to fuel mix, new services, and suppliers' access to bottleneck facilities like electricity transmission, gas pipelines, and the "last mile" in telecommunications. But outside regulation, "diversity" and "discrimination" refer to societal relations. As our nation's population mix is growing more diverse, so is the mix of people depending on utility service. What is a utility's responsibility to reflect this diversity in its employees and contractors? What is the regulator's role?

Some utilities are addressing diversity voluntarily, such as through the admirable Utility Market Access Partnership organized by the National Association of Regulatory Utility Commissioners. But voluntary means voluntary. It means non-mandatory, as in "if I care enough," "when I get around to it," or "if it doesn't cost too much." If the goal is to reduce the gap between utility-workforce diversity and societal diversity, "voluntary" isn't enough. The gap persists. Suppose we made the question tougher: Should diversity be mandatory, meaning mandated by the regulator? Should a utility franchise—a government-granted, government-protected, government-supported legal right to operate a profitable business free of competition—include an obligation to create a diverse work force and contractor base? And an even tougher question: Does that obligation exist already? Does a commission's traditional legal authority include any authority to mandate particular efforts or results?

Thirty-six years ago, the U.S. Supreme Court examined a toenail on this full-bodied question and answered it mostly negatively. The National Association for the Advancement of Colored People (NAACP) had petitioned the Federal Power Commission (FERC's predecessor) to issue a rule prohibiting utilities from racially discriminating against their employees. The proposed rule would have required the Commission to "(a) enumerate unlawful employment practices; (b) require regulatees to establish a written program for equal employment opportunity which would be filed with the Commission; and (c) provide individual employees the right to file discrimination complaints directly with the Commission." (As summarized in Chief Justice Burger's concurring opinion). The NAACP argued that (a) the FPC's substantive statutes (the Federal Power Act and Natural Gas Act) both declare that the electricity and gas businesses are "affected with a public interest," and (b) racial discrimination by utilities conflicts with the "public interest." The statutes, they argued, therefore authorized and obligated the FPC to bar racial discrimination by its licensees.

The FPC rejected the request, saying, in effect, "That's not my department." Both the Court of Appeals for the D.C. Circuit and the U.S. Supreme Court agreed with the FPC. As the Supreme Court explained:

> [T]he use of the words "public interest" in a regulatory statute is not a broad license to promote the general public welfare. Rather, the words take meaning from the purposes of the regulatory legislation.
>
> ...
>
> [T]he principal purpose of those Acts was to encourage the orderly development of plentiful supplies of electricity and natural gas at reasonable prices .... The use of the words "public interest" in the Gas and Power Acts is not a directive to the Commission to seek to eradicate discrimination, but, rather, is a charge to promote the orderly production of plentiful supplies of electric energy and natural gas at just and reasonable rates.[61]

Sympathetic to the petitioners' purpose, the Supreme Court stressed that if a utility's discriminatory practices triggered fines, back pay awards, litigation fees, or "illegal, duplicative or unnecessary labor costs," the Commission should

---

[61] *National Association for the Advancement of Colored People v. Federal Power Commission*, 425 U.S. 662, 669 (1976).

disallow those costs when setting "just and reasonable" rates. Those actions fell within the agency's domain; regulating employment practices did not.

Is that the end of the road? Are we limited to utility voluntarism or does the Court's decision leave room for mandates? (Technically the opinion binds only FERC, but its reasoning could resonate with any regulatory statute, federal or state.) Here are some thoughts:

**Suppose a state commission finds that a utility's hiring or subcontracting practices discriminate by race, ethnicity, sex, national origin, sexual orientation, or age.** Could the commission find that this discrimination reduces the utility's responsiveness to the public? Or that it inflates the utility's cost structure because its workforce and contractor corps were deprived of high-quality people? These findings would require factual investigation, comparisons among work forces and real cause-and-effect linkages between workplace discrimination and utility performance. But an affirmative answer is plausible. Armed with these factual findings, a commission could solve two legal problems left unaddressed by the *NAACP* opinion. First, the commission would not be exercising some "broad license to promote the general public welfare"; it would be carrying out its core purpose—policing the performance of public utilities and setting rates accordingly. Second, the commission would have rooted its decisions in factual findings rather than in a general desire to improve society. Courts defer to factual findings when based on substantial evidence.

**Having found utility performance impaired by discrimination, what steps could the commission take?** Could the commission calculate cost savings lost due to discrimination and disallow that amount from rates? Impose penalties for the performance shortfall? Condition the utility's continued franchise right on immediate actions to solve the problem? Revoke the franchise in favor of a company less likely to discriminate? If the commission linked these consequences factually and reasonably to the company's discriminatory actions, would the commission be safe from legal challenge? Better yet, might the possibility of financial consequences spur more "voluntary" efforts so that the gap closes more quickly? And having found an indisputable link between discrimination and performance, could the commission now require the utility to take specific actions aimed at eliminating the discrimination, such as active recruiting, training of human resource staff and supervisors, whistleblower processes, and other practices used by model companies? How would these regulatory actions differ from the rulemaking sought by the NAACP but blocked by the courts? By basing the regulator's actions on utility performance rather than some "broad license to promote the general public welfare," we may have created some space for a commission mandate.

I admit this approach could cause backlash. There will be some who agree with Chief Justice Burger's concurring opinion (somewhat sourpuss, in my view), arguing that the alleged costs from discrimination

> could not be quantified without resort to wholly speculative assumptions that would be unacceptable for ratemaking purposes. It would be quite impossible, for example, to measure or determine with any exactitude "the costs of inefficiency among minority employees demoralized by discriminatory barriers to their fair treatment or promotion." Nor is it likely that "the costs of strikes, demonstrations, and boycotts aimed against [a utility] because of employment discrimination" ... could ever be determined with sufficient reliability .... [I]t would not be in the public interest to allow intervenors to delay the orderly progress of rate proceedings in the vain hope that such costs might, after protracted litigation, be quantified.

Fair enough: Commission decisions need factual bases. But a commission could, after hearing from experts, create a rebuttable presumption that discriminatory practices sacrifice savings and cause costs, then require the utility that engages in these practices to show otherwise or suffer a disallowance.

**If we know that racial discrimination can cause utility inefficiency, what bars a commission from acting affirmatively to prevent it?** Rather than waiting for discrimination to occur, making findings, and then imposing penalties, could a commission require all utilities (not only utilities accused of discrimination) to (a) report periodically on their hiring and promotion practices and results, (b) explain any lack of progress, and (c) institute best practices as determined by the commission? If these requirements are linked to operational performance, what could be the legal arguments against them? How would they differ from standards for outages, dropped calls, or water quality?

Unlike running the Girl Scouts or the Red Cross, regulating utility performance is not about asking for volunteers. Effective regulators mandate quality standards and base compensation on performance. We do it for outages, dropped calls, and water quality. As long as we link it to performance, we can do the same for diversity.

# 31
# "All of the Above" Is Not a National Energy Policy

> History teaches us that men and nations behave wisely once they have exhausted all other alternatives.
>
> Abba Eban

A **rational national energy** policy should (a) transparently balance long-term goals and short-term needs, certainty and risk, experimentation and stability; (b) continuously question legacy policies to make room for new ones; (c) have roots in benefit-cost analysis; and (d) favor idea-makers over wheel-squeakers.

Our national energy policy, described these days as "all of the above," fails these tests. This gap between the ideal and the real has at least five causes.

## Stating Goals without Resolving Conflicts

Our politicians declare six goals (become energy-independent, reduce pollution, maintain total reliability, create jobs, lead the world in technology, empower consumers) while promising three conditions (lower prices, lower taxes, personal privacy). Now add our personal goals and conditions: We want to live in quiet neighborhoods but use loud leaf blowers, drive everywhere but have uncongested roads.

These equations don't balance, because the conditions conflict with the goals. They recall a New Jersey Senate race in the 1980s, where after hearing his opponent's long list of promises—strong defense, clean environment, great universities, safe cities, pleasant parks, no potholes, *and* lower taxes, the incumbent said: "That's not pie in the sky; that's a whole floating bakery."

Stating goals without resolving conflicts does not make an energy policy.

## Zero-Sum Battles for Market Share

Whether the fight is for federal research grants, loan guarantees or tax credits, our policy debates are often zero-sum battles for market share: coal against nuclear against gas against renewables, renewables against each other, producers against energy efficiency. This circular firing squad produces policies that leave the Man from Mars scratching his head: subsidies for X to counteract the subsidies for Y. Renewables have a hard time competing with oil, gas, coal and nuclear in part because those sources have long enjoyed subsidies: accelerated depreciation and intangible drilling expensing; taxpayer-borne Persian Gulf presence; carbon's exemption from emissions taxes; and nuclear's half-century historic debt to federal research and development, its 10,000-year future debt to citizens who have to guard the waste sites, and its Price-Anderson cap on accident liability. Rather than reduce the subsidies on legacy sources, we grant subsidies to new sources, just to keep the fight fair. This raises the price for everyone.

## False Dichotomy: Regulation vs. Competition

Our discourse on regulation's role too often descends into dichotomy. Supporters of regulation are accused of "command and control," a phrase whose staying power owes more to alliteration than accuracy. Supporters of competition are accused of "letting markets run over people," an attack that ignores the life-savers (medicine, food) and life-enhancers (air travel, baseball, the Beatles) that markets make for people. It is not clear whether the disagreements are philosophical or financial, since so often the latter are framed as the former.

"Regulation vs. competition," like "Hatfield vs. McCoy," has lost its link to the facts. Theoretical bipolarity is undermined by daily reality: We like regulation when it protects; we dislike regulation when it obstructs. This view is less hypocritical than practical. Every utility industry needs, and has, a mix of regulation and markets. Some regulation is necessary to support markets—like licensing nuclear plant operators so that performance errors don't lose the public's loyalty. Some regulation is necessary to correct markets—like price caps that block the price and supply manipulators during shortages.

Regulation and competition, these apparent opposites, thus have a common purpose: performance for the consumer. Regulation regulates business activities, but as Peter Drucker wrote, "The purpose of business is to create a customer." All legitimate business activities perform for the customer. The same is true of regulation. Regulation performs for the consumer. The conversation, therefore, should be less about how regulation reduces profit, less about how markets abuse consumers, and more about how to design regulation and markets as parts of a single machine, one that performs for the consumer.

## Disagreement over the Role of Government

The philosophical–financial dispute between regulation and competition reflects disagreements over government's role. My cause is an investment; your cause is a subsidy. Consider current attacks on the Environmental Protection Agency for enforcing clean air statutes against coal plants. The EPA does what it does—controls power plants directly—because carbon emissions are underpriced. It's simple economics: Pollution's cost is not reflected in the pollutant's price. But plenty of people oppose the EPA's rules and oppose a price on carbon, while offering no other answer. These passive-aggressives want to pollute for free. Since polluting has a cost, polluting for free necessarily means that someone else—some asthmatic child today, some drought-bearing African village tomorrow—pays for your pollution. A "free market" that is free for some but costly for others is hard to defend on either philosophical or financial grounds. It's government's job to correct that error.

## Blurriness over the Meaning of "Cost-Effective"

All participants in the energy policy debate claim allegiance to cost-effectiveness (biggest bang for the buck), but the agreement ends there. Whose bang and whose buck? Local buck and national bang, or national buck and local bang? Who gets and who pays—the parents or the children? My children or your children? Elections make it harder: Every politician wants a positive bang-to-buck balance in every electoral cycle. But in the energy business, investments are often experiments, taking years to stumble to success. Cost-effectiveness doesn't occur biannually.

## Conclusion

"All of the above" has a place, but not as a policy. Where no single solution is certain, trying multiple approaches makes sense—if each "try" is defined as an experiment, designed with purpose, limited in scope, compared with control groups and assessed based on outcomes, then kept or discarded accordingly. "Try everything" fails if it means competing paths, non-intersecting, like track runners in their lanes, each out to beat the other. The better metaphor is building a house, with a plan based on satisfying needs while avoiding regrets; with foundation, walls, windows, floors and stairs, each piece fitted to the others. Any plan needs to honor two principles. First, the foundation has to be wise use: making energy efficiency the foundation, so that we can maintain comfort and productivity at lower cost than "producing more." Second, we need to pair every cost-causer with a cost-bearer so that no fuel source wins by hiding facts.

With these principles in place, production options can support each other, either as transitions while new technologies mature, or as complements (like the gas–wind relationship). Competition among sources still can occur, to fill slots in the plan. But there must be a plan.

# 32

# Supporter-as-Critic: An Expanded Role for Regulatory Professionals

> Everyone connected with the national defense program should have a patriotic interest in seeing that it is properly carried out.
>
> Senator Harry Truman, February 10, 1941

> The committee—often at odds with the military services—became a "sympathetic critic" of the War Production Board and helped raise public confidence in the way the war was being managed.
>
> *Harry S. Truman: His Life and Times*, available at www.trumanlibrary.org/lifetimes/senate.htm

**The Truman Committee,** formally named the Senate Special Committee to Investigate the National Defense Program, made criticism a form of patriotism. The Committee saved not only dollars but lives, exposing leaky aircraft engines and cost-plus contracts. Can we apply this concept to regulation? Consider nine examples.

**If you support "regulation,"** you conserve your regulatory actions. You choose regulation only when necessary and use it no more than necessary. Regulation is necessary when private behavior, unregulated, conflicts with the public interest. (Think speed limits.) Limiting regulation to those situations conserves the credibility that regulation needs to survive its inevitable errors and opponents. You shape regulation to solve those situations, then adjust as facts change. To protect children from sweatshops, regulation came down hard. Now regulation focuses more on children's schooling and diet. But even when abuse has abated, alert regulators keep the regulatory muscles supple rather than allowing atrophy. The alternative is bust–boom, ignoring gas pipes for decades, then piling on after a fatal explosion.

**If you support "deregulation,"** you avoid inconsistency by checking the nearest mirror. Most attitudes toward regulation are double-edged: We seek its protections but oppose its obstructions. The food we eat, the pills we swallow, the restaurants we visit, the cars we drive and the roads we drive on, the doctors we see, the companies whose stock supports our retirement, the house we live in, even the cemetery we'll end up in—all would have less value and more risk were there no regulation.

**If you support "consumers,"** you avoid entrenching a culture of "keep rates low" that has pressured decades of regulators and utilities to delay improvements and repairs to our 1950s-era infrastructure, a culture that resists exposing consumers to the costs they cause.

**If you support "shareholders,"** you cease disguising self-interest as political philosophy. You don't deride "government regulation" when it imposes responsibilities but embrace it when it excludes competitors. You resist casting rate cases as zero-sum conflicts where a customer's benefit is a shareholder's loss. You view the company's core constituency not as "ratepayers" who pay money captively but as citizens who deserve choices about what, when, and from whom to consume. You advise shareholders to recognize that their short-term interests often diverge from the public interest. Then you recognize that, over the long term, this divergence of interests is neither healthy nor inevitable. A healthy equity return requires a healthy customer base and a trusting public; both of which can exist only if the utility is accountable to regulators.

**If you support "states,"** you respect the other states as much as your own. You practice the Golden Rule: You prevent policies that shift your costs to other states, that disfavor suppliers from other states, that hoard your land for your own state's needs while blocking its use for other states' needs. You view as "pro-state" those national policies that preempt states from discriminating against each other; and you view your nation, the United States, as a body you contribute to and not only take from. (And you avoid the phrase "states' rights," which is both historically blemished and constitutionally inaccurate; states don't have rights, they have powers—powers that are both granted and limited by a U.S. Constitution designed to protect us from our provincialism.)

**If you support good government,** you help your governor make good decisions. Consider this example: A governor dislodged a respected switch-hitting lawyer-economist with 35 years of regulatory experience, a national reputation, and enough objectivity and flexibility to win trust from all factions, replacing him with a legislator friend whose key qualification was enough honesty to admit he had "little expertise" in utility regulation. If you support good government, you point out the irony of using the gubernatorial soapbox to attack "public employees" when you've just appointed one utterly unprepared for his job.

**If you support renewable energy,** you want the public to accept a cost increase in the near term to create cost decreases in the long term. So you avoid laws that lack logic: laws that mandate renewable purchases without regard for cost, and laws that block imports that could lower total cost. You criticize candidates who call for "green" but don't disclose the cost. You insist on cost-effectiveness: calculating the public's tolerance for rate increases, budgeting for purchases accordingly. Then you make renewables compete on the merits.

**If you support "nuclear,"** you own up to the half-century of hypocrisy that sells this source as a free market miracle, when its economic survival has depended on taxpayer billions for research and government protection from disaster liability. You reserve the term "conservative" for those who conserve, not for those who promote an energy source whose radioactive waste still has no home, and which will require bunkers and guards for more millennia than human history has yet recorded. (See *Into Eternity*, a documentary about ONKALO, Finland's tunnel system, designed to store their nuclear waste for 100,000 years undisturbed—assuming their descendants can read, and will heed, the signs that warn against disturbance.)

**If you support "competition,"** you recognize its inherent contradiction: Every competitor wants to be the last one standing, indispensable to consumers. Every competitor aspires to be a monopolist. That aspiration spurs some to manipulate, hoard and abuse—behaviors that require regulation to prevent and redress. But others seek indispensability through discoveries that change life, like the polio vaccine or the Stradivarius violin, breakthroughs that then inspire others to compete. (See David Brooks, "Confusing Capitalism and Competition," *New York Times* (Apr. 24, 2012).) Because competition, like humanity, is capable of good and bad, a supporter of competition uses the term carefully. "Competition" is not mere rivalry, a struggle among the sharp-elbowed, each focused on making someone else lose. "Competition" is a market structure, one with many sellers, none of whom has unearned advantages and all of whom have access to non-replicable "bottlenecks"; it is a market structure that forces prices down and quality up, with no one contestant able to influence outcomes. A supporter of competition insists on market structures in which parties win on their merits alone, by playing fair, bearing their own costs, and being satisfied with "some" rather than with "all."

# PART FIVE

# Jurisdiction:
# Power Is a Means, Not an End

The U.S. Constitution gave America split-level government. Our regulatory statutes reflect that decision. Enacted mostly in the early 20th century when utilities were local, those early statutes made most utility regulation local. In the ensuing decades, the nation's interconnectedness has required larger federal roles. In response, state policymakers have both challenged the growing federal powers and sought ways to exempt or protect themselves from federal decisions. Meanwhile, federal and state legislators, usually acting independently of each other, have layered on new mandates without reexamining the federal–state regulatory relationship.

Complicating this unstable jurisdictional architecture are two other factors: ideological shifts that accompany elections, and states' efforts to use their powers to benefit their local constituents. The risk today is of policymakers focusing more on turf than on performance, more on allocating costs than on reducing costs.

The essays in this Part Five catalogue the causes of jurisdictional strife and offer solutions. The effective regulator aims to align jurisdiction with mission, even if her own powers diminish. She focuses less on turf than on results.

# 33

# Legislatures and Commissions: How Well Do They Work Together?

> The meeting of two personalities is like the contact of two chemical substances. If there is any reaction, both are transformed.
>
> Carl Gustav Jung

Legislatures delegate powers to commissions. To delegate is to decide: Which problems are best addressed by the legislature, and which by the commission? Regulatory statutes often answer this question suboptimally. Here are three examples and three common causes, followed by two principles for effective legislature–commission relations.

## Legislative Delegation: Three Examples of Suboptimality

**Low-income families:** For our poorest citizens, cost of service exceeds ability to pay. Legislatures underspend on reducing poverty. Regulators with hearts then allocate more fixed costs to variable charges, to cut bills for low-usage customers. This practice conflicts with economists' view that recovering fixed costs through variable charges lowers efficiency, reducing resources for all. Performing the political function of redistributing wealth—here, helping the poor by lowering their bills—diverts regulators from their duty to induce efficient performance. Could we avoid this diversion by improving the legislature–regulator relationship?

**Pollution:** Electricity production pollutes. The cause of electricity production is electricity consumption. Consumers would pollute less if prices reflected pollution's cost. But regulators face conflicting pressures: Reduce pollution but keep prices low. The solution requires a mix of the political with the technical. The political challenge is to convince customers of their responsibility to bear the costs of their consumption. If legislatures act to meet this challenge, commissions then can use their technical expertise to design rate structures and efficiency programs that reduce the long-term cost of the political decision. Legislative silence, in contrast, leaves the commission exposed to political attack when it should be free to solve the technical problems.

**Market structure—Can we make competition work?** How does a legislature authorize competition after decades of monopoly? Competing for attention are multiple bases for decisionmaking: *ideology* (markets or regulation?); *political expediency* (By Election Day, will prices rise or fall?); *pressure group placation* ("stranded cost" recovery for incumbents? high "shopping credit" to help new competitors? price capped service for non-shoppers?); and *facts* (Do economies of scale, reliability and efficiency increase or decrease with de-integration?).

Industry structure must serve industry purpose. An industry's purpose is to serve customers. Whether a given industry structure will serve customers well is a factual question. Answering factual questions requires objectivity and open-mindedness. Ideology, expediency, and placation belong at the margin. When deciding an industry's structure, what then is the best mix of legislative and commission powers? Should the legislature change the structure itself, or should it delegate the "whether" and "how" to an expert commission?

I would draw the political–technical boundary as follows: The legislature makes the political judgment that a century-old structure requires rethinking. The commission makes the technical judgments about which new market structures are likely to work best. In retail electricity competition, most state legislatures blurred these lines. Legislatures made political declarations that "competition" best served the public, then translated those declarations into fixed starting dates. But the workability of those declarations depended on technical facts about economies of scale, reliability and readiness. The spottiness of effective retail competition shows that legislatures are not well suited to determine, and calibrate policies to, technical facts.

## Legislative Suboptimality: Three Causes

**Legislative staff resources:** Recurring subjects like budget, taxation, education, health care and public safety have permanent legislative staff. Because utility legislation arises infrequently, staff faces steep learning curves.

**High political component:** With a modest push from interest groups, technical regulation slips easily into bipolarity and zerosumsmanship: shareholder vs. ratepayer, economy vs. environment, incumbent vs. newcomer, residential vs. industrial, technocrats vs. equity advocates. Since legislators specialize in compromise, they find ways to make a majority. But like a house's concrete foundation, which allows no compromises, regulation's technical foundations of reliable service, economic efficiency and performance standards are weakened by political balancing.

**Short-term stimuli:** Utility planning is long-term, but legislative stimuli are often short-term: A rate increase looms, a pipe bursts, a manufacturer departs, some existing regulatory practice bothers someone. This mismatch produces short-term fixes not well connected to long-term missions.

## Effective Legislature–Commission Relations: Two Principles

1. **Align responsibilities with comparative advantage.** Legislatures make the big tradeoffs. They establish the exchange rate among competing values, interest groups, and time periods. Guns vs. butter, schools vs. manufacturers, and today vs. tomorrow are legislative judgments. Regulators are better at the technical judgments: defining efficient performance, calibrating rewards and penalties to produce that performance, quantifying tradeoffs, and identifying solutions that avoid tradeoffs. Regulators also design legal procedures that produce objectivity—the engineering, accounting, and finance objectivity supporting the public's expectation that lights will turn on, water will flow, and phones will ring.

2. **Make the legislature–commission relationship a team relationship.** Since the legislature creates and empowers the commission (constitutional commissions excepted), oversight is inevitable. But the effective legislature–commission relationship is less supervisory than cooperative: shared goals, coordinated action, mutual trust, and two-way critique.

Shared goals require a shared definition of the public interest—a common view of that combination of economic efficiency, sympathetic gradualism, and political accountability that best serves the community.[62] With coordinated action and two-way critique, the two bodies can determine who does what best (with emphasis on separating political from technical). If a legislature wants the commission to implement competition, but the commission finds that high economies of scale or technical impracticalities make competition inefficient, the commission should say so. If the legislature caps "default service" (sometimes called "standard offer service" or "last resort service") at a below-market price, the commission should explain how that distortion kills competition. The legislature should expect and invite these critiques. If the statute requires that mergers satisfy the long-term public interest but the commission approves mergers based on short-term rate freezes, the legislature should say something. That's two-way critique; that's teamwork.

---

[62] See Chapter 1.

# 34

# It's April—Do You Know Where Your Legislatures Are?

> Work hitherto badly done, spasmodically done, superficially done, and too often corruptly done by temporary and irresponsible legislative committees, is in future to be reduced to order and science by the labors of permanent bureaus, and placed by them before legislatures for intelligent action.
>
> Charles Francis Adams, quoted in Thomas K. McCraw, *Prophets of Regulation: Charles Francis Adams, Louis D. Brandeis, James M. Landis, Alfred E. Kahn*

April brings showers, flowers—and legislation. State legislatures want their commissions out of wireline but into green power; they want electric rates lower but electric reliability higher; they want water rates stable but water quality better. They want utilities to improve outage performance, but they won't fund enough commission staff to oversee that performance. These inconsistencies make regulatory life difficult. To solve the problem, consider three questions.

## How Should We Allocate Decisions between Legislatures and Commissions?

Policymaking has five steps: (1) Define the problem, challenge, or goal; (2) identify, assess, and select solutions; (3) apply the solutions to specific problems; (4) create and sustain public support for the solutions; and (5) evaluate, critique and adjust. Now imagine a two-dimensional matrix: Make these five steps the rows; make Legislature and Commission the columns. Who does what? You would likely select every cell, making political and regulatory bodies overlap on every step. That's our reality.

Without principles for sharing responsibility, these overlaps can cause confusion and conflict. Part of the problem comes from the difference between the politician's world and the regulator's world. Squeezing the problem into press-release format produces pressure to solve it by Election Day. Blaming the biggest target lets everyone else off the hook. A public led to expect easy answers won't want to pitch in. Politics favors those who oversimplify and sound certain. Effective regulators, in contrast, acknowledge complexity, uncertainty, and the need for humility. But they also need to make decisions in a timely manner and communicate them comprehensibly.

## What Is the Right Mix of Predictability and Flexibility?

To attract serious investment dollars, policymakers must commit predictable constituent dollars. Exhibit A in the rogues' gallery of unpredictable policies is the production tax credit (PTC) for wind production in the U.S., where investors endure a biennial waiting game to see if the PTC survives another budget cycle.

While investors need predictability, regulators need flexibility. They need to adjust their bets with changes in facts: facts about cost structures, levels of competitive entry and exit, technological breakthroughs and stumbles, customer resistance. A decade ago, retail electricity competition statutes failed the flexibility test. They (a) fixed the start dates, regardless of the market's readiness; and (b) gave non-shoppers a "default service" price that was artificially low, deterring competitive entry. Now a new set of legislators is repeating their predecessors' errors, enacting renewable purchase quotas regardless of prices, transmission capacity, or availability of lower-cost alternatives. Encasing answers in concrete before facts are clear prevents regulators from doing what they do best: shaping options to reach goals cost-effectively.

## Does Legislative Intervention Necessarily Undermine Regulatory "Independence"?

In the relationship between legislatures and commissions, "independence" has multiple meanings. Some want independence to equal isolation: Regulators should wait while legislators legislate; the baton then passes to the regulator and the legislator retires, the regulator carrying out the legislature's judgments without further political involvement. But to equate commission independence with an absence of political involvement is to miss the difference between interference and guidance. Isolation leaves the political body without objective, technical advice on feasibility and cost, while the commission loses the political cooperation needed to re-calibrate statutes once experience reveals their inevitable imperfections.

Regulatory isolation can serve political purposes. New legislative policies have unknown effects: The incumbent could lose business, foreign investment could replace domestic investment, rates could rise. Given these possibilities for disruption, dislocation and disappointment, some politicians will prefer that their constituents aim their irritation at the regulators and at regulation in general. So after enacting a regulatory statute, they move on.

But independence-as-isolation is unrealistic. No decisionmaker is truly independent—from the financial markets, from economic cycles, from citizen irritability, from judges who insist on facts, procedures, and rationality.[63] Politics and regulation are not separate planetary systems whose only commonality is the big bang of national conception. Instead of conflating independence with purity, we might define independence differently: as avoidance of pressures to distort, deceive, or substitute political gain for professional judgment. This form of independence means aiming for the right answer first, then using politics to build support. Rather than asking "Whom do we need to please?" ask "How do we get this right?" With this definition of independence, legislature and regulator each sees and deploys its independent value. The political process can build solutions on technical foundations; the regulatory process can serve the political function of achieving legislators' goals. Independence is not sacrificed; it is respected.

## Recommendations for Regulators and Legislators

Legislatures and commissions differ in many ways: how their members are selected, how they make decisions, how they communicate their decisions, how they are held accountable, the boundaries on their discretion, the personality attributes that bring success. Despite these differences, a productive relationship is possible, if they emphasize their joint responsibility to serve the public. Here are three thoughts.

**Consult continuously, from conception through implementation:** While the legal relationship between legislature and commission is delegator–delegatee, the practical relationship should be more like architect–engineer or composer–soloist—one emphasizing grand design, the other making it work, both immersed in the other's field. The baton may change hands, but the runners have a common plan.

**Emulate each other's best qualities:** Politicians can think more like regulators by understanding the technical side, accepting constraints rooted in cost and technology, pressing position-takers to use facts and logic, and proceeding incrementally until the factual fog clears. Regulators can think more like politicians,

---
[63] See Chapter 4, "Independent."

talking to the public in ways they can understand. On this latter point, see the extraordinary opinion of the West Virginia Public Service Commission, explaining to recession-suffering citizens, in non-technical terms, the reasons and reasoning for a $50 million rate increase.[64] (Also eye-catching is the Commission's decision to subject a unanimous "settlement" to a full evidentiary hearing, then to reduce the settlement revenue requirement by $10 million. "Settlement" is the parties' misnomer for their proposal to the Commission.[65])

**Take joint responsibility for results:** Joint responsibility emphasizes results over roles, each party assisting the other's success. It beats blame-shifting ("I've done my part; the failure is your fault."). Because each party performs its legal role, independence remains relevant, but that role-independence is a contributor to the result; it is not its own result.

---

[64] *Appalachian Power Company and Wheeling Power Company,* Case No. 10-0699-E-42T (Mar. 30, 2011).
[65] See Chapter 48, "Regulatory 'Settlements': When Do Private Agreements Serve the Public Interest?"

# 35

# More on Legislative–Regulatory Relations: Layers, Protections and Cost-Effectiveness

> Nobody talks more of free enterprise and competition and of the best man winning than the man who inherited his father's store or farm.
>
> C. Wright Mills

**The preceding essay** addressed the blurry boundary between legislating and regulating. Uneasiness arises from three uncertainties: Who should make which decisions? Where is the sweet spot between predictability and flexibility? When does legislative oversight of regulation shift from amicable intergovernmental cooperation to an attack on regulation's objectivity and independence?

These uncertainties accumulate as we learn more about how utility services affect our economies, our personal lives, and our grandchildren. Addressing these uncertainties, we sometimes add new layers of law that sit uneasily on what lies underneath. At other times, we enact forms of constituent "protection" that undercut our aims. And we struggle with the concept of cost-effectiveness, which should be central to these decisions.

## Policy Layers: Are They Consistent?

Responding to each era's urges, we tend to layer policies without accounting for redundancies, contradictions and gaps. Consider our renewable energy experience. Over 35 years, the nation's efforts to boost renewables have produced four separate structural policies, each dating from a different political era but all aimed at the same subject: relationships among renewable generators, utilities and consumers. *PURPA*, a federal statute, requires utilities to purchase from eligible cogenerators and renewables producers. The price is the utility's "avoided cost." *Net metering*, a state law concept, allows consumer-producers to "run their meters backwards," with utilities required to accept the output. The compensation is not the utility's avoided cost, but the full retail rate—a rate exceeding avoided cost because it recovers both fixed and variable cost. *Renewable portfolio standards*, currently a state law concept, require utilities to buy a specified percentage of total requirements from eligible producers. These statutes usually specify neither total quantity, nor specific price, nor total cost. *Feed-in tariff*, the newest entrant, is a state law concept obligating the utility to buy unspecified output from eligible renewables producers, at a price designed to attract sufficient providers to meet the state's goals. The price is not the utility buyer's avoided cost but, in effect, the renewable seller's opportunity cost.

These policies overlap, duplicate, and at times conflict on key variables: eligible sellers, seller compensation, and interconnection rights and obligations. Notice especially the four different approaches to compensation: utility avoided cost, seller opportunity cost, retail rate, and none-of-the-above. That's hardly a rational, cost-effective approach to renewable power.

Beneath, or on top of, these policies are other efforts to send money to renewables developers, from either taxpayers or ratepayers. These efforts include *direct taxpayer or ratepayer funding* (e.g., grants, leases, loans, loan guarantees, systems-benefit charges, return-on-equity adders) and *tax benefits* (e.g., accelerated depreciation, capital-based tax incentives, production-based tax incentives, sales- or property-tax relief, manufacturing and other tax credits). The final layer contains *efforts to influence customer behavior*, efforts like retail rate design, home efficiency programs, and offers to buy demand reduction.

Selecting the funding source—taxpayers or ratepayers—is a separate issue, often decided by this principle: One gets more political mileage from enacting a benefit than from assigning a cost—which is why so many policies are promulgated by legislative action but funded through regulatory action.

How do these overlapping policies interact with each other? Do they duplicate, undermine, or reinforce? The absence of answers—or much traction on the question—seems attributable to at least one of two causes: We don't know what works, so we try everything; or every interest group wants something, so the easiest approach is to placate every petitioner rather than make the hard calls.

## Do Some "Protections" Undercut Our Aims?

We consistently hesitate to raise rates to reflect real costs, especially during economic downturns. We worry that our poor can't pay or that industries can't compete. So we delay increases and even grant discounts. But the overconsumption induced by these discounts benefits no one in the long run. Overconsumption leads to overinvestment; then stranded costs, stranded investors, stranded taxpayers, and cynical citizens who lose faith in their governments because their high rates are compensating for their parents' low rates. Is not the obviously better approach to set prices properly and help people learn the effects of their behavior, while using other resources, like taxpayer resources, to assist those needing our help?

## Do We Define Cost-Effectiveness Clearly?

It's easy to define cost-effectiveness: It's biggest bang for the buck. But whose bang and whose buck? Is the relevant bang local, state, national, or global? Who gets the bang—this year's voters or next century's citizens? Who pays—the parents or the children? And if we insist on a perfect bang–buck balance in every electoral cycle, is cost-effectiveness ever possible?

Clouding the cost-effectiveness calculation is the myth of the "self-made man." In U.S. energy policy, there is no such thing. Every technology has multiple helpers—loan guarantees, accelerated depreciation, tax credits, caps on producer liability, bankruptcy protection and more. (This long list of government assists no doubt reminds some readers of C. Wright Mills: "Nobody talks more of free enterprise and competition and of the best man winning than the man who inherited his father's store or farm.") When the technology succeeds commercially, how do we assess the value of each contributor? How do we know which help to withdraw, on the grounds that technology can succeed without it?

And—do we realize that aid to one technology can increase the cost of another technology? Spending money to invent new technologies is one thing; but aiming aid to make existing technology "competitive" is another. We subsidize nuclear power, oil, and coal, giving pricing advantages over wind, solar, and geothermal. Then we subsidize wind, solar, and geothermal to make them "competitive" with nuclear, oil, and coal. Does this approach make cost-effectiveness sense?

## Recommendations

The most alert regulators not only look ahead; they evaluate past policies too. Contrast merger policy. Since the mid-1980s, dozens of electricity and telecommunications utilities have merged: horizontal, vertical, and conglomerate mergers, even some none-of-the-above mergers. Each merger applicant predicted "synergies," often carbon copies of prior mergers' claims. A quarter century later, after billions have been spent on acquisition premiums, we have no studies testing these claims against reality. Merger policy is only one example of gaps between assertions and evidence.

It sounds sleep-inducing, but a continuous study process, organized by legislators and regulators together, is one solution. It would produce more improvement than "sunset reviews" that ask only about budget and bureaucracy. Injecting also the perspectives (not the positions) of regulated entities, users, investors, technologists and academics, all aimed at an agenda of objectivity and cost-effectiveness, would smooth out policy evolution. Then we can avoid the lurches and overreactions that reduce public trust in both legislators and regulators.

# 36

# Federal–State Jurisdiction I: Pick Your Metaphor

> There can be hope only for a society which acts as one big family, and not as many separate ones.
>
> Anwar Sadat

**C**ats and dogs, gridlock, peaceful coexistence, parallel play, lamb lying with lion, hand in glove. Those are some metaphors for federal–state jurisdictional relations, in ascending order of effectiveness. The next five essays sort through our jurisdictional experiences, seeking to explain successes and failures. This first essay sets the context. Our regulated industries are multistate industries serving both local and multistate markets. Simultaneous federal and state roles are unavoidable. Each is necessary to the other's success. Why does this interdependence produce so much irritability? Understanding the reasons will assist improvement.

## No Escape: When Regulated Industries Are Interstate, Federal–State Simultaneity Is Unavoidable

Until the 1980s, state regulation usually coincided with effective regulation, because infrastructural assets, corporate boundaries, business activities and relevant markets were primarily intrastate. No longer. Electric and gas consumers depend on production from distant states, brought by transmission lines and pipelines that traverse states; consumption in one state pollutes the air and water in other states. Local water users benefit from (and pay for) national water quality standards. Local phone callers depend on a national market of providers who use an interstate telecommunications infrastructure.

"Interstate" is not a burden to bear; it is an opportunity to exploit. In this interstate context, "effective regulation" is no longer synonymous with "exclusively state regulation." I once heard a state commissioner say, "If we are not for preserving state regulation, what are we for?" He had it wrong. The mission is not to preserve jurisdiction, but to make it effective. Jurisdictional effectiveness requires roles defined rationally, aimed at a single purpose: to induce regulated industries to perform at their best. To produce performance, regulatory responsibility should align with industry activity.

A focus on industry improvement rather than on jurisdictional gains and losses helps avoid a related error: isolating one regulatory actor from another, attacking and enjoying while oblivious to the irony. This behavior exists outside regulation: decrying "Hollywood" but enjoying its movies; deriding "New York" but tuning in to Letterman and Leno; complaining of federal "subsidies" while driving on the interstate; the skinhead whose favorite food is burritos.[66] And it happens within regulation: complaining of the Northwest's control of low-cost hydropower while baking its salmon; downplaying the broadband deficit in rural America while roasting its corn. There can be no principled disagreement with the reality of "interstate." Then why is "federal–state tension" the norm? Why is "federal–state cooperation" emphasized so often, like Shakespeare's Queen who "doth protest too much"?[67]

## Why Does the Interdependency Produce So Much Irritability?

Simultaneous federal and state presences are inevitable, but permanent irritability and tension are not. The relationships shift, depending on the issue and the facts. Four examples follow.

1. **When national and in-state interests clash.** Consider the siting of electric transmission and gas pipelines, where the nation's interest in efficient transactions and reliable supply conflicts with state interests in preserving natural resources and aesthetics. The tension is natural. It is hard for a state to weigh its wishes against the nation's needs objectively, and it is hard for a distant federal regulator to value local passion fully. The tension is unavoidable, but we could drop the expressions of shock and dismay. Over 200 years ago, the people approved a Constitution whose Commerce Clause sought to convert the continent from 13 colonial economies into one nation of commerce. Subsequent Supreme Court decisions have reminded state legislatures that the Commerce Clause prohibits a state-as-regulator

---

[66] Skinhead source is essayist Richard Rodriguez, *McNeil-Lehrer Newshour* (Nov. 2, 1995); see www.pbs.org/newshour/bb/race_relations/race_relations_11-2.html.
[67] *Hamlet*, Act 3 Scene 2.

from hoarding its resources (including its land, scenic and environmental resources) to the detriment of other states.[68]

2. **When the federal-vs.-state issue is, at bottom, a state-vs.-state issue.** There seems no end to state-vs.-state cost allocation battles, resolved finally at FERC, with the winner praising the "nobility of the federal neutral," and the loser attacking the "arrogant federal preemptor." It reminds me of my seventh-grade math teacher, Mrs. Fitzpatrick, who once said, "I know how you kids talk about grades: If it's a B or above, it's 'Look what I got!' But if it's C or below, it's 'Look what she gave me.'"

3. **When the federal agency makes decisions that raise costs for state-jurisdictional customers.** The EPA sets water quality standards, FERC approves transmission "adders," the FCC approves a cost-increasing universal service modification. These decisions benefit the nation in the long term, but they raise costs for local customers in the short term. The political distance of decisionmaker from affected people is the source of the tension. But it may also be the strength of the solution: Political distance increases political insulation, enabling the decisionmaker to "do the right thing."

4. **When the federal and state agencies differ over the role of regulation.** Here the two levels of government differ not over their role, but over regulation's role. We see this most often in disputes over "deregulation."[69] States often criticize FERC and the FCC for the view that competition is sufficient to support a reduction in regulatory presence. This is not a dispute over state–federal jurisdiction; it is a difference over regulatory outlook and technique, and for some, regulatory conscientiousness.

But when the anger is high enough, the disagreement over policy sours into one over trustworthiness and turf. Former FERC Chairman Pat Wood sought to introduce regional transmission policies and regional organized markets. His goals were to increase and guide infrastructure investment, diversify customer choices, increase market accountability, and reduce long-run costs. Plenty of people, based on their market positions, had predictable reasons to support or oppose him. That's regulation. What devalued the debate was the hyperbole, as when one state commissioner, perhaps unaware of the unfortunate historical overtones, accused Wood of coercing states into a "forced march."

---

[68] See *Philadelphia v. New Jersey*, 437 U.S. 617, 624 (invalidating New Jersey's ban on imports of out-of-state garbage; "where simple economic protectionism is effected by state legislation, a virtually per se rule of invalidity has been erected.").

[69] For a discussion of this term's deficiencies, see Chapter 23, "The War of Words: Competition vs. Regulation I"

## Conclusion

Our regulated industries perform many services, some near the customer, some distant; some local, some multistate. Regulation's purpose is to induce high-quality performance. The allocation of regulatory roles requires us to ask: What specific actions we do want from our regulated industries? What regulatory agencies are best positioned to produce that performance? Effectiveness over turf, substance over emotion: Those are the emphases most likely to ensure success.

# 37

# Federal–State Jurisdiction II: Jurisdictional Wrestling vs. Coordinated Regulation

> No man is an island entire of itself; every man is a piece of the continent, a part of the main.
>
> John Donne

**The preceding essay** noted that for interstate industries, federal–state simultaneity is unavoidable—and good for consumers. Why, then, does this interdependency produce so much irritability? One illustration of irritability is when what appears to be "federal vs. state" is actually state vs. state. A good example is some states' discomfort with FERC jurisdiction over "resource adequacy."

When a car driver selects his speed, he pursue his private interests—dentist appointments, warm dinners, court appearances, soccer games. So do airlines—on-time departures, lower labor costs, avoiding turbulence. Because these self-interests often diverge from the public interest, we regulate: with speed limits and traffic lights for car drivers, safety rules and air traffic controls for airlines.

Buyers and sellers of electricity also pursue their self-interest. Consumers want lighting at reasonable cost, retail utilities want stable revenues, generation owners want maximum output at maximum price, no one wants blackouts. In an interconnected, interstate transmission system, individual, unregulated, self-interested decisions would produce electrical instability. So we regulate: FERC certifies reliability entities, approves regional transmission tariffs, and allocates multistate transmission costs.

That FERC regulation includes mandating capacity adequacy requirements. FERC has approved regional transmission tariffs that require "load-serving entities" (retail entities legally obligated to serve loads that depend on the regional transmission system) to have available a specified quantity of generation capacity exceeding their customers' load requirements. This on-hand reserve reduces the probability of blackouts in the event of unanticipated consumer demand or equipment breakdown.

Some states oppose not only the magnitude of these mandates but also FERC's authority to impose them. They raise a question of statutory interpretation: Does FERC's exclusive statutory jurisdiction over wholesale sales in interstate commerce, and transmission service in interstate commerce, include authority to require these retail entities to comply with generation adequacy requirements?[70]

Statutory interpretation aside, the policy question is clear: When unregulated, self-interested uses of an interconnected system would cause reliability problems for others, is there a need to regulate? The question compels a "yes" answer. Regulating in-state behaviors that affect interstate adequacy is unavoidable.

Who, then, should do the regulating? It cannot be the state commission. Regulation is necessary when private behavior diverges from public interest. In an interconnected transmission system, divergence occurs because some transmission users, pursuing their private interest, can cause problems for others. Just as airlines can't be air traffic controllers, transmission users can't be adequacy regulators.

A state commission is not a transmission user, so why can't it be the regulator? For the same reason that a single state cannot decide air traffic priorities for multistate air space. A state commission, it is true, is a regulator. But it regulates to induce its in-state utility to serve its in-state customers at the lowest feasible cost. To impose adequacy requirements in-state is to increase costs in-state. In an interconnected system, the benefits of that in-state cost inevitably flow in part to other states. This is the classic "positive externality" in which each individual state will underinvest because it does not receive the full benefits of its investment. The sum of each state's self-interest actions, therefore, will not yield regional adequacy. And no consumer would want to live in a region whose reliability depended on the sum of each state's voluntary actions. Someone above the fray needs to take charge and assign obligations.

That leaves only the federal level as a regulator of generation adequacy. Some states accept this reality. These states still might object to FERC's techniques and procedures, but not to its jurisdiction. Other states, bothered by their

---

[70] The question was answered affirmatively by the U.S. Court of Appeals for the District of Columbia Circuit in *Connecticut Department of Public Utility Control v. FERC*, 569 F.3d 477 (D.C. Cir. 2009) (upholding FERC's authority to approve regional transmission tariffs that allocated responsibility for capacity reserves among the region's load-serving entities).

FERC-assigned reliability share, blame FERC and Congress for their "impairment of the state prerogative." How do we get out of this box?

The choice is between (a) allowing "local control" to supersede the national interest, and (b) pursuing the national interest with sensitivity to local facts. The legitimate concern is not with a national regulatory entity prescribing results within the state, because some super-state prescription is unavoidable. The legitimate concern is that in prescribing results, the prescriber will ignore local concerns. There cannot be "local control" of decisions that affect non-local interests; but the federal forum must take into account local facts and local values. "Take into account" does not mean "be bound by" or "honor at all costs." It means "weigh along with other facts and values."

Is that not what happens now? Can anyone persuasively assert that states lack opportunities to be "heard" by FERC? There are official proceedings, mutual visits to each other's national and regional conferences and workshops, joint studies, countless informal meetings. States are heard. A federal regulator is not "ignoring state concerns" just because it weights them less heavily than one might wish, or decides that some states seek the unfair result of benefitting from reliability paid for by others.

## From Jurisdictional Irritability to Bi-Jurisdictional Policymaking: Three Thoughts

**Improve each other's hearing.** In any conversation, what improves hearing is speaking to each other's concerns.[71] A state speaks to the federal agency's concerns if it speaks as a co-regulator seeking solutions to multistate problems, rather than as a market participant seeking the protection only of its own residents. The federal agency speaks to the state's concerns if it describes its purpose as seeking to serve the sum of legitimate in-state values.

**Recognize interdependencies and mutual benefits.** By approving terms and conditions for intra-regional transmission, FERC creates opportunities for state-regulated utilities to shop the regional market. Each state's approval of terms and conditions for retail service allows utility-as-shoppers to create demands that stimulate wholesale competitors to sell. Each jurisdiction can shape the market positively. With mutual recognition, each jurisdiction can help the other to do its job—a better result than seeking the other's removal through appellate attacks on jurisdiction.

---

[71] See any book by the Georgetown linguistics professor Deborah Tannen, such as *You Just Don't Understand: Women and Men in Conversation*; *Talking from 9 to 5: Women and Men at Work*; *The Argument Culture: Stopping America's War of Words*; *You're Wearing That?: Understanding Mothers and Daughters in Conversation*; and *Conversational Style: Analyzing Talk among Friends*.

**Focus less on "national interests" and "state interests," and more on what matters: industry performance.** We measure industry performance in terms of economic efficiency, reliability, product innovation, customer satisfaction. The relevant economic actors—the manufacturer choosing a plant location, the generation investor selecting technology and site, the load-serving utility designing its supply portfolio—do not think about federal vs. state; they think about results. So should our regulators.

## Conclusion

There are not two interests, national and state. There is a single goal: high-quality industry performance. To produce that performance, there may be a national role and a state role, but there is not a national interest and a state interest.

# 38

# Federal–State Jurisdiction III: Jurisdictional Peace Requires Joint Purpose

> Through the evolutionary process, those who are able to engage in social cooperation of various sorts do better in survival and reproduction.
>
> Robert Nozick

Since our utility industries are interstate, federal–state jurisdictional overlap is unavoidable; yet this interdependency still produces irritability.[72] Outcomes will improve if the state commissions act as co-regulators rather than consumer advocates.[73] Having described the problems, let's start toward solutions, using a simple principle: Jurisdictional peace requires joint purpose.

## Avoid Oversimplification by Understanding the Jurisdictional "Why"

People talk of the "federal–state relationship" as if there were only one. There are at least five. If we understand the "why" behind each relationship—the mix of national purposes and local values—we can replace tension with jointness. Consider these different federal–state relationships:

1. **Federal law directs states to take specified actions to carry out national policy.** Section 210 of the Public Utility Regulatory Policies Act of 1978 requires each state to administer its utilities' obligation to purchase wholesale power from "qualifying" generating facilities (renewable energy producers and cogenerators), at state-approved rates based on each utility's

---

[72] Chapter 36, "Federal–State Jurisdictional Relations: Pick Your Metaphor."

[73] Chapter 37, "Federal–State Jurisdiction II: Jurisdictional Wrestling vs. Coordinated Regulation."

"avoided cost." *Why?* Congress decided to diversify the nation's electric generation, in terms of fuel types and supplier types, but saw states as experts on utilities' supply alternatives and costs.

2. **Federal law establishes national policy, recognizes the need for state involvement, but limits states' range of motion.** In 2005, Congress added Section 215 to the Federal Power Act of 1935. Section 215 made FERC the master of electric bulk power system reliability, allowing state regulation of reliability only if "consistent with" federal rules. *Why?* Congress wanted a national entity (a FERC-certified "electric reliability organization") to establish national standards for users, owners and operators of the multistate, interconnected grid, while viewing state-level variations as helpful provided they did not undermine the national standards. Allow multiple chefs in the kitchen, if the extra activity does not spill the soup.

3. **Federal law precludes state activity entirely.** In Section 201 of the Federal Power Act, the 1935 Congress granted FERC exclusive jurisdiction over "unbundled" transmission of electric energy in interstate commerce.[74] *Why?* The interconnected, interstate grid knows no state boundaries. Electrons entering the highway in one state affect traffic in other states. As our Framers foresaw in the 1780s, a nation of commerce cannot yield to conflicting state preferences.

4. **Federal law conditions federal benefits on state actions.** We have federal transportation grants for states if they enact speed limits and right-turn-on-red rules. We have federal stimulus grants for states that investigate electricity rate design. *Why?* National tax revenues should serve national goals—here, reduction in fossil fuel use.

5. **Federal law leaves states free to act without limit.** Section 201 of the Federal Power Act of 1935 denies FERC authority over retail sales of electric energy, leaving states free to act as they wish. *Why?* Congress believed that (a) retail use equals local use, and (b) local use has only local effect. True in 1935, false today. One state's waste is another state's burden. If one state's retail rates cause an unnecessary contribution to peak load, the extra capital investment for transmission and generation costs the region. Unnecessary consumption also causes more fuel-burning, raising the price of fuels and emissions allowances for all. Markets for fossil fuel and emissions are multistate markets. Unnecessary demand raises market prices; a decrease in demand lowers market prices. Each state would prefer that its neighbors decrease demand. Back to jurisdiction: What once was local now is national. So we see Congress and FERC entering the retail territory, addressing retail

---

[74] See *New York v. Federal Energy Regulatory Commission*, 535 U.S. 1 (2002). "Unbundled" means made available for sale separately.

rate structure and demand-side management. "Trampling state values," or protecting states from each other?

## Define the Joint Goal, Then Allocate Duties to Achieve It

To produce jurisdictional collegiality, there are three prerequisites:

**Find the shared mission, identify the necessary tasks, then define who does what best.** Consider the hospital operating room or the Habitat for Humanity construction site. Workers focus on purpose and performance, their roles determined by expertise. No one argues about jurisdiction.

**Think clay, not concrete.** My state colleagues often say that states do "consumer protection," while the feds do—something else. Aren't the roles more malleable? There is nothing state-only about "consumer protection." There are numerous examples of an exclusively federal presence. Take food and drug safety. Nothing could be more "local" than an individual's ingestion of potatoes and pills, but food and drug safety is regulated nationally. *Why?* Because a local scare would up-end national markets. (Spinach contamination on the West Coast unloaded shelves on the East Coast.) Radioactivity poisons persons—more local effects. But nuclear safety is exclusively federal. (Three Mile Island: one local event, an entire nation loses confidence for decades.) An industry's integrity needs a federal footprint.

**If the purpose of regulation is performance, place jurisdiction where performance risk arises.** Take pharmaceuticals: Some risks arise in research, design, production and labeling—national markets, national regulation. Other risks arise in prescription, marketing and sales—local activities, so the states license physicians and pharmacists. No one disputes these common-sense allocations. In water, capture, storage, treatment, delivery and sale are largely local, thus regulated in-state. Water quality has both national and local causes and solutions, so its regulation occurs at both levels (requiring federal-state consistency and coordination).

Perhaps the dialogue's problem is the very phrase "consumer protection." Protection from what? If regulation is about performance, then "protection" means protection from subpar performance. Regulate performance where it occurs: Performance affecting national markets needs national regulation; performance affecting only local markets needs only local regulation.

## Solve the Problems at Their Source: Congress

In electricity, telecommunications, and gas, jurisdictional disputes have come to the courts. But courts cannot fashion solutions where old laws have lost their logic; they can only pick winners and losers among parties disputing those old laws. Courts do not ask, "What is the best allocation of jurisdictional roles?"

They ask only, "In the case before us, who wins and who loses?" Courts cannot solve the problem.

Today's jurisdictional roles arise from 75-year-old federal statutes designed for a simpler world. We have amended them episodically and opportunistically, rather than comprehensively and objectively. Only Congress can re-craft a solution. Does Congress have the capacity? We all know congressional members and staff of high intellect and integrity. The problem is not Congress. The problem is those of us who pull Congress in multiple, inconsistent directions, producing statutes containing multiple inconsistencies without direction. Joint purpose and allocation of roles will eliminate inconsistencies and give us direction.

# 39
# Federal–State Jurisdiction IV: A Plea for Constitutional Literacy

"A victory for the Tenth Amendment," declared Arizona's Governor—about a Supreme Court opinion that never mentioned, and had nothing to do with, the Tenth Amendment, and which struck most of the state statute.

At issue was the Supremacy Clause, not the Tenth Amendment. Addressing Arizona's 2010 immigration statute, the Court struck three provisions as preempted by federal law. The fourth provision? The Court did not decide its validity, because "[t]here is a basic uncertainty about what [it] means and how it will be enforced." The Court allowed that provision to take effect—which is different from finding it constitutional. The Court did not affirmatively find *any* provision constitutional.[75]

What does Arizona immigration have to do with utility regulation? Federal–state jurisdictional issues like immigration, arising under the Supremacy Clause, Commerce Clause and Tenth Amendment, pervade the electric, gas and telecommunications industries. A century ago, states granted hundreds of utilities the right to serve, often as state-protected monopolies. Accompanying that privilege to serve were obligations to perform: reliably, safely, and non-discriminatorily, at just and

---

[75] See *Arizona v. United States*, 132 S.Ct. 2492 (2012). The Court struck as preempted three sections of the state statute: Section 3, making it a state law misdemeanor to fail to comply with federal alien registration requirements; section 5(C), making it a misdemeanor for an unauthorized alien to seek or engage in work in the state; and section 6, authorizing state and local officers to arrests without a warrant any person "the officer has probable cause to believe ... has committed any public offense that makes the person removable from the United States." The fourth provision requires state police officers, when conducting a stop, detention or arrest, to try, in some circumstances, to verify the person's federal immigration status. The Court, without finding it constitutional, allowed this provision to stay in effect until state courts could determine its meaning. The quote from Arizona Governor Jan Brewer is at www.foxnews.com/politics/2012/06/25/brewer-supreme-court-arizona-decision-victory-for-rule-law/.

reasonable prices. But state regulation alone proved insufficient to produce the necessary performance. The utilities' interstate features, and their indispensable role in a growing nation's infrastructure, led Congress in the 1930s to design a distinct federal regulatory presence. Our dual regulatory structure has depended for its success on clear legal boundaries, and on regulators who cooperate with common purpose and consistent policies.

It's been a bumpy ride. Federal–state jurisdictional disputes permeate at the agency policymaking level; plenty end up in court. Nuclear power, universal service, dialing parity, area codes, customer premises equipment, unbundled network element pricing, transmission siting, multistate cost allocation, corporate structure limits, environmental values: This is a short list of jurisdictional jams that judges have had to sort out because regulators could not. (As of this writing, the federal courts are hearing federal–state disputes over regional transmission planning, state generating capacity rules, demand response compensation, and relations between utilities and qualifying facilities under the Public Utility Regulatory Policies Act.) The bigger the costs, the bumpier the ride.

It is worth the time to re-examine whether a 1930s jurisdictional relationship is sensible in a 21st-century world. Co-regulation requires shared purposes, fact-based flexibility, allocation of regulatory responsibility based on comparative competencies, and respect for the legitimate but different needs of Main Street and Wall Street, of local business and international capital. All these factors change over time. Smart, dedicated people can come to different answers. Arguing is unavoidable and helpful. What is avoidable and unhelpful is rhetoric rooted in constitutional illiteracy. "States' rights," "Tenth Amendment," "sovereignty," "encroachment": These terms often have oratorical resonance disproportionate to their constitutional relevance. Most federal–state questions boil down to one or more of four questions. The first two address limits on federal powers; the second two deal with limits on state powers.

1. **Has Congress exceeded its interstate commerce powers?** The Constitution's Commerce Clause grants Congress the power to regulate interstate commerce. Federal preemption of states is possible only if Congress is acting within its powers. Remember, though, that if in-state activity affects interstate commerce, even indirectly, it's still interstate commerce. (Just ask the Ohioan Roscoe Filburn, a farmer who just wanted to grow extra wheat for his family; and the Alabaman Ollie McClung, who thought Congress had no business ordering his Ollie's Barbecue to serve all races. Both lost their cases.)[76]

---

[76] See *Wickard v. Filburn*, 317 U.S. 111, 127-28 (1942) (federal regulation of farmer's in-state wheat production is permissible where his production, combined with all others similarly situated, has non-trivial effect on interstate commerce); *Katzenbach v. McClung*, 379 U.S. 294 (1964) (federal regulation of small restaurant's racial discrimination is permissible where restaurant bought products in interstate commerce). Every law student learns these cases.

2. **Does the federal statute interfere with reserved state powers?** The Tenth Amendment provides that "powers not delegated to the United States by the Constitution, nor prohibited by it to the States, are reserved to the States." This is a mirror image of the Commerce Clause. If Congress is acting on a matter that is not interstate commerce, yet purporting to preempt states, it is interfering with powers reserved to them. The Tenth Amendment also prevents Congress from "commandeering" state legislative machinery to carry out federal aims.[77]

3. **Does the state regulatory program violate, discriminate against, or unduly burden interstate commerce?** Congress's Commerce Clause power reflects the Framers' vision of a nation unified by commerce. Implicit in that vision, made explicit by the courts, is a "dormant Commerce Clause" with two features. First, it prohibits provincialism. A state may not erect trade barriers, discriminate against sellers or buyers from other states,[78] or hoard its natural resources for its own citizens,[79] unless the state itself is a "market participant."[80] Second, a state may burden commerce with regulation, but the regulation must bear a reasonable relationship to the in-state benefits.[81]

4. **Did Congress intend to preempt the state law?** As the Court said in its Arizona immigration decision, "from the existence of two sovereigns follows the possibility that laws can be in conflict or at cross-purposes." Provided Congress acts within its constitutional powers, the Supremacy Clause allows it to preempt state laws. On the spectrum from national uniformity to state experimentation, Congress's elected members get to pick the point. Preemption can be express or implicit, but it always flows from congressional intent. There is no reader of this essay, no United States citizen, who has not benefited from national consistency, due to Congress's power to preempt.

* * *

These are the four ways to think about federal–state legal relationships. Within each category, decisionmakers balance values, none of which is absolute. A century of utility regulation has produced cases in all four categories. That gives us

---

[77] See *New York v. United States,* 505 U.S. 144 (1992) (Congress may not force states to regulate disposal of nuclear waste according to federal criteria or, failing to do so, take title to the waste).

[78] See *Wyoming v. Oklahoma,* 502 U.S. 437 (1992) (State may not limit coal imports by requiring coal-burning utilities to use at in-state coal for at least 10 percent of their needs).

[79] See *New England Power Co. v. New Hampshire,* 455 U.S. 331 (1982) (state may not ban the export of hydro power produced in the state).

[80] See *Reeves v. Stake,* 447 U.S. 429 (1980) (South Dakota did not violate the Commerce Clause when its Cement Commission's policy confined sales from the state-owned cement plant to in-state residents).

[81] *Pike v. Bruce Church, Inc.,* 397 U.S. 137, 142 (1970).

a body of law—literature even—that can discipline our dialogue, soften the hard edges of dispute, and avoid the absolutist positions that delay compromise.

The Constitution is—pardon the oxymoron—sacred political language. Literacy prevents demagoguery. The winner is democracy.

# 40

# Intra-Regional Relations: Can States' Commonalities Outweigh Their Differences?

> To give entrance to [protectionism] would be to invite a speedy end of our national solidarity. The Constitution was framed under the dominion of a political philosophy less parochial in range. It was framed upon the theory that the peoples of the several states must sink or swim together, and that in the long run prosperity and salvation are in union and not division.
>
> *Baldwin v. G. A. F. Seelig,* 294 U.S. 511, 523 (1935)

**This fourth picture** in the federal–state gallery addresses a prime tension-contributor: state-vs.-state conflict, more politely called "intra-regional relations."

## Contrasts in Community Commitment

Beneath the friendships and trust gained from residence in this state regulatory community, the subsurface has plenty of growling, teeth-baring, and logic-suppressing. Examples of questions people ask about each other:

1. Why do coal states insist on a right to charge and pay low rates, when those low rates stimulate electricity consumption that causes pollution costs for other states?

2. Why do the states with hydroelectric dams insist that the low-cost power is "theirs," when this power source's low cost owes more to nature, geographic

serendipity, federal taxpayers and 1930s laborers than to any efforts and innovations made by those states' current residents?

3. Why do residents of nuclear power states complain about federal rules requiring them to bear the cost of burying their nuclear waste, when without careful burial the environmental costs will burden others for millennia?

4. Why do states that see wind power as in-state economic development and improved local air quality work so hard to have other states fund the transmission investment?

5. Why do we work harder at allocating costs to others than at understanding—and owning up to—our own responsibility?

6. FERC Order No. 719 requires each regional transmission organization to allow "aggregators of retail customers" (ARCs) to bid demand response into the RTO's organized market—unless the state prohibits the retail customer's participation. But a state that prohibits participation causes the region to forgo a leftward shift in the demand curve—a fancy way of saying that if one state blocks efficient demand response, the region's prices stay higher than necessary. Why is this behavior considered "OK" as a matter of "state prerogative"? (Separate question: Why would a national regulator, with a statutory obligation to advance benefits for all consumers, invite and accommodate state policies that reduce benefits for consumers?)

7. Why do so many urban power plants end up near low-income neighborhoods?

*Contrast* these examples of states that offer their wealth to others:

1. Some states cause their ratepayers to pay extra to attract renewable energy or increase energy efficiency, even though the benefits of supplier diversity, emissions reduction and demand reduction will produce lower costs and prices for non-residents.

2. Some states subsidize education for the next generation of power engineers, line workers, and pipe hangers so that the nation's lights stay on, even though some of these students will take their skills to other states.

3. Some states are generous with low-income assistance, according dignity to our poorer citizens, making the entire nation more civilized.

4. Some western states are working to integrate information on population patterns, resource richness, environmental vulnerability and political cost tolerance into a regional electricity solution that recognizes the commonality of risk and opportunity.

## Causes of Intra-Regional Tension

Why do we have more examples of opposition than cooperation? Two related reasons are incrementalism and an attitude of "no losers, ever." In regulation, incrementalism is inevitable. We make many decisions case-by-case: this asset in rate base, that cost allocation, this transmission adder, that rate increase. In Major League Baseball's 162-game season, every game is win-or-lose. Similarly, every regulatory decision gets strip-searched for negative attributes. While every state wants to "collaborate" and "compromise," no one wants to lose, not even once, even if a loss today can produce a gain later. Yet long-term benefits require short-term hits. So by salami-slicing our decisionmaking, we distort vision and depreciate value. A "no losers, ever" test produces real loss.

The problem also comes from confusion over words and actions. Consider the phrase "states' rights." A focus on "rights" creates a mindset of entitlement, leading to worry about winning. There is no such thing as "states' rights." Individuals have rights; states have powers. (See the U.S. Constitution, Tenth Amendment: "The *powers* not delegated to the United States by the Constitution, nor prohibited by it to the States, are reserved to the States respectively, or to the people." [emphasis added].) In regulation, the relevant powers are the powers to regulate industry performance.

With powers and performance in mind, consider now the difference between state-as-stakeholder (i.e., when it advances its residents' interests over non-residents' interests) and state-as-regulator (i.e., when it focuses on improving industry performance). If we focus less on stakes and more on performance, we focus less on loss and more on benefit.

## Solution

States want deference from federal agencies. Which group of states is more deserving of deference: the cost-shifters and baby-splitters, who emphasize the internal and the short term; or the planners and pie-expanders, who emphasize the external and the long term? Would states deserve—and gain—more credibility with federal regulators if they were seen—and acted—less like states protecting their consumers and more as co-regulators seeking to solve a national problem?

Maybe the answer lies with marshmallows. In the 1960s, researchers started longitudinal studies with a group of four-year-olds. They gave the children a choice: one marshmallow immediately vs. two marshmallows 15 minutes later. Those who managed to defer gratification for 15 minutes had, on reaching high school, better grades and SAT scores; and, decades later, better body mass indices, better careers, better lives. While attributing the inter-child differences in part to "wiring," the researchers did not give up on the immediate gratifiers. There are ways to "re-wire" children—to teach techniques that strengthen the will muscles. (You had a better chance of surviving the 15-minute wait if you simply turned away from the marshmallows or covered your eyes. Other techniques included "kicking the desk, or tug[ging] on their pigtails, or strok[ing] the marshmallow as if it were a tiny stuffed animal.")[82]

Similarly, constituencies that learn to defer gratification live better lives—as do their successors. What has this to do with regulators? Regulators can teach "re-wiring." Regulators are the issue experts. While regulation is political (its decisions assign obligations, benefits, and costs), it is one step removed from politics. Its practices and procedures emphasize fact-finding, principles, and consistency over grab bags, power struggles, and happenstance. (Not to mention desk-kicking, pigtail-tugging, and marshmallow-stroking.) Regulators have the institutional credibility to help citizens grasp the need for deferred gratification. That is why election-year governors who pressure their commissions to "get rates low" have it wrong, while the New England governor who told his commission chairman, "Leave the politics to me; you focus on the long term" had it right.

---

[82] Jonah Lehrer, "DON'T! The Secret of Self-Control," *The New Yorker* (May 18, 2009).

# PART SIX
## Practice and Procedure

---

Procedural law can be confining. Commissions must respond to submissions, grant hearings, and issue orders on time. But a regulator is not a short order cook, racing to serve what his guests have ordered. Effective regulators plan the menu, guide the ingredients, and serve meals that sustain.

The essential step is to take charge of framing. Applicants frame their cases to advance their private interests. Effective regulators reframe these cases to make central the public interest. They also recognize the power of defaults, the non-decision decisions that flow from inertia. Like nations that make organ donation "opt-out" rather than "opt-in" (saving thousands of lives), effective regulators establish policies that promote the public interest when utilities or customers fail to act.

It all comes down to a focus on performance. By establishing and enforcing standards, regulators can design procedures to produce the right results. For effective regulators, a rate case is not just a request for revenues; it is a test for performance. In contrast, putting rate increases on autopilot, through so-called "formula rates," "riders," and "surcharges," induces a trance that is the enemy of alertness.

Current regulatory procedure has two elements that undermine effectiveness. One is the notion that every request deserves a hearing at which every party has its say, regardless of time consumed and merit offered. This pervasive "right to be heard" creates a species of Garret Hardin's "tragedy of the commons": dockets and hearing rooms so crowded that no one has time or place to think. A separate problem is the constant pressure for "settlements." The term is a misnomer, because in regulation, parties can't literally settle cases; commissions decide cases. Settlements (meaning, then, agreements that parties propose to commissions) are useful when only private interests are at stake. But when "settlements" affect the public interest (in regulation, that is nearly always so), they often mirror the aims of the best-resourced parties, those most able to "hold out" for their position. To passively adopt settlements is to preside rather than lead. A commission can encourage settlements and still lead, however, by establishing the principles that potential settlers must pursue.

The most prominent example of regulatory passivity is the continuing, unthinking acceptance of the incumbent monopoly as permanent office-holder. We talk often of competition as the means to make sellers accountable. If competition has this merit, why not have a periodic competition for the right to be the monopoly?

# 41

# "Framing": Does It Divert Regulatory Attention?

> Framing a discussion appropriately is "an ethically significant act."
>
> Robert Frank, "The Impact of the Irrelevant," *The New York Times* (May 30, 2010) (quoting psychology professors D. Kahneman and A. Tversky)

> ... [D]escription is prescription. If you can get people to see the world as you do, you have unwittingly framed every subsequent choice.
>
> David Brooks, "Description is Prescription," *The New York Times* (Nov. 26, 2010) (discussing Leo Tolstoy)

**Most regulatory proceedings** are initiated by utilities who seek, in some way, to increase their profitability. Profitability being part of the public interest, these submissions deserve our attention. But what if these filings are "framed" to divert our attention—away from our public interest mission?

Robert Frank, a Cornell University economics professor, writes about the difference between false advertising and "promotional puffery." Our laws ban the former but allow the latter. The premise, says Frank, is that citizens are "suitably skeptical." But recent behavioral research says we should be skeptical about our skepticism. Frank describes a psychology study conducted in the 1970s. The subjects had to spin a wheel, then guess what percentage of African countries were members of the United Nations. The subjects assumed the wheel was neutral, but it was rigged: For one group of subjects it always stopped on 10, for the other group it always stopped on 65. On average, the first group guessed that the percentage of African countries in the UN was 25 percent; the second group guessed 45 percent. The irrelevant wheel influenced judgment. The psychologists concluded, in a 1981 paper, that "the adoption of a decision frame is an ethically significant act."

A utility proposal is not necessarily "promotional puffery," but it is an exercise in framing—framing a private interest quest (profitability, market share maintenance) as a public interest question (viability, reliability, "synergies"). Does this framing determine, or at least influence, which problems receive regulatory attention, and which solutions win approval? Does private interest framing divert us from our public interest mission?

For three common utility filings, I'll describe the frame, the proposal, and the risk of diversion. What comes through is a false conflict: between the framer's private interest mission and the regulator's public interest mission. By locating and eliminating the false conflict, we can avoid the diversion. Then the needs of the utility and the public can be served simultaneously.

## Formula Rates

Frame: "We face rapidly rising costs, so we need expedited cost recovery."

Proposal: "Formula rates"—a mechanism by which most cost increases flow through to ratepayers without a general rate case.

Diversion risk: If costs are rising, the better question is: Is our utility making all possible efforts, using the most effective practices, to identify and control cost drivers? Are we basing compensation on the utility's wishes or the utility's performance? Focusing on cost recovery alone diverts attention from accountability.

False conflict: There is no conflict between expediting cost recovery and insisting on best practices. We do need to decide, though, which goal is the minimum condition. "Prove use of best practices, then we will expedite cost recovery" is a better approach than "We'll expedite cost recovery because you asked."

## Inter-Regional Utility Merger

Frame: "We need to be 'more competitive' by producing 'synergies.'"

Proposal: A merger between southeastern and midwestern utility holding companies.

Diversion risk: Most regulators do not wake up each day saying, "The path to performance is to merge—let's tell our utilities to seek mergers." Despite dozens of mergers over the last two-and-a-half decades, no one has proved that beyond a certain minimum size, large company combinations have lower per-unit costs, higher rates of innovation, or better customer service, or that a reduction in the number of players improves competition. A merger proposal easily occupies 6 to 12 months of regulatory resources—time better spent identifying best practices and inducing the local utility to adopt them.

**False conflict:** Mergers can be efficient. Many utilities' service area boundaries were determined more than 70 years ago. Technological progress in power production and telecommunications certainly has changed economies of scale and scope. Whether those changes favor smaller companies (by allowing the efficient separation of presently integrated functions) or larger companies (by allowing the integration of distant assets and activities) deserves more attention. A merger, or a divestiture, allows regulators to explore these questions. But an opportunistic merger proposal, framed as "approve it by September or the deal dries up," precludes such reflection.

## "Pre-Approval" of Investment in a Major Power Plant

**Frame:** "We need 400 MW of long-term firm capacity, to be ready in five years. Without cost recovery certainty, granted now, we cannot finance the plant and get it built on time."

**Proposal:** Pre-approval of a decision to build a major power plant, along with a regulatory commitment to allow recovery of construction costs.

**Diversion risk:** By insisting that the regulator focus on a specific project—its costs, financing and timing—the utility diverts attention from the larger questions: Has the utility investigated all options? Has the utility empowered its customers to take all cost-effective measures to reduce demand and consumption? Has the commission designed rates to induce efficient usage? Did the utility paint its regulators into a corner by waiting so long to propose the project that there is no time to study alternatives?

**False conflict:** There is no inherent conflict between inducing efficient consumption and building new capacity. The conflict arises if cart precedes horse—build now, address efficient consumption later. One avoids the conflict by establishing preconditions: "We will approve projects that emerge from an investigation that investigates all reasonable scenarios and ranks all options by cost effectiveness."

\* \* \*

Framing happens so frequently we almost don't notice it. And framing works (for the framer, that is), for three reasons: (1) It depends not on deception but on diversion, on emphasizing something important to the framer and de-emphasizing what is important to the public. (2) Every framed proposal has some public interest component: Cost recovery shouldn't lag behind expenditures, mergers can improve efficiencies, new power plants can avoid blackouts. Unlike the psychologists' wheel, the utilities' frame is rarely irrelevant. (3) Framing rearranges regulators' priorities, since utility filings tend to trigger statutory deadlines while commission-initiated cases do not.

**Solutions:** We can insist we're neutral, that framing has no effect. But the behavioral researchers say we're probably wrong. An obvious solution is to recast private interest proceedings as public interest inquiries—by asking deeper questions, by consolidating narrow cases with broader investigations, by conditioning private approvals on public commitments. Legislatures can help too, by enacting statutes that make commission-initiated proceedings no less mandatory than utility-initiated proceedings. And if a commission lacks sufficient resources to pursue its own priorities, it needs to inform the legislature—whose constituents, if informed, would not tolerate public tax dollars being spent only on private submissions.

# 42

# Decisional Defaults: Does Regulation Have Them Backwards?

**R**ead the book *Nudge*, by Richard H. Thaler and Cass R. Sunstein (2008). Its contribution to regulation is potentially profound. In a section entitled "Defaults: Padding the Path of Least Resistance," the authors assert:

1. "[I]nertia, status quo bias, and the 'yeah, whatever' heuristic are pervasive."

2. "All these forces imply that if, for a given choice, there is a default option—an option that will obtain if the chooser does nothing—then we can expect a large number of people to end up with that option, whether or not it is good for them."

3. "Defaults are ubiquitous and powerful. They are also unavoidable in the sense that for any node of a choice architecture system, there must be an associated rule that determines what happens to the decisionmaker if she does nothing."

4. "Of course, usually the answer is that if I do nothing, nothing changes; whatever is happening continues to happen. But not always."

Their illustration is organ donation. Germany and Austria have different defaults. Germany's is "opt in": a citizen's consent to donation must be explicit. Austria's is "opt out": The law presumes a citizen's consent unless he declines explicitly. In these two adjacent nations, what portion of the population consents? Germany, 12 percent; Austria, 99 percent. Difference in lives saved? Thousands.

The authors argue for an apparent paradox: "libertarian paternalism." They want public policy to give people choices (libertarianism) but guide them toward the "right" choices (paternalism). Public policy need neither ignore people's foibles nor coerce their choices; it can "nudge." Nudging requires policymakers to design the right defaults.

In our field, what happens when inertia takes over, when regulators should decide something but don't? Do our defaults make sense? Five examples follow.

## Energy Efficiency

Consumers underinvest in energy efficiency. They overvalue upfront costs and undervalue long-term benefits; they require too short a payback period; they will passively pay 18 percent interest on a credit card balance but not act to earn an 18 percent return on an efficiency investment. Inertia is powerful—and it harms our consumers and environment.

Yet for most energy efficiency policies, the default—the "choice" if the consumer makes no choice—is to do nothing, i.e., to continue inefficiency, to make us worse off. True, programs are available. But to trigger their benefits, the consumer has to act: find, hire, and pay an energy auditor; choose among multiple thermostats, hot water heater covers, insulation types, window replacements; do the advanced math necessary to learn that paying now produces benefits later; find a bank and fill out loan papers; write a big check. Who on earth does any of these things, when there is soccer to play and *SpongeBob* to watch? Opt-in is our default; as an energy efficiency policy, it fails.

Why not make "opt-out" the default? Opt-out means that unless you say otherwise, a commission-selected, independent auditor will visit your home, determine the cost-effective investments, procure the contractors and the financing, and arrange matters so that the stream of savings exceeds the stream of costs, leaving the resident's wallet untouched but the residence's efficiency increased. Why is our default backwards?

## Retail Competition

Ten years ago, some states passed statutes introducing retail electricity competition. The goal was to have multiple retail suppliers competing on price, customer service and product innovation. These experiments had to scale two interdependent obstacles: incumbent dominance and customer inertia.

In most states, the default was backwards. If a customer selected no supplier, her supplier would be the incumbent. Since most residential customers made no selection (inertia), incumbent dominance continued. The default undermined the entire statutory purpose. This failure was unnecessary. Without eliminating the incumbent option (libertarianism), we could have designed a default that advanced the statutory purpose (paternalism). Why not have non-choosing customers default to the new entrants, based on one of the following criteria: (a) in proportion to the new entrants' market share; (b) randomly; (c) in proportion to benefits offered by the new entrants, such as payments into a low-income fund; (d) according to merit criteria determined and applied by the regulator?

Each of these options has its problems, but so did the default to the incumbent, whose dominant market share was the problem motivating the legislation to begin with. In many jurisdictions, retail electricity choice failed to produce retail electricity competition—a vibrant market with multiple viable suppliers, at least for residential consumers. This default-to-the-incumbent approach, requiring opt-in rather than opt-out, was one reason why.

## Rate Structure

Embedded cost rates are average rates, calculated by dividing the utility's revenue requirement by its expected sales. They are the same rates for every hour of the year. Because actual costs vary by time of day, week and year, average rates do not send accurate price signals; time-of-use rates do. Accurate price signals produce efficient behavior, conserving resources for all citizens. Some states do have optional time-of-use rates, but inertia remains powerful. If embedded cost is the wrong rate and time-of-use rate is the right rate, which is the better default?

## Commission Staffing

How well do we staff our state commissions? The default structure consists of positions designed decades ago, when markets and transactions were different. Our industries face new challenges, but the default is still shaped by civil service rules and budget limits: We tend to shift people to new areas without sufficient education, rather than bring in new people expert in the new issues. The default should not be a static, reactive structure but anticipatory analysis: What are the new challenges? What skill sets will best meet those challenges? Should we retrain our existing people or must we find new people? Hiring procedures should be as flexible as industry change requires.

## Statutory Authority

Competitive business and nonprofit organizations assess their opportunities continuously, restructuring their priorities, staffing and resources to be at their best. The default is alertness, assessment, adjustment and re-invention—aligning decisions with demands.

A commission's statutory authority needs the same constant attention. Legislatures and commissions, combining their comparative advantages,[83] must identify industry structures to encourage, standards of excellence to establish, economic risks to manage, innovations to induce. But our default is different. Our default is

---

[83] See Chapter 33, "Legislatures and Commissions: How Well Do They Work Together?"

a century-old statute, changed only when some political urgency or interest group pressure moves a legislature to amend it—usually adding responsibilities without resources. These episodic interventions do not always produce a coherent whole.

A better default would be a legislative requirement that every two years, commission and legislature produce a joint charter and plan. These documents would describe the challenges faced by each regulated industry, then assess the fit between industry structure and industry performance, between commission responsibility and commission authority, and between commission obligations and commission staffing. Accompanying the document would be a statutory change that reflected all these needs. This default would adjust commission authority to ensure public interest achievement.

# 43

# Utility Performance: Will We Know It When We See It?

[T]he instantaneous textbook solution to achieving better quality has for too many years been to hire more quality inspectors. Unfortunately, it is simply not possible to "inspect-in" or "audit-in" quality. Quality must be designed-in and built-in.

Norman R. Augustine, *Augustine's Laws*

In a single three-month period during my tenure as Executive Director of the National Regulatory Research Institute, our experts addressed a telecommunications bankruptcy, a proposed $2.4 billion integrated gasification combined cycle facility, a 40-state effort to guide multi-utility transmission planning, and a utility's hundred-million-dollar rate increase request. Common to these cases was performance—a term we hear far less frequently than "pre-approval," "cost tracker," "construction work in progress," "revenue requirement" and "rate relief." We seem to pay more attention to dollar flows than to performance standards.

To address this imbalance, NRRI produced that year (2010) three technical papers on utility performance: *How Performance Measures Can Improve Regulation*; *Utility Performance: How Can State Commissions Evaluate It Using Indexing, Econometrics, and Data Envelopment Analysis?*; and *Where Does Your Utility Stand? A Regulator's Guide to Defining and Measuring Performance*. Those papers address the problem conceptually. This essay will look at the problem strategically. It identifies eight obstacles on the path to performance, and five ways to reach a better balance.

## Eight Obstacles on the Path to Performance

**Docket control:** Most docket items arise from utility proposals, which commissions must process within a statutory time limit. These factors combine with resource constraints to crowd out commission-initiated performance reviews.

**Commissioner turnover:** With terms averaging under four years, commissioners have less experience than the utility executives whose performance they must judge. That inexperience combines with humility to blunt the performance-assessment tool.

**Expertise gap:** A credible performance reviewer needs expertise equal to the utility. Because performance review has not had historical priority, this expertise level is not part of the regulatory infrastructure.

**Resource gap:** It remains regulation's unaddressed irony that commissions face hiring freezes and budget cuts to save taxpayer money, while utilities can hire the experts they need using ratepayer money. The resulting resource gap limits performance reviews. (For more on this problem, see Chapters 50 and 51, entitled "Regulatory Resources I: Why Do Differentials Exist?" and "Regulatory Resources II: Do the Differentials Make a Difference?")

**Judicial restrictions:** Some courts have limited commissions' authority to challenge or prescribe utility activities, citing the "managerial prerogative."[84] At their most confining, these judicial statements cause regulators to forsake setting standards for performance. But then when the utility performs poorly, regulators hesitate to penalize, for fear of weakening the utility financially.

**Performance–finance tension:** Utilities need capital, and sources of capital require predictable returns. Performance penalties make capital markets frown. How to signal capital markets that ratepayer dollars will flow, while conditioning that flow on high-quality performance, is a chronic struggle for regulators. The investment community's golden fleece is the "hospitable regulatory environment." Financial analysts strip-search commission decisions for evidence of dollar flow, unobstructed. There is a tendency to equate assessment with animosity, inquiry with inhospitability. This tendency, associated with short-term financial metrics, can discourage commissions from assessing long-term performance.

**No consensus on standards or metrics:** There is no regulatory consensus on to how to define or measure performance.[85] Credible metrics are hard to design, and data hard to gather. These difficulties deter efforts to compare performance

---

[84] See Scott H. Strauss, Jeffrey A. Schwarz and Elaine Lippmann, *Are Utility Workforces Prepared for New Demands? Recommendations for State Commission Inquiries* 28-38 (National Regulatory Research Institute 2010).

[85] See Evgenia Shumilkina, *Where Does Your Utility Stand? A Regulator's Guide to Defining and Measuring Performance* (National Regulatory Research Institute 2010).

among utilities, or to track their improvement or degradation over time. The problem perpetuates itself: Absent consensus on performance parameters, there is no performance conversation; absent conversation, there is no progress on measuring and improving performance.

**The competition–confidentiality connection:** Even utilities with monopoly service rights face competitive entry—some dramatically so (such as wireline incumbents facing competition from wireless sellers). For these utilities, survival as monopoly providers can depend on their competitive success. Sharing data on their strengths and weaknesses creates competitive risk.

## Five Ways to Reach a Better Balance

These eight factors cause great variation in the attention commissions pay to performance. The risk is that performance review occurs not continuously, incrementally and professionally, but only after a major outage or cost overrun—when headlines and political intervention can distract from analysis. Here are some options for improvement.

**Define the desired performance.** Performance covers many subject areas—safety, customer service, financial ratios, operating cost, plant output, innovation, asset management, management vision, workforce efficiency. Because advancing some objectives can detract from others, specifying priorities involves tough trade-offs. But the exercise produces mutual expectations, enabling the commission to hold its utilities accountable.

**Condition approvals on performance.** Rate increases may be required by statute, but so is performance. To grant rate increases when asked but assess performance only when things go wrong is asymmetrical. Every utility request—a certificate to build, a rate increase, a merger or divestiture—should be accompanied by a promise of improvement. Every commission approval, then, should be conditioned on evidence of achievement.

**Embed performance in commission organization and processes.** Successful businesses have divisions and processes devoted to quality control. This practice is worth replicating within commissions. A commission can put each utility on a public schedule for performance reviews, tracking improvement over time. Within a region, especially a region served by the same multistate company, commissions can create interstate committees that construct a common vocabulary, then pool their knowledge and processes, even as the states vary in their weightings. This takes money—and statutes that enable the commission to raise that money.

**Frame regulatory proceedings as performance inquiries; frame regulatory opinions as performance assessments.** A commission is not a supermarket where parties shop for benefits. A commission is a regulatory agency, obligated to establish and enforce performance standards. It is true that statutes entitle parties to make requests and require commissions to respond. But the commission's response need not be confined by the party's request. That is the central difference between courts and commissions. Courts are confined to the parties' presentations; commissions are obliged to advance a larger public interest.[86] It takes extra work, but on receiving a request for rate increase, a commission can require not only evidence of cost of operations, debt, and equity but also evidence of improvement in performance factors.

**Bring Wall Street along.** An Oregon utility executive once said, "Thank goodness for regulators; they save us from ourselves." In the long run, investor interests and ratepayer interests are aligned. Investors don't benefit from performance failure, or from a regulatory system that overlooks it. Because no monopoly position is permanent, strong performance becomes market protection. If regulators send clear signals about expectations and consequences, this rigor will produce more benefit than cost.

---

[86] See Chapter 11, "Commissions Are Not Courts; Regulators Are Not Judges."

# 44

# "Prudence": Who's Minding the Store?

> This was no time to be asking fundamental questions—certainly not in the formative stages of a project.
>
> Norman R. Augustine, *Augustine's Laws*

## Excitement Causes Costs

Regulation has its equations: for the annual revenue requirement, for rate design, for cost of capital, for "grossing-up" taxes. Here's another:

$$PE + PIO + URR + CC = CO,$$

where PE is policy excitement, PIO is private investment opportunity, URR is under-resourced regulators, and CC is captive customers. CO is, of course, cost overruns. Also known as "taking risks with other people's money," the equation predicts accountability slippage and dollar disappointment when four factors exist: (1) Policymakers want something badly; (2) private investors are eager to assist; (3) regulatory resources are unavailable, distracted or overworked; and (4) captives are stuck with the bet. The equation works in both regulated and unregulated markets, where the "captives" are ratepayers and taxpayers, respectively.

There's plenty of historical data to fit the equation: nuclear power in the 1970s, savings and loans in the 1980s, banking and housing in the aughts. These historical examples have their current counterparts. Here are seven cost drivers and their advocates' arguments.

## Are We at Risk Today? Seven Possibilities

**Nuclear power:** "We need more baseload plants, coal is dirty, clean coal is speculative, and renewable is unreliable. Nuclear has learned from its mistakes."

**Transmission:** "We've starved transmission investment for two decades, the new renewable power sources are remote from loads, and baseload generation needs to reach growing population centers."

**Clean coal:** "Coal is America's dominant resource, renewables cannot serve baseload demands, and nuclear remains technologically speculative, stuck in waste storage disputes and dependent on taxpayers to cover catastrophes."

**Smart grid:** "It will help utilities operate more efficiently and reliably while cutting carbon emissions, cause customers to consume less, improve utility planning, and grow jobs."

**Shale gas exploration:** "We can become the 'Saudi Arabia of gas,' cut our foreign energy dependence, and build a low-cost 'bridge to the future,' buying time for nuclear and clean coal."

**Broadband:** "It's today's equivalent of the U.S. mail: Our economy, our educational future and our civic society require that everyone be connected, regardless of location and income."

**Water infrastructure:** "Our pipes and pumping stations are a half-century old, water treatment is becoming more complex, and our population is growing while our water supply is fixed. We need to fix our plumbing."

Plenty of powerful interests, all pressing for approval of their prudence. Is regulation ready?

## Does "Prudence" Get Sufficient Attention? Seven Concerns

To prevent excess costs, we must insist on utility prudence. We have legal tools: the "just and reasonable" standard and its cousin, the "prudence" review. But there are seven obstacles.

**Unclear expectations:** "Just and reasonable" and "prudence" are only chapter headings. Commissions define "prudent" as "what a reasonable person would do." What would a "reasonable person" do with a billion-dollar choice among nuclear, clean coal, transmission and demand response? Courts have defined prudence circularly, as avoiding "unreasonable costs," operating at "lowest feasible cost," and "operat[ing] with all reasonable economies."[87] Regulatory expectations range from "tolerable" to "average" to "excellent." Clarity is needed.

**Intra-agency tension:** Legislatures want regulators to boost favored resources while also ensuring their prudence. That places regulators in a tough spot. An agency tasked by law to propel clean coal cannot easily couple support with skepticism. Two more examples: Federal Power Act Section 219 directs FERC to boost transmission with "incentives." But prudence requires that any transmission solution beat the non-transmission alternatives. How does an agency judge that contest if it's charged with boosting one of the contestants? Similarly, the FCC has declared broadband a national priority. Can it now risk discouraging investors by probing the prudence of broadband plans?

This is not a new problem. The old Atomic Energy Commission had the dual role of advancing nuclear power while ensuring its safety. The resulting role tension caused Congress to separate the functions; the Nuclear Regulatory Commission now handles safety while the U.S. Department of Energy funds nuclear research. The Food and Drug Administration is pressed by the pharmaceutical industry to approve drugs rapidly, even as the public expects protection from unsafe products. The Department of Agriculture publishes dietary guidelines that advise against excess fat and calories, even as its mission includes helping beef and cheese producers.

**Prudence skeptics get marginalized:** When excitement and money surround a solution, supporters caricature prudence skeptics as mission opponents, marginalizing them for having "other agendas." And some have other agendas, like competing solutions—or, just as bad, have no agenda, no alternative, no obligation to grapple and decide, just a habit of saying "no."

**Asymmetry of expertise:** Assessing prudence requires deep knowledge of engineering and project costing. Absent internal expertise equal to the expertise of the planners and builders, a commission will hesitate to judge severely. It's a question of humility.[88]

**Insufficient benchmarks:** We are betting billions on new things—new technology, new forms of financing, new expectations for customer behavior. Newness means the costs and benefits are unknown. Prudence review depends on comparisons, but with new products and few suppliers, and with custom design a constant feature, it is hard to comparison-shop.

---

[87] See, respectively, *General Telephone Co. of Upstate New York, Inc. v. Lundy*, 17 N.Y.2d 373, 377, 218 N.E.2d 274, 277 (1966); *Potomac Electric Power Co. v. Public Service Comm'n*, 661 A.2d 131, 138 (D.C. App. 1995); and *El Paso Natural Gas Co. v. FPC*, 281 F.2d 567, 573 (5th Cir. 1960).

[88] See Chapters 50 and 51, "Regulatory Resources I: Why Do Differentials Exist?" and "Regulatory Resources II: Do the Differentials Make a Difference?"

**Prudence review is no fun:** There is no good time to determine prudence. Pre-expenditure, we lack the perspective and facts needed to make binding decisions on cost caps or cost approvals. Commissions don't like making ratepayers the risk-bearers of unknown outcomes. Post-expenditure, prudence disallowances hurt the utility, and they risk attacks on regulation itself—the clichés of "20-20 hindsight," "Monday morning quarterbacking" and "hostile regulatory environment." Then there's the "too big to fail" dilemma, where assigning the appropriate cost consequence could damage the only company we have. The temporal middle ground—continuous prudence decisions during the construction phase—has its own awkwardnesses, by drawing the commission into monthly project management decisions before it has enough perspective to judge prudence.

**Rhetoric and ideology:** Regulation produces conflicting feelings. We want its protections but resent its obstructions. This dichotomy invites demonizing and demagogueing by the oversimplifiers who accuse the regulatory advocates of "command and control" and the de-regulators of letting "markets run amok." It is better to concede that for untested technologies, both markets and regulation have their weaknesses: A market is effectively competitive only if consumers have substitutes, but new technologies often lack substitutes; while regulation looks skeptically at the suboptimal outcomes that experiments inevitably produce.

*\*\*\**

Excitement has a cost, especially if prudence review is marginalized. How do we bring prudence back to the center? That is the next essay's subject.

# 45

# Rate Case Timing: Alertness or Auto-Pilot?

> How frequently should we reset rates? Regularly—say every two years? Only when someone asks? Or when some trigger gets pulled, like a new plant entering operation?
>
> From a thoughtful regulator

**This question has** a technical side: Are the large cost drivers growing or shrinking? Are riders, surcharges, and adjustment clauses dominating the revenue picture? Is the utility over-earning or under-earning relative to the authorized return on equity?

But there is more to this matter than technique. Try rephrasing the question: "When setting rates, which works better—alertness or auto-pilot?" Then consider these four thoughts.

## Commission Role: Umpire or Initiator?

**Tutorial for regulatory newcomers:** A utility's "annual revenue requirement" is the total dollars the utility needs annually to pay its prudent expenses, invest prudently in infrastructure, pay down debt principal, pay interest on debt, and earn a reasonable return for shareholders. To get rates, we allocate the revenue requirement among customer classes, then divide each class's revenue requirement by the predicted sales to that class, yielding a rate of dollar/unit of sales.

A utility's revenue requirement is a prediction, the sum of hundreds of cost accounts, some reflecting costs already occurred (the sunk capital costs), but many based on estimates. At any point in time, actuals vary from estimates. Traditional ratemaking assumes that these deviations balance out. When there is imbalance, sustained and unidirectional, someone notices, then initiates a rate case—either the utility seeking a rate increase or a consumer intervenor seeking a rate decrease (or the commission initiating a rate investigation). The process works, as long as someone notices the imbalance and acts.

The alert regulator therefore has a continuous monitoring system, distinguishing bumps from trends. When she sees the trend, she starts the rate case. While other entities can initiate a case as well, the regulator's alertness allows her to lead. Then the rate case is not a contest between parties with the regulator keeping score; the rate case is an inquiry led by the regulator, using the parties' information and expertise to produce a public interest answer.

## Commission Leadership: Will Customers Accept Rate Increases?

If a commission is initiator rather than umpire, does it risk appearing responsible for rate increases? Is this a bad thing?

Utility cost increases are inevitable.[89] Long-deferred capital needs, renewables-induced transmission demands, broadband investment, gas pipeline safety, and aging water mains are facts we cannot ignore. We want the public to view these facts as public obligations to embrace, not utility profit-seeking to resent. The commission-as-initiator is better positioned to make this case. The regulatory leader treats customers not as victims to protect but as public interest partners to persuade.

Commission-as-risk-taker has a second benefit: an incentive to mitigate unavoidable rate increases by finding cost decreases. In traditional ratemaking, the utility seeks to cut costs between rate cases, because a dollar saved is a profit earned. But during a rate case, the utility's incentive is the opposite: Argue that expenses are high, to create a cushion for cost-cutting between cases. Knowing this, the commission can lean forward, instructing the utility to bring in ideas on operational efficiencies. The commission is not compelling the company to self-incriminate; the utility can argue against the efficiencies it has identified. But this self-exam will make the record richer. When else in regulation do we press for cost-effectiveness?

## Commission Focus: Revenue or Performance?

The typical rate case is about rates: lining up revenue with cost. It treats the public as ratepayers. But if we view the public as customers rather than ratepayers, we can use rate cases to test performance—to ensure that customers get what they pay for. If we time rate cases based on cost factors only, we focus more on revenue than on performance.

---

[89] Chapter 27, "Low Rates, High Rates, Wrong Rates, Right Rates."

To erase this asymmetry, why not call for rate cases not only when actual costs trend away from the predicted, but also when we learn of new cost-saving opportunities? By requiring the utility to report on the industry's newest best practices, regulators will have a basis for ordering rate decreases to reflect achievable cost savings. We can make performance the attention-equal of revenues by asking two annual questions: "What are the five main improvements that your industry has made in utility operations, planning, and investment?" and "What actions have you taken to embed those improvements in your company's culture and practices?" Rate cases will no longer be about revenues only.

Summing up: A utility initiates a rate case to have its revenues raised, not to have its performance assessed. The reactive regulator falls into line, addressing revenues only. The active regulator will also pursue performance.

## Commission Calibration: Are the Protagonists Aligned with the Public?

To regulate, we calibrate: We intervene as necessary, and only as necessary, to align a utility's business interest with the public interest. In the rate case context, consider the two possible scenarios:

**When rates are high relative to cost:** The utility is not likely to propose a rate reduction. If the utility has better cost information than does the regulator, this situation—producing actual returns above authorized returns—can last indefinitely. This behavior is neither unlawful nor immoral; it is plain vanilla pursuit of profit. But it diverges from the public interest. (Some utilities do offer rate decreases, especially when necessary to retain customers.) So the alert regulator intervenes, by establishing rate case timing.

**When rates are low relative to cost:** One would expect utilities to seek rate increases timely. Like all public actors, though, utilities make political judgments, including delaying rate increases when the public is irritable. These decisions may seem public-spirited, but they can end up weakening the utility's finances or producing balloon increases later. Gradual, small rate increases are less disruptive to personal finance and public trust than infrequent but larger ones. So when rates are too low, the alert regulator again intervenes.

*\*\*\**

What seemed like a mechanical question—"How should we time rate cases?"—raises challenging questions of commission posture and preparedness. Connecting all the possible responses are two nouns—revenue and performance; and four verbs—initiate, lead, focus, and align.

# 46

# Interconnection Animus: Do Regulatory Procedures Create a "Tragedy of the Commons"?

> Picture a pasture open to all.... As a rational being, each herdsman seeks to maximize his gain. Explicitly or implicitly, more or less consciously, he asks, "What is the utility to me of adding one more animal to my herd?"... [T]he rational herdsman concludes that the only sensible course for him to pursue is to add another animal to his herd. And another; and another.... But this is the conclusion reached by each and every rational herdsman sharing a commons. Therein is the tragedy. Each man is locked into a system that compels him to increase his herd without limit—in a world that is limited. Ruin is the destination toward which all men rush, each pursuing his own best interest in a society that believes in the freedom of the commons. Freedom in a commons brings ruin to all.
>
> Garret Hardin, "The Tragedy of the Commons," *Science* (Dec. 13, 1968), available at www.garretthardinsociety.org/articles/art_tragedy_of_the_commons.html

**No one disputes** the benefits of interconnectedness: accessible air travel, job mobility, telecommuting, economies from interregional trade. Yet regulatory efforts to increase electrical interconnectedness draw opposition, seemingly reflexive, always intense. Embedded in regulatory practice and culture, this behavior is not cost-free; public benefits are delayed and diminished. Can we make adjustments, or is opposition inevitable?

## Procedural Narrowness Yields Zero-Sum Relationships

Consider the battle over new, extra-high-voltage electric transmission facilities. In the Virginia-to-Ohio region, FERC allocated their costs on a "postage stamp" basis (all users pay the same rate regardless of location or specific benefit, on the grounds that everyone benefits somehow). Challenged in the Seventh Circuit by Ohio, Illinois, and other Midwestern interests, FERC lost. The Court found insufficient evidentiary support and inconsistent FERC reasoning.[90]

The case is but one of many cost allocation battles, state against state, producer against consumer, utility against independent, East against West. Despite the national benefits of new infrastructure, controversy persists over who should pay. Two reasons are statutory and cultural. Regulatory statutes—in this case the Federal Power Act—always grant opportunities to litigate: New facilities require new costs; new costs require rate filings; rate filings attract proponents and opponents. Our litigation culture adds the sharp edges: Victory-seeking clients hire victory-promising lawyers; these party-pairs join the battle if the litigation cost is below the value of winning multiplied by the probability of winning.

One more ingredient makes conflict inevitable: the narrowness of the typical proceeding. A 500-kV transmission facility looks like a "big project." But for a nation with 300 million citizens who rely on electricity for everything from incubators to funeral homes, a single transmission facility is a small contributor to life's daily costs. Yet it gets its own proceeding, in which participants then focus on winning benefits and avoiding costs associated with that single facility. *Procedural narrowness is the key ingredient in the recipe for a zero-sum dish.* By isolating each proposal from its benefits context, our procedures promise a showdown between win-seekers and loss-avoiders.

## Facility-Specific, Party-Centric Litigation Produces a Procedural "Tragedy of the Commons"

Once a proposal reaches the cost allocation stage, its prudence is presumed. Prudence means that over a time horizon sufficiently long, and over a geographic territory sufficiently wide, the benefit-cost ratio is sufficiently positive to justify the investment relative to alternatives. The only question remaining should be, "How do we allocate the net benefits so that no one is worse off and everyone is better off?"

---

[90] *Illinois Commerce Commission, et al. v. FERC*, 576 F.3d 430 (7th Cir. 2009).

## INTERCONNECTION ANIMUS: DO REGULATORY PROCEDURES CREATE A "TRAGEDY OF THE COMMONS"?

In Litigation Land, that positive approach is a rarity. Narrow, proposal-specific proceedings mean that even if the proposal is part of a net-benefits package, a party has a right to oppose it if, for that project and that party, the benefit-cost ratio is negative. This right to a hearing, project-by-project, causes waste and distraction. There is an expectation that every proposal must have a positive outcome for every party, that a proposal is "bad" if it makes anyone worse off. How logical is it, how useful, to slice-and-dice regulatory decisions into a series of win–lose polarities? No clear-thinking citizen (i.e., one uninfected with regulatory experience) would insist that every public policy benefit him personally. Otherwise, we would cease funding for multiple sclerosis because not everyone contracts it, eliminate the local crossing guard because not everyone crosses there, eliminate the Air and Space Museum because not everyone goes there, and eliminate every other program for which the cost bearers differ from the benefit receivers.

Oddball examples? They do not differ logically from oppositional responses to cost allocation proposals for utility infrastructure. These oppositions, each one rational individually, draw out regulatory proceedings, delay benefits, add costs, and kill projects. Under our regulatory procedures, the sum of individually rational litigation decisions yields a societally irrational result.

Welcome to regulation's "tragedy of the commons," where the commons is not Garrett Hardin's pasture, but the "right to a hearing" for every cost-causing project. We slice proposals so narrowly that someone always has a reason—and a right—to oppose. The sum of all these individual rights, vigorously and expensively exercised, creates policy gridlock and Hatfield-vs.-McCoy animus.[91]

Hardin points out that "the commons, if justifiable at all, is justifiable only under conditions of low population density. As the human population has increased, the commons has had to be abandoned in one aspect after another." This reasoning applies to regulatory procedure. When administrative litigation was simple—buyer and seller arguing over rate levels—there was sufficient aural and temporal space to air all concerns. That simplicity is gone. A typical transmission case can have a dozen parties, arguing about total cost, allocated cost, need, alternatives, rate design, intergenerational equity, environmental effects, eminent domain and more. As with Hardin's pasture, the problem grows geometrically, because (a) there are multiple cases simultaneously and (b) every party's "right to be heard" begets a counter-right in that party's opponents. These factors shrink the supply of problem-solving resources: time, money and goodwill. The result is Hardin's tragedy of the commons.

---

[91] See Mark Twain, *The Adventures of Huckleberry Finn*: "A feud is this way: A man has a quarrel with another man, and kills him; then that other man's brother kills *him*; then the other brothers, on both sides, goes for one another; then the *cousins* chip in—and by and by everybody's killed off, and there ain't no more feud. But it's kind of slow, and takes a long time."

So regulators call for "consensus" and "cooperation." This reliance on voluntary restraint, on what Hardin calls "conscience," produces a Darwinian result: The victorious are the holdouts—the ones who resist consensus and cooperation. As Hardin concludes, "Conscience is self-eliminating."

## Solution: Broaden Proceedings' Scope So That Benefits Exceed Costs

To save our regulatory commons, we must break out of zerosumsmanship. We need proceedings whose substantive scope ensures that total benefits exceed total costs.

A transmission system benefits not only the generation and loads it connects, but also the regional economy it supports. "Just and reasonable" ratemaking does not always count that broader benefit. Ratemaking merely identifies a revenue requirement and the rate levels necessary to produce it. There is no mention of employment growth, industrial location attractiveness, or environmental values, even though the right transmission proposal can enhance all three. It is this singular focus on revenue requirement and rate levels that produces zero-sum thinking. As any attendee of multistate, multiparty regional transmission "settlement" discussions will testify, calls for "consensus" do not work well in a zero-sum context.

Ratemaking's confines need not condemn us to endless cost allocation disputes. The key is to broaden the decisional context. There is usually some combination of transmission proposals, covering broader geographic areas or long time horizons, for which total benefit exceeds total cost. By replacing zero-sum proceedings with positive benefits proceedings, the parties can fight over benefits rather than cost. The result: more cooperation, more speed, more results.

# 47
# Interconnection Animus: The Readers React

**The preceding essay** prompted an unusual number of responses. I am grateful for this thoughtfulness, examples of which appear below. All the writers emphasized that they spoke only for themselves, not for their organizations or clients.

Several writers noted the coincidence of an essay on Hardin's "Tragedy of the Commons" appearing in the same week that the Nobel Committee awarded the Economics Prize to Dr. Elinor Ostrom. One person wrote that she won the prize "primarily for her research in dissecting the 'Commons Problem' and advancing the idea of sustainability. She is also the first woman to win this coveted prize. Hardin is indeed the 'father' of the Tragedy concept, but Ostrom gave it new life."

On a wonderful personal note, Indiana Commissioner **Larry Landis** wrote:

> [W]hen I told you earlier that I had been introduced to Garret Hardin's essay nearly 40 years ago, it was by the professor with whom I took the last class required for my master's in political science, a crossover political science/economics class ... [T]hat professor was Elinor Ostrom of Indiana University, who this week was named co-recipient of the Nobel Prize in economics. And by the way, the class was phenomenal. Life is amazing that way.

Finance expert **Stephen Hill** wrote:

> One reason for the electric transmission building "boom" is FERC's change in the allowed return rewards. They elected to provide profit levels above the cost of equity to encourage such building and have based the cost of equity on market-based estimates of integrated utility costs (DCF/CAPM). However, FERC also allows those operations to recover their costs through a "formula rate," in which the allowed return on equity (profit) is recovered monthly, without fluctuation, like a cost. A steadily earned profit is not a risky income stream, and the yield of such an income stream to an investor would have to be substantially less than

that appropriate for a publicly traded integrated company. My point here is that the Commons Tragedy you reference, I believe, has been set in motion by misguided regulatory policy at FERC. I don't have a problem with profit incentives (i.e., letting the "market" work); it seems to me that what's being allowed, due to the manner in which transmission equity returns are collected, far exceeds the actual cost of equity capital for those firms.

**Dr. Ken Zimmerman** of the Oregon Commission staff wrote:

Scott, perhaps you miss the point here. Perhaps the issue is not cost allocation per se but rather who, by what parties, and by what process that allocation should occur. In other words, are regulators, courts, hearings, and the like the best (in whatever sense of the word) parties/process to construct either the pie to be allocated or the allocations themselves? I would suggest not. Perhaps we need to turn the process and parties around. We could begin from the bottom up and build both the understanding of the projects/operations and the costs involved, as well as the goals they will serve and the consequences of not moving forward with the work. This process still has the chance of failure, but it would help reduce the "zero-sum gaming" you mention, as well as the opportunistic last-minute "shots across the bow" of old adversaries.

**Edith Pike-Biegunska** of Regulatory Assistance Project wrote:

You claim (and I agree) that important societal considerations are disadvantaged in the current ratemaking process. The battle that most recently culminated in the Seventh Circuit decision in *Illinois Commerce Commission v. FERC*[92] illustrates the type of drawn-out controversy that current ratemaking procedures often yield. Your discussion uses this as an example of how the narrow interests of a few stakeholders can waylay projects that are, in fact, beneficial to society at large. While your essay focuses on procedure as the main culprit in thwarting socially constructive proposals, I wonder whether the problem does not actually lie in the substantive statutory provisions of the FPA.

In the last section of your essay, you highlight the fact that "just and reasonable" ratemaking does not take into consideration important factors such as environmental values and employment growth. Do you think that one way to address this problem might be by amending the FPA itself to directly apportion societal resources to projects with the types of benefits that the current system ignores? The FPA might, for example, mandate "clean first" policies. Clean first policies would provide access

---

[92] *Illinois Commerce Commission v. FERC*, 576 F.3d 470 (7th Cir. 2009).

to clean energy generation ahead of traditional, fossil fuel-intensive generation through: (1) rate design; (2) new interconnections; and (3) transmission access. Such an approach might avoid the need to curtail stakeholders' rights to contest proposals, while ensuring that environmentally and socially beneficial policies are considered. I wonder whether this sort of substantive amendment to the FPA itself would address your concerns.

**Jason Zeller** of the California Public Utilities Commission staff added:

A couple of possible changes might improve the transmission approval process: one would be the creation of interstate compacts between adjacent states that would establish rules for cost allocation for lines that cross state lines. For example, one could posit developing a single criterion for evaluating the merits of new lines, such as a positive cost/benefit ratio. The compact or the individual state commission would approve established values for enhanced reliability, transfer capacity, access to renewable resources, economic development opportunities, increases in property taxes, and reductions in line losses. NARUC [National Association of Regulatory Utility Commissioners] or NRRI [National Regulatory Research Institute] could provide some economic and technical expertise for modeling these values. Concerning siting, the inherent conflict between the localized effects and dispersed benefits of new transmission projects could be mitigated by developing compensation formulas that are targeted to affected communities. Compensation for affected communities could become part of the transmission tariff itself, e.g., a mil per kWh. Finally, any transmission approval process should include a mandatory ADR component with a dedicated facilitator to resolve conflicts prior to formal litigation.

And this from **Ron Edelstein** of the Gas Research Institute:

We often face similar issues on justifying public or consumer interest R&D. It turns into a contested rate case, with multiple parties, consumer advocates, large industrials, commission staff, and gas companies, even before it gets to the commissioners. Free riders (like electric utilities, who benefit from O&M cost reduction and supply R&D but don't have to pay for gas R&D) abound. Questions of "Will this R&D happen anyway without ratepayer funding?", "Why should my consumer class pay?", and "Why should my state pay?" are all raised. Benefit/cost ratios are discussed and can be quantified, but how much of the benefit goes to the gas company and how much to the consumers, how much to manufacturers of equipment, how much to producers and service companies, and how much to the general public (like clean air) are contentious issues.

So good R&D programs go unfunded or underfunded, and all, including the consumers of all classes, the general public, the gas companies, and the nation, pay the price in lost opportunities. EPRI faces a similar problem, and of course Bellcore was eventually sold by the baby bells to SAIC when they started competing with each other.

**Larry Nordell**, an economist with the Montana Consumer Counsel, said:

Scott, I think you are wrong on this one—at least you are painting with way too broad a brush. The arguments for spreading the costs of new transmission over all customers is a favorite one of resource developers, who want access to markets without paying the costs of transmission and who know their projects will look cheaper to the purchasing utilities if they are not tied to transmission expansion costs. And the arguments are a favorite for renewable advocates who simply assert that the benefits are obvious and don't want to be bothered with details. But in fact, (and my experience is in the west and may be different from the eastern interconnection) there are usually clear beneficiaries for most of these transmission lines and clear target markets for the generation projects. Why should those who don't benefit have to subsidize them? If wind developers in Montana want transmission to market to California, shouldn't they have to get the agreement of California buyers to pay for their power and the transmission costs before the lines are built? Your proposal would have such lines built, and the costs spread over the western interconnection, without any hard look by California utilities at whether they want the energy—that is, whether the benefits are great enough to warrant the costs, given the available alternatives. That is a basic tenet of economic reasoning, and it is not helpful to discard it simply by raising the specter of the tragedy of the commons.

Further, I find your use of the "tragedy of the commons" analogy to be ironic. The usual formulation is that when people do not face the costs of their resource use they tend to overuse it. Spreading the costs of new transmission to all parties and separating transmission costs from the resource decisions leading to the need for the new lines will lead exactly to that result.

The west has a long history of cooperation on interstate lines that belies your claim of regulatory myopia, a cooperation that would be sorely tested by trying to force the non-benefiting states to pay for the lines as well as to accept the impacts. Here's the reasoning Northern Tier

Transmission Group (which I have worked with) has used with regard to cost allocation: preferable cost allocation proposals are those that have the voluntary support of the parties on whom costs are proposed to be allocated. In the event that a party asks Northern Tier Transmission Group to devise a cost allocation for a project which has not been able to gain voluntary acceptance, costs will be allocated in accordance with beneficiary pays and cost causer pays. But the parties are cautioned that estimates of benefits are uncertain and subject to risk, and turning estimates into a mandatory cost allocation is not a simple technical exercise. I should note that Northern Tier Transmission Group does not have authority to do anything more than recommend a cost allocation to the relevant Commissions. MISO, which does have that authority, appears to be heading in a similar direction.

It is entirely too easy, when one is proposing that one's favorite project be paid for by others' money, to succumb to optimism in projecting benefits and to ignore risks and less favorable outcomes. The best and most careful judges of how big and how likely benefits will be are the people whose money is at stake. Mandatory cost spreading would lead to bad judgments on which lines to build, how big to build them, and when to build them. This would be an irresponsible outcome for the regulatory community. And that leads to my final comment: Your essay reads like a position of advocacy by an enthusiast for a favored result. In my view, it is an inappropriate position for you to take as the head of NRRI. There is a full court press on currently promoting the spreading of transmission costs without regard to benefits. We need well reasoned responses from the regulatory community, and we need and expect your help.

**Hannes Pfeifenberger** of Brattle wrote:

Scott—very much true and very well put … The RTOs' formulaic cost–benefit and cost-allocation approaches … have pretty much undermined transmission investment for anything but reliability reasons. Luckily, the industry has figured that out now. The only question is whether we can find the vision and political will to do something about it. I think not even the state commissions working together will get us there. It may require regional governors to get together.

# 48

# Regulatory "Settlements": When Do Private Agreements Serve the Public Interest?

> It is the policy of this commission to encourage settlements.
>
> Multiple sources

> Settlements seem somehow to reach the lowest common denominator in many instances, and often end up defying the public interest. They are often used to tie commissioners' hands, not to help them resolve vexing problems.
>
> Former state commission chair

**State commissions are** seeing more filings: rate cases, requests for pre-approvals of major capital investments, corporate restructurings. Commissions also are starting proceedings themselves, investigating carbon reduction options, transmission construction, and renewable energy.

At the same time, commission staffs are shrinking due to hiring freezes and retirements (many were hired in the 1970s when energy was "big"). With rising workloads squeezing shrinking staffs, settlements are attractive as work-reducers. But settlements are double-edged swords: They have positive value if they solve public interest challenges, negative value if they edge the commission out of its statutory role. This distinction is not always easy to see.

**"Settlement" is a misnomer.** First, a clarification of terms. A regulated utility may conduct no commerce—provide no service, charge no rates—without commission approval based on filed documents. That is the law in nearly every jurisdiction. This "filed rate doctrine" distinguishes utility regulation from ordinary commerce. In regulation, therefore, a "settlement" cannot set policy. It is only the "settling" parties' proposal to the commission. A settlement settles nothing.

## Benefits of Settlements

**Informality:** Settlements involve informal exchange. Informal exchange enhances understanding of each entity's technical problems and private goals. Both effects spiral upwards. As technical fluency grows, commissions defer to the parties' solutions, encouraging more informal exchange, more technical understanding, and more commission deference. Mutual exposure to parties' private goals spurs settlement solutions that align private interest with public interest—if the commission has established public interest parameters first.

**Expedition:** Settlements can save time. Two caveats: First, when there are resource differentials among the parties and the settlement process is unguided by commission principles, large parties can grind down the small, making "settlement" a euphemism for "take it or leave it." Litigation, when disciplined and efficient, can make resource differences less relevant, because alert hearing officers can weed out the time-wasters. Second, saving time is not an end in itself; success is measured in the quality of outcomes, not the number of dispositions.

## Risks of Regulation-by-Settlement

A settlement culture can induce regulator passivity. Regulators who wait for the parties to settle (a) engage less mentally, (b) learn less about the regulated businesses, (c) build less confidence, and (d) become less relevant. A stance of "Let's see what the parties say" leads to "Let's see what the parties want" and, ultimately, "Who are we to stand in the way of their deal?" There is risk of atrophy: Muscles unused become muscles less able. This spiral points downward: As the commission becomes less engaged and less alert, it becomes less respected and less relied upon, leading to more settlements and more atrophy.

## Settlements Confuse Commissions with Courts

A court's jurisdiction is limited to a case or controversy initiated by a plaintiff. A settlement eliminates the controversy. *Plaintiff vs. Defendant* becomes *plaintiff and defendant*, the parties agreeing that they no longer need the judge. The court has no general "public interest" power independent of the dispute as defined by the parties.[93]

---

[93] Caution: In disputes with a large public interest component, a court could reject a plaintiff-defendant motion to withdraw, especially if intervenors remain dissatisfied. The court's powers still are bounded, however, by the original complaint.

But a commission is not a court.[94] A commission's powers are defined not by the case-as-filed, but by the substantive statute that enables, creates and empowers the commission. The commission's baseload duty—to ensure reliable service at reasonable prices—does not vary with parties' private decisions to initiate or "settle" disputes. The regulatory purpose is not inter-party peace but public interest advancement.

## So When Are Settlements Appropriate?

Settlements are appropriate when they help a commission carry out its public interest obligations. Examples: (1) The settlement subject demands technical proficiency, (2) the parties' proficiency exceeds the commission's, and (3) the parties' private interests are aligned with the long-term public interest.

**But beware of gaps, in the settlement process and the outcome.** If the settlement process is missing segments of the public interest spectrum, such as future generations, workforce quality, environmental responsibility, management efficiency or technological innovation, the settlement's claim on the public interest is incomplete. And the mere presence of these segments does not necessarily mean *effective* presence. As noted, the mantra that "settlements are more efficient than litigation" has holes when there are resource differentials. Undisciplined settlement processes favor large parties: They can attend more meetings, produce more studies, bring more staff, pay more lawyers to talk longer and louder. In contrast, strong judges using efficient litigation procedures can make resource differentials diminish. Abstract preferences for settlement ignore these points.

## What Evidentiary Support?

A commission order makes policy. A settlement-approving order is no different. Credible policies require credible evidence. A settlement therefore needs testimony supporting the signatories' public interest assertions. That settlement testimony must have the same rigor and comprehensiveness as litigation testimony. "We negotiated hard and this is our agreement" is not public interest evidence.

The record should contain both the evidence that supports the settlement, and the evidence that preceded the settlement. Settlements often require each signatory to withdraw its initial testimony, mainly because that testimony contradicts the settlement outcome. A party now asserting that "the settlement ROE of 12.5 percent is sufficient" prefers no reminder of his prior statement that "anything below 14 percent will cripple the company." No party wishes to be heard saying, "As my chances of victory vary, so does my view of the truth." Testimony is a statement under oath; it is not mere choreography, to revise as the music

---

[94] See Chapter 11, "Commissions Are Not Courts; Regulators Are Not Judges."

changes. Credibility is the coin of the regulatory realm. Respect for the realm diminishes if the commission abets testimonial hide-and-seek. Leaning in the other direction—recording all filed testimony, pre- and post-settlement—disciplines parties to take public interest positions to begin with.

## Recommendations

Regulatory settlements are joint proposals for commission action. They advance the public interest when the "jointness" arises not from short-term baby-splitting, not from one-party dominance masked as compromise, but from expert idea-sharing. (Settlements also work for compromises of private commercial matters that do not affect non-parties, present or future.) The likelihood of public interest results rises, therefore, if the commission focuses not on an abstract preference for harmony, but on two criteria. First, a settlement proposal must be backed by principles and evidence aligned with commission priorities. Second, the resources, expertise, and alternatives available to each party must be roughly equivalent. Under these conditions, no one party's view of "the public interest" prevails for reasons other than merit.

# 49

# Competition for the Monopoly: Why So Rare?

> [T]he public has an obvious interest in competition, "even though that competition be an elimination bout."
>
> Hecht v. Pro-Football, Inc., 570 F.2d 982, 991 (D.C. Cir. 1977) (quoting Union Leader Corp. v. Newspapers of New England, Inc., 284 F.2d 582, 584 n.4 (1st Cir. 1960))

**Storms bring outages,** outages bring anger, and the angry ask: Can we replace the utility? During the 2011–2012 outages, Long Islanders asked it about the publicly owned Long Island Power Authority; D.C. area residents asked it about the investor-owned Potomac Electric Power Company. During their 1999–2001 price and supply crisis, Californians asked it about their utilities. Crises are bad times to make long-term decisions, but good times to ask big questions, like "Why do we do things this way?"

Commissions revoke franchises rarely—those of major utilities (as opposed to small water companies) nearly never. To raise the question is to lose credibility. It's "politically unrealistic." It's "never been done before." "The devil we know is better than the devil we don't." "It'll upset Wall Street." "The Governor will have our heads." So many ways to say "no."

This mental blockage, this consensus against curiosity, undermines the cause of regulation. It creates an expectation as entrenched as it is unstated: that the incumbent's tenure is lifelong. The common penalty for inadequacy is a small fine and a second chance: the fine calculated to sting but not disable, the second chance wrapped in a rate increase to fund the fix, a combination of knuckle-rap and back-pat, a regulatory reflex described by Peter Bradford (paraphrasing a former New England Chairman) as "And if you do that again, we'll clobber you."

If we award profits for adequacy rather than excellence, the utility's inevitable slippages will be departures from adequacy rather than excellence. In real markets, markets with alert, active consumers, sellers walk on the high wire. Their choice is simple and stark: Excel or lose. How might regulators of monopolies replicate this performance pressure? One answer is to host a periodic competition for the right to be the monopoly. The competition would have five components.

1. **Term of years:** With no specified term there is no election day: no challenger, no competition of ideas, no sense that survival depends on excellence. That is why most utilities have stayed in office for a century. Accountability would be enhanced by a stated franchise term: some period long enough to deter distorted decisionmaking (e.g., putting off capital expenditures to keep rates low—like cutting funds for schools and road repairs, it lowers taxes now but raises costs later ), and short enough to ensure responsiveness to customers' needs. The 20- to 30-year range makes sense. (To clarify: The goal is not to term-limit the incumbent but to make it compete to keep its job.)

2. **Bidding procedure and ranking criteria:** Pre-qualification standards would screen bidders for experience, skill, and financial strength. Then come the subjectivities: Is there a corporate culture plan that places public service first, that accepts the mission and role of regulation? Is there a business plan that identifies the products and services customers need and the cost-effective means to design and deliver them? (The commission will need to provide prospective bidders all essential data about the service territory and customer base; otherwise the incumbent will have an unearned advantage.)

3. **Clear regulatory policies:** No investor wants a pig in a poke. Before the bidding, the commission and legislature must give guidance on expectations, rewards, and penalties. While policymakers should not pour cement around their policies—change over 20 to 30 years is inevitable—they should promise that prudent costs incurred to accommodate changes are recoverable.

4. **Path for property transfer:** This is where discussions bog down: How does the bid winner get control of the incumbent's infrastructure? The property transfer path must be predictable and litigation-free, the buyout price known at the time of the bid. This is not hard, if one follows mainstream regulatory principles. Utility infrastructure has two key features: (1) It is immobile, so its value depends on using it for the franchise purpose; and (2) the utility's customers have paid for it through their rates, so they deserve to receive its remaining economic value. Given these features, the proper price for the incumbent's property is depreciated book value. This price gets the incumbent its constitutionally guaranteed "just compensation": recovery of and return on its investment. (Anything more is, technically, an economic

windfall: a payoff exceeding the investors' legitimate expectation.) Since this same departure payment will apply both to the current incumbent and new franchisee when the latter's term ends, bidders will face no uncertainty about recovering their prudent investment. And this fixed price principle prevents a bidding war for the target company. Competitors can design their bids to serve the public rather than to please incumbent shareholders—a marked difference from utility acquisition strategy today.

The preceding paragraph assumed the new franchisee would own the infrastructure. The alternative is a one-time transfer from the incumbent to the state or local government. The government-owned infrastructure then is operated by the winning franchisee. Each approach—private and public ownership—has its pros and cons, all needing more study. Plenty of U.S. utilities are owned by governments, whether local, state, or federal. On the one hand, government ownership reduces customer cost by using tax-exempt financing and eliminating return on equity investment (and income taxes on that profit). It avoids the classic shareholder–customer struggle, known as the "Averch-Johnson" effect, whereby all else equal, utilities prefer actions that grow the profit-earning rate base over actions that reduce total customer cost. (The non-asset-owning franchisee can still profit handsomely from its performance; the key is to design the franchisee's compensation to align shareholder and customer interests rather than make them adversaries.) On the other hand, government ownership, even with operations in private hands, creates risk that investment and maintenance decisions will be distorted by political pressures, like pressures to lower costs for current voters at the expense of future voters, or to "create jobs" through investments that are not cost-effective.

5. **Financial uncertainty:** The prospect of losing its franchise will make the franchisee's business profile riskier (although unlike non-utilities, it knows it will recover its prudent investments). That higher risk means higher capital costs. But there are ways to reduce risk, at no cost to customers. To reduce lenders' risk, the bidding process can make clear that (a) physical collateral for the loans (the physical assets used to provide utility service) will remain in place and in use (with prudent cost recovery assured) regardless of the franchisee's identity, (b) any loan obligations will transfer automatically to the new franchisee (whose financial ability to take on those loans would be among the selection criteria), and (c) all prudent outstanding debt will be reflected in rates.

Shareholder uncertainty is another matter—assuming the new franchisee is shareholder-owned. The company's cost of equity will reflect the risk that it might lose its franchise (but not its investment) after 20 years. That cost is legitimate; customers must pay for it. So policymakers must compare that cost to the performance gains from franchise competition.

\* \* \*

And that is the unknown. Would shareholders, facing the risk of losing the franchise, elect different kinds of board members, who in turn would hire different kinds of executives and managers, to lead these companies? Would those board members and executives make the utility more dedicated to performance for the customer, so that the utility generates ideas for innovation rather than requests for "rate relief"? Would regulators, knowing it was their job to select the best, become more active in pressing for improvement? Regulators are gaining experience with using competition to supply essential franchise services formerly the incumbent's responsibility. Maryland, New Jersey, Ohio and others oversee the bidding from wholesale supply of capacity and energy. Hawaii, Maine, Oregon, and Vermont have selected new franchisees to supply energy efficiency services. Maine is investigating alternative suppliers of smart grid services.

There is no intent here to spell out all possible facets of a franchise competition process. Employee rights, customer-financed expertise built up within the company, liability for unknown environmental damage committed by the predecessor: All these factors, and more, require attention. But a predictable, periodic competition for the franchise could change a service territory's psychology. Today, franchise revocation is the nuclear bomb in the regulator's arsenal of accountability, never to be mentioned, let alone used. Better to view franchise competition as a mainstream means of extracting best practices, by attracting the companies most likely to invent and use them. The legal and political burdens should not be on the regulator to justify replacing the incumbent; the burdens should be on the incumbent (and any prospective replacement) to justify their privileged role. That way, franchise competition can align the interests of all: regulators, customers, executives and investors.

# PART SEVEN
# Regulatory Organizations

---

The first six Parts have focused on regulators as people. But organizations matter also. Regulatory commissions face immense organizational challenges. Asymmetry of resources between the regulator and the regulated is so chronic and pervasive that insiders treat it as inevitable despite its inanity. The situation is intolerable, yet few speak out. And the resource gap is growing, as legislators impose new duties while budget-balancers maintain old staff levels.

Regardless of resources, a commission owes its public explanations of its merit. Commissions need to measure their effectiveness and justify their budgets. They must position themselves, just as private interests do, "branding" their work in ways that educate citizens about regulation's purposes and needs.

# 50

# Regulatory Resources I: Why Do Differentials Exist?

> ... [S]trategies are not something you *hope* for; strategies are something you *work* for.
>
> Peter F. Drucker, *The Daily Drucker* p. 340 (2004) (emphasis in original)

**Effective regulation should** aim for excellence. Regulators establish standards, design rewards and penalties, then evaluate and assign consequences. The process should induce continuous improvement in utility performance.

Judging utility performance requires experts in utility performance. Utility responsibilities are frighteningly varied. They have to replace infrastructure, reduce environmental effects, induce efficient customer behavior, discover and deploy new technologies, redefine universal service, and raise capital from a skittish investor community. To assess all these actions—assessing being the regulator's main job—requires expertise no less deep and broad than the utility's. Regulatory expertise requires, in turn, personnel with the training, experience, and support sufficient to set and apply new standards, in a way that earns credibility from those who are judged.

The open secret is that most utilities have more expertise than most commissions. That differential undermines regulation's purpose, because it causes regulators to view utility efforts deferentially rather than skeptically. (A true skeptic is not an opponent; she is willing to be convinced but insists on being convinced.) When deference replaces skepticism, the roles of regulator and regulated are reversed. The standards, and the pace of improvement, get established by the regulated and accepted by the regulator.

This essay asks three questions: Are there differentials in resources and expertise? Why do they exist? Why do they persist? The following essay then asks three more questions: Does the differential make a difference in regulation's quality and credibility? Why does it receive so little political attention? How might we solve the problem?

## Are There Differentials?

Why debate it? Does anyone really think that, outside of the largest states, commission staff is the resource equivalent of the utilities? The differential is everywhere.

**Hearing room:** In a typical rate proceeding, the utility has a separate witness for each of five to ten major issue areas, with each witness supported by one or more number crunchers, technical writers and reviewers. Representation is usually by outside counsel with decades of experience, backed by younger associates and inside counsel. The commission staff has much less.

**Audits:** The utility will bring a separate expert for each cost center, backed by underlings and the outside auditor. The commission staff has much less.

**Career paths and continuity:** For each major position within the utility corporation there is a "farm team" of up-and-comers preparing, and being prepared, to take over. Commissions can rarely afford such redundancy. More common is that a commission loses a 30-year veteran who is the organization's expert-on-almost-everything, with no comparable person to carry on. (This is happening now. People first hired in late 1970s and early 1980s, recruited to handle Arab oil embargo implications, nuclear power, gas pipeline unbundling and telecommunications foment, are retiring in an era when no one runs for political office on a platform of hiring top-notch government regulators.)

**Professional development:** After hundreds of speaking engagements at all manner of industry conferences, I can testify that the majority of attendees come from the industry, often using funds from utility budgets funded by utility customers.

## Why Do Differentials Exist? Why Do They Persist?

**Legislative discretion exceeds commission discretion:** In most jurisdictions, the commission's budget is sized by the legislature, whose discretion is limited only by politics. The utility's budget comes before the commission, whose discretion is limited by statute and Constitution. So the legislature can line-draw—between spending and cutting, between effective regulation and ineffective regulation—according to its preferences (and the pressures that form those preferences). But regulatory law views a utility's regulatory expenditures as a customer responsibility, meaning that if the total is reasonable, the commission must approve it. The utility's expenditure is not unreasonable merely because it is larger than the commission's.

**Staffing practices, commissioner terms and commission workload favor inertia:** Staff sizes, job classifications and salaries have roots in the 1970s and 1980s. Then regulatory life was simpler: Rate cases and audits were the norm, consumer advocates and utilities were the lone parties. Regulatory life has grown more complex, but staff infrastructure has not kept pace. Further, most commissioners enter office without utility regulation experience; many stay fewer than four years. Commission chairs are no different. Add the crush of case processing, and it is nearly impossible to acquire the time and mastery necessary to restructure an agency.

**Legislatures are more likely to enact mandates than to fund them:** State commissions will receive (some have already received) multiple utility requests to approve the construction of nuclear power plants, with total costs in the hundreds of billions of dollars. What state legislature has recognized this reality by authorizing state commission hiring of nuclear construction experts? Similarly, over a dozen state legislatures have directed their utilities to purchase renewable energy in increasing quantities. Meeting these mandates will require physical and economic integration of diverse power sources into an electric transmission system constructed long ago based on different assumptions. What state legislature has backed this mandate with new state commission staff experts in integration?

Contrast this federal example: The Energy Policy Act of 2005 vested in FERC a new reliability role: the duty to review and approve (or disapprove) enforceable standards for the use, ownership, and operation of the nation's bulk power electric system. Congress authorized FERC to hire hundreds of engineering professionals with reliability expertise. Resources kept pace with requirements.

**The political culture tends to favor private expenditure over public expenditure:** It happens every election cycle: Politicians promise cuts in public spending while urging increases in private spending. This culture carries over to utility regulation. If an electric, gas, telecommunications, or water utility asserts shortages of, respectively, control room operators, safe dig monitors, pole attachment experts, or chemicals testers, no one argues. But if the commission seeks staff to set standards for these same activities, the legislative response is, usually, "Make do." Ironic addition: As I write, multiple commissions are receiving, simultaneously, utility requests for rate increases (increasing company spending), and gubernatorial commands to cut staff (decreasing commission spending).

**Utilities and their financial allies do not make regulatory resources a priority:** There should be a unity of interests here. Utilities often call for "less regulation." Instead of focusing on more vs. less regulation, we should focus on effective vs. ineffective regulation. Less regulation does not help a utility if understaffing, inattention and overwork lead to regulatory error. Attentive, objective regulation creates clear signals, lowers uncertainty, and rewards high performance. Those results are good for both consumers and investors.

Yet there is rarely a vocal constituency for regulatory resources. Utility management, shareholder associations, bondholder organizations, rating agencies—these groups tend to "rate" commissions based on whether specific commission orders favor specific economic interests, not on whether commissions have the right resources.

**The political culture warns against "regulation" and "turf building":** In our political culture, we favor regulation when it protects; we disfavor regulation when it obstructs. Regulatory resource-seekers bear the burden of proof, while their opponents accuse them of turf-building. These factors discourage commissions from trying.

Three tough questions: Are there differentials in resources and expertise? Why do they exist? Why do they persist? The next essay asks three more: Do the differentials make a difference? Why do they receive so little political attention? How might we solve the problem?

# 51

# Regulatory Resources II: Do the Differentials Make a Difference?

> Agencies do not need to conduct experiments in order to rely on the prediction that an unsupported stone will fall.
>
> *Associated Gas Distributors v. Federal Energy Regulatory Commission*, 824 F.2d 981, 1027 (D.C. Cir. 1987) (reasoning that regulators need not conduct factual hearings to learn that monopolists will act in their self-interest)

**The preceding essay** argued that "[e]ffective regulation should aim for excellence...." The process should induce continuous improvement in utility performance. Absent equivalent expertise and sufficient resources, regulators cannot assess performance credibly. Comparing utilities' and commissions' expertise and resources, I asked three questions: Is there a differential? Why does it exist? Why does it persist? The present essay addresses three more questions: Do the differentials make a difference? Why do they receive so little attention? How might we solve the problem?

## Do the Differentials Make a Difference?

Resource differentials weaken two of regulation's most important verbs: evaluate and anticipate.

**The effective regulator evaluates:** Conscientious evaluation requires substantive mastery. Under-resourced regulators can evaluate only what they know. When they don't know, they defer. It's natural, but it's wrong. An evaluator of performance does not defer to the performer. As a young musician I played many auditions and competitions. No judge deferred to my judgment. They judged me in relation to objective standards and to my competitors. Regulation should proceed similarly.

Some utilities oppose evaluation, including the necessary regulatory resources, on grounds of "the managerial prerogative," i.e., management decisions are the utility's exclusive domain. This reasoning is wrong. The prerogative allows utilities to choose how to perform; the regulator still must decide how well they perform.

**The effective regulator anticipates:** Effective regulation aligns private behavior with public interest. To align, one must anticipate: How might private behavior, absent regulation, diverge from public interest? Without a speed limit, how fast will people drive? How do we channel private behavior without blunting its positive attributes?

Anticipation involves strategy: a plan of action that accounts for the actions of others. Consider industry structure. Industry structure addresses who sells, what they sell, whether we should have monopoly or competition, what factors constitute competitiveness. The regulatory process of converting a market from noncompetitive to competitive, and keeping it competitive, requires strategy. If a market structure is effectively competitive, it should align private behavior with public interest: The sum of every competitor's self-interested actions should yield maximum consumer welfare. So say the textbooks. But theory confronts reality: Every rational competitor aspires to be a monopoly. Regulation must anticipate this tension, between the purpose of competition and the purpose of competitors. Regulation thus requires strategy: It must prepare to act and adjust as players pursue their purposes. And strategy—its development, execution and assessment—requires resources.

**From stimulator to skeptic:** Absent sufficient resources to evaluate and anticipate, the regulator can only react. Reactivity is a range, from canvasbackery to skepticism.[95] Skepticism has its own range, from "No" to "Yes, grudgingly." In merger cases, "Yes, grudgingly" sometimes takes the form of "We approve this merger, with conditions." But "Yes, grudgingly" is still reactivity; it is not leadership. The anticipatory regulator would have articulated, prior to any merger proposal, a vision for market structure, then pursued a strategy to produce that structure. That change in attitude and ambition makes the difference between producing benefit and avoiding harm.

## Why Do Resource Differentials Receive So Little Attention?

Let's go down the list of players, asking why they say so little about a problem so obvious (and so readily resolvable). There will be more questions than answers.

---

[95] Terminological credit to Peter Bradford; see Chapter 3, "Decisiveness."

**Regulators:** Do they want to avoid accusations of turf building, or admissions of unpreparedness? Do they see their job as presiding rather than leading, with presiding requiring fewer resources?[96]

**Utilities:** Do they treat "regulation" as something to diminish rather than strengthen? Something to make ineffective rather than effective? Do they equate more regulatory resources with more utility accountability, preferring less of each? Do they see regulation as a contest, with regulators being an opponent?

**Consumer advocates:** Do they see the fiscal equation as zero-sum—the more resources for the regulator, the fewer for the consumer advocate? Do they see the regulator as an opponent? Or as a clerk, stamping "approved" on deals that parties arrange off the record?

**The public:** The regulatory resource differential is like underground water pipes: The depreciation is known by the experts but unseen by the public. The public sees a stream of official orders, long legal opinions, and procedural formalities. From these indicia of activity, one would not likely infer the overwork and thin-spreadedness endemic to many commissions.

**Legislators:** "Effective regulation" has no well-organized political constituency. There is no perceived crisis. Budget and taxation, education, poverty, crime, hazardous waste spills: These are the political urgencies that fill the calendar of the overworked state legislator. Crises of confidence in regulation (such as, in the electric industry, the public ire in California, Illinois, Ohio, and Maryland over experiments in retail competition) occur irregularly. And while these events sometimes produce new policies (or returns to prior policies), they do not seem to stimulate soul searching on regulatory resources.

## How Might We Solve the Problem?

We need an open conversation about these questions: What distinguishes effective regulation from ineffective regulation? What are examples of each? What roles do resources play? To start the conversation, here are five ideas.

1. **Match challenges with resources.** Implement a systematic, continuous process for (a) identifying regulatory challenges, and (b) determining the professional skills necessary to meet those challenges.

2. **View regulatory budgets as investments in utility performance.** Successful investments make the economy more efficient, more responsive, more accountable. It does not make sense to cut the Internal Revenue Service's

---

[96] See Chapter 5, "Commissions Are Not Courts; Regulators Are Not Judges."

auditing budget if the return on the investment is positive. The same goes for regulatory staff.

3. **If we add responsibilities, add resources.** A staff too small to handle the many rate cases filed cannot also handle the renewables portfolio statute, broadband expansion, investigations of nuclear power, and the proposed leverage buyout of the incumbent electric utility.

4. **Eliminate the political distinction between ratepayer dollars and taxpayer dollars.** Utility regulatory affairs budgets are paid with ratepayer dollars. These amounts are tiny relative to total rates, unnoticed, uncomplained about. Regulatory budgets, usually funded by taxpayer dollars, receive multiples more scrutiny and skepticism. This differential does not make sense.

5. **Lose the adversarial attitude.** Regulation is not a battle, defined by rate-case victories and losses. Regulatory effectiveness assists utility performance, producing satisfied customers, legislators and owners. Why oppose what benefits everyone?

# 52

# The Resource Gap Grows: What Are a Commission's Duties?

> Commissions ... might scientifically study and disclose to an astonished community the shallows, the eddies, and the currents of business, the why and the wherefore of the shoaling of channels, the remedies no less than the causes of obstructions.
>
> Charles Francis Adams, quoted in Thomas K. McCraw, *Prophets of Regulation: Charles Francis Adams, Louis D. Brandeis, James M. Landis, Alfred E. Kahn*

**The preceding two** essays argued that a utility–regulator differential in resources undermines the regulatory mission. The risk is that performance standards, and the pace of innovation, are established by the regulated and accepted by the regulator—the opposite of what the public interest requires.

The problem is getting worse. In a recent six-month period, my expert witness duties amounted to a final exam on frontier issues: an $80 million "incentive" proposal authorizing supra-normal returns; a multistate merger combining two holding companies, three utilities, and a host of trading and marketing affiliates that had recently escaped bankruptcy; a rate case addressing the "return on equity" effects of riders and pre-approvals; and a "formula rate" proposal under a statute mandating billions in new utility spending. These cases exposed regulation's soft underbelly: a growing gap between political demands and regulatory resources.

We can solve the problem if we (1) recognize that with regulatory workloads that are new and growing, a differential in resources has consequences for quality; and (2) articulate the obligations of legislators, commissions, utilities and ratepayers to reduce the differential and ensure quality.

## Workloads: New and Growing

A time traveler from even five years ago would be struck by the diversity and immensity of regulators' responsibilities. Our commissions (a) design new performance standards to reflect climate change concerns and customer-empowering technologies; (b) predict cost uncertainties associated with environmental upgrades, infrastructure modernization and terrorist protection; (c) reconcile utilities' exercise of their eminent domain powers with landowners' disgruntlement; (d) allocate the risk of bad luck—the inevitable divergence of actual from predicted costs; (e) monitor billion-dollar construction projects to keep those divergences to a minimum; (f) stimulate and oversee renewable power procurement; (g) evaluate wholesale market competitiveness to enable build-vs.-buy decisions; (h) monitor immature markets at retail to ensure that new entrants face no barriers erected by incumbents; (i) educate consumers so that the billions in "smart grid" investments are matched by changes in customer behavior; and (j) position commissions to distinguish mergers that advance the public interest from those aimed only at acquiring and aggrandizing.

These efforts arise from obligations imposed by legislatures, yet these bodies rarely accompany their new laws with new resources.

## Consequences for Quality

The resource shortage reflects not only a growing absolute gap (between the commission's duties and its resources) but also a growing relative gap (between the commission's resources and the utility's resources). Why the relative gap? We fund a commission by asking: "What are legislators willing to allocate from a limited pool of taxpayer funds?" The commission's needs compete with every other budgetary demand. For the utility, there is a different question: "What are your reasonable needs?" This question is constitutionally commanded, because a utility is entitled to recover from ratepayers the reasonable amount of dollars necessary to educate the commission on the utility's expenses and capital requirements. There is no competition from other resources. The two questions produce two different answers. Hence the relative gap.

Compounding the resource gap is an information gap, further undermining the regulatory purpose. Compared to a commission, the utility has greater knowledge of its costs and cost-saving opportunities. Absent comparable access to and mastery of this utility information, the commission cannot credibly determine whether the utility's costs reflect cost-effectiveness. (Adding to the information gap is the expertise gap, since to judge the utility's performance credibly one must oneself be an expert in that performance.)

## Legislators' Obligations

If the purpose of regulation is performance, regulators need the resources to assess performance. The legislative obligation is simple: Pay for what you pass. A commission is not a reservoir of unlimited expertise and staff, poised to administer every new program and solve every new problem. To impose new duties without budgeting new staff, to claim credit for "greening the electric supply" while "limiting the growth of government," is misleadership, because it misleads. Worse, it infantilizes the electorate, leading them to expect public improvements without paying for them.

## Commissions' Obligations

The commission's obligation is also simple: Speak up. Not every legislator understands the labor intensity of utility regulation. Regulation involves a long series of mental verbs: identifying questions, inviting ideas, organizing expertise, processing participation, deliberating options, drafting possibilities, publishing decisions, defending in court, monitoring compliance, enforcing against violators. All this takes time, expertise and money. Legislatures need to know.

A second commission obligation is equally simple: Don't approve what you can't monitor. Commissions often approve mergers subject to conditions. The merger cannot satisfy the public interest if compliance with conditions is uncertain or if harm could go undetected and unpenalized. This logic train means a commission can, and must, condition its approvals on having enough staff to ensure compliance. A condition like this quickly makes the utility applicant a commission's ally in obtaining resources.

## Utilities' Obligations

A utility can meet its burden of proof only if its commission has mastered the evidence. If the commission commits to this principle, and if it then commits to disapproving proposals when it lacks the resources to evaluate them fully, the utility's need for approvals matches up with the commission's need for resources. The utility then has several options. It can use its political clout—much of which derives from the government's grant of a century-long monopoly—to press for commission resources. Or it can skip the legislative process by volunteering to collect through rates the resources the commission needs. No one is asking the utility to pay from its pocket. Shareholders have no obligation—other than through normal income taxes—to fund their regulators. But refusing to volunteer to collect funds from ratepayers, while insisting on ratepayers paying for the utility's own regulatory costs, would strike any objective person as inconsistent and indefensible.

## Ratepayers' Obligation

Someone, whether ratepayers or taxpayers, needs to pay for regulatory resources. But some resist this responsibility. One common argument is "The utility got this statute passed; the shareholders should pay for the necessary staff." That argument fails because it taxes the utility for exercising its First Amendment right to petition the government. I also hear "Our commission is the utility's doormat; why fund it?"—a statement whose downward spiral of illogic needs no explanation. Then there's the general "we need to reduce government spending" canard, a viewpoint whose disconnect from benefit-cost reality is disassembled by Cornell Professor Robert Frank in his 2011 book *The Darwin Economy* (showing, among many other examples, that failing to fix roads now costs more later).

This ratepayer-taxpayer resistance can be removed if those who know better—legislators, regulators, utilities, and ratepayer representatives—share that better knowledge.

# 53

# Commission Effectiveness: How Can We Measure It?

If you can't measure it, you can't manage it.

What's measured, improves.

Peter Drucker

... [I]f I have quick access to key metrics every day, my creativity stays within certain bounds—my ideas all center on how to achieve our goals.

Paul Allen

A **commissioner asked me** "How can I assess my commission's performance? What are the metrics?"

Regulators are realizing that their legacy practices—processing retail utility filings and intervening in federal cases—are too reactive. They wish to display more purposefulness, more decisiveness, more independence from the stakeholders, more leadership.[97] How can they plot their progress? First, some suggestions of metrics, arranged by three major objectives. Then, a critique of "traditional" metrics; and finally, a question: Is the term "metrics" even useful?

---

[97] See Chapters 1, 2 and 4.

## Objective: Clarify and Embed the Commission's Regulatory Purposes

Metrics must reflect purpose. Regulation's purpose is to align private behavior with public interest. The regulator must establish performance standards for utilities, then enforce those standards. Setting standards requires multiple value judgments. Two examples: (1) What is the appropriate performance standard—average, superior, state-of-the-art, better-than-the-neighbor? (2) Where there are vectors in tension, like economic efficiency vs. affordability, economic development vs. environmental sensitivity, speedy decisions vs. participatory procedures, what are the right resultants? These conflicts call for courage, in the form of decisiveness. Being everything to everyone—what Garry Wills calls "omnidirectional placation"[98]—precludes purposefulness.

> *Metrics for this objective:* Has the commission made the necessary value judgments? If you asked each of your commission's employees (California has 800) to state the commission's regulatory purpose, performance standards, and tension resolutions, would the answers be consistent? Does the commission have clear expectations for each utility's performance, in terms of cost-effectiveness and innovation? Does each utility's performance meet those expectations? Would that utility's employees all answer the "purpose" question consistently?

## Objective: Identify the Regulatory Challenges

Gas and electric challenges include climate change, energy efficiency, rate design, and regional power supply planning. Water industry challenges include small water company finances, compliance with federal water quality standards, the prospects for consolidating scattered service territories, and the reality that Earth's water supply is fixed while its population is growing. Telecommunications challenges include redefining the responsibilities of the "carrier of last resort," ensuring the cost-effective spreading of broadband, resolving the persistent scuffles between incumbents and new entrants, and being candid (i.e., factual) about the competitiveness and price efficiency of "deregulated" markets.

Added to those industry-specific challenges are those cutting across all sectors: market structure (Do we want competition or monopolies?); corporate structure (Do we want leveraged buyouts, conglomerates, and non-integrated asset collections; or do we want local companies focused on providing essential services?); infrastructure sufficiency (Will we pay for our own wear and tear, or will we leave those costs to our offspring?); rate design (Is it time to remove the average-cost mask, exposing the true hourly cost of consumption?); technological

---

[98] Garry Wills, "Behind Obama's Cool," *The New York Times* (Apr. 7, 2010) (reviewing David Remnick, *The Bridge: The Life and Times of Barack Obama*).

advances (Who should fund the demonstration projects that produce both dry holes and breakthroughs?); and workforce replacement and modernization (Where do we find the next generation of pole planters, tree trimmers, and substation designers?).

> *Metrics for this objective:* Has your commission identified the main challenges? Has it assigned resources to them?

## Objective: Shape the Regulatory Infrastructure to Meet the Challenges

Regulatory excellence requires a regulatory infrastructure. There are five parts to that infrastructure, each with its own metrics.

1. **Authority to act:** Prehistoric regulatory statutes need systematic modernization, not piecemeal revision. Enacted a century ago, then layered with amendments responding to episodic urgencies and opportunities, our statutes have gaps, redundancies and asymmetries that weaken regulatory authority.

    > *Metrics for this objective:* Given the challenges described above, do we have the statutory authority we need to produce the performance we need? Are our relations with legislators productive? When legislators think about revising laws, do they ask the commission first?

2. **Information necessary to act:** Information reaches regulators unevenly: if they ask, if they have time to ask, if they think to ask, if someone chooses to supply it, if the information supplied is truthful and evenhanded.

    > *Metrics for this objective:* Do we have the information, and the information-gathering processes and resources, necessary to make good decisions? Do the utilities have a duty to inform? Does the commission learn of its options sufficiently early to make decisions timely and carefully? Do they fulfill that duty timely and objectively? Is there trust?

3. **Expertise necessary to act:** Traditional commission expertises are silo-based: accountants, economists, engineers, lawyers; electric, gas, telecomm, water; rate cases, mergers, service quality investigations. These knowledge bases remain essential, but there is a risk of hammers seeing only nails. The new challenges are multidisciplinary and long-term.

    > *Metrics for this objective:* Do our commissioners and staff have skills in multidisciplinary thinking and multi-year strategizing?

4. **Decisionmaking leading to action:** Many legacy procedures emphasize the reactive—awaiting utility filings at the state level, intervening as supplicants in federal venues. Reactivity risks prioritizing by pressure from parties. Utilities initiate proceedings to advance business objectives. That's understandable and acceptable. But the sum of these entrepreneurial efforts does not equal public interest policy. Reactivity makes regulators captive.

   Marshall McLuhan (*Understanding Media: The Extensions of Man* (1964)) offers an analogy. If "medium is the message," then procedure is the policy. The context (e.g., cinema, television, comic book, traditional book) defines the intensity of a person's participation. The procedure (e.g., adjudication, investigation, rulemaking, cross examination, multi-party panels, informal discussions, "collaboratives," commission-directed submissions) defines the level of commission alertness—and the quality of its leadership.

   *Metrics for this objective:* Policymaking is both proactive and reactive. Are we getting the mix right? Do the present procedures and workloads allow the commission to lead, or only to react? Do our proceedings focus on the commission's priorities or the stakeholder's priorities? Are we disposing of dockets or producing performance?

5. **Continuous re-evaluation:** Effective regulation is continuously self-critical: It examines and re-examines its infrastructure to ensure the best fit of purposes, authorities, information, expertise, and procedures to the challenges at hand.

   *Metrics for this objective:* Have we defined regulatory excellence? Are there re-evaluation criteria and procedures? Is there a process for making mid-term corrections? When a commission approves a merger based on specified expectations of benefits, does a later commission assess the results?

## Other Metrics: Useful and Not-So-Useful

I have identified above three main commission goals—clarify purposes, identify challenges, shape infrastructure—and several metrics by which to assess progress. Here are more metrics that together test achievement of these goals.

**Advocates' performance:** Useful. Do the advocates appearing before regulators address commission priorities or their own objectives? Do they offer balanced positions that apply their expertise to the commission's needs, or do they insist on their clients' advancement regardless of context? Do they use facts and logic, or adjectives and adverbs? Do they advance propositions that are absolute and unprovable? (See Mark Twain: "An adjective habit, or a wordy, diffuse, flowery habit, once fastened upon a person, is as hard to get rid of as any other vice." Letter to D. W. Bowser, March 20, 1880.)

**Commissioner and staff time allocation:** Useful. How do we spend a majority of our time—reading objective material or reading stakeholder advocacy? Meeting with experts or meeting with parties?

**Docket disposition:** Not so useful. "We process cases expeditiously" is basic competence; it goes without saying. If we were evaluating a young musician for admission to a music conservatory, we would not say, "She plays in tune."

**Rate levels:** Not so useful. "Our rates are lower than comparable states" tells us nothing about performance. Are they lower because commission policies produce better utility performance, or because the utility has deferred maintenance by shifting costs to future ratepayers and difficult decisions to future commissioners?

\* \* \*

We now can see the inadequacy of the term "metrics." The term connotes quantifiability. But none of the useful metrics is quantifiable. A commission is not a consulting firm (metrics: billable hours and quarterly profits); regulation is not an election contest (metrics: I lowered taxes, you increased the deficit). Even in the worlds of consulting and campaigning, real public value is unrelated to these common quantities. Measurement of value is necessary, but the currency of value remains elusive. Let's keep thinking.

# 54

# Commission Budgets: How Do We Know When We're "Worth It"?

> Facts are stubborn things; and whatever may be our wishes, our inclinations, or the dictates of our passions, they cannot alter the state of facts and evidence.
>
> John Adams

**Government budget-cutters want** commissions to justify their costs. How can commissions respond?

Traditional, quantifiable benefit-cost criteria don't work, because the benefits of great regulatory decisionmaking aren't readily quantifiable. Number of dockets opened and closed, decisions issued, hearing days per proceeding: These facts signal the need for resources but they do not measure worth, because they do not distinguish effectiveness from ineffectiveness. Rate levels are poor indicators of regulatory quality as well. Two equally effective agencies could have different rate levels for many reasons. Their utilities' embedded cost-based prices could reflect rate bases of different vintages. Their capacity surpluses could differ due to different time points on the capacity-demand curve. The commissions might be raising current rates to avoid future costs—for example, investing in demand management actions or renewable energy, to avoid future generation needs or environmental penalties.

Quantification difficulties aside, the public deserves to know how commissions earn their keep. But how? There are two main questions: Are we doing the right things and doing them well? Are our actions having a positive effect? Reversing the sequence: What effects do we want to have? What actions are most likely to have those effects? Are we taking those actions and acting effectively? Measuring effectiveness boils down to identifying the outputs we want and inputs we need.

## Outputs and Inputs

The purpose of regulation is performance. The evidence of regulatory effectiveness, then, is the performance of our utilities and their customers. Are the utilities carrying out best practices and doing so cost-effectively? Are consumers behaving responsibly, i.e., do they understand the costs they cause, do they bear those costs, do they act to minimize their costs, and do they avoid behaviors that cause costs for others?

Given those outputs, what are the essential inputs? What decisions do regulators have to make to produce the outputs? Here are six question areas to help commissions probe their priorities and practices.

**Best utility practices:** Does the commission research, identify, and publish, regularly and continuously, utility practices that represent excellence? For each of the major areas—operations, capital planning, construction, financing, safety, quality of service, customer relations—has the commission (1) identified the top performers and top practices and (2) induced its utilities to adopt those practices cost-effectively?

**Best customer practices:** Same questions. Customers are not passive recipients of utility services. They create the demand that causes utilities to incur costs. Just as individual driving habits ease or impede the traffic flow, smoothing or slowing everyone else's trip, customer consumption influences the utility's cost structures, operations, capital plans and financing. Alert customers help make markets competitive, while indifferent customers support inertia—that powerful force that keeps the incumbent in place. Does the commission regularly research and identify the best customer practices, then act to induce those behaviors?

**Customer trust:** To influence customer behavior, commissions need customer trust. Testing that trust will be tough decisions on cost increases, infrastructure (like water and gas pipes, advanced meters, and broadband), and new rate designs needed to induce behavior change.[99] There is risk of resistance, leading to legislative trimming of commission authority. Whereas resistors see a commission hurting the public; the commission must show how each policy serves a public goal. Persuasion requires more than packaging; it requires understanding how customers and their neighborhood networks absorb and share information. (And misinformation. Much citizen anger about "advanced meters" flows from misunderstandings, multiplied and inflamed by the speed and breadth of social

---

[99] For more thoughts on customers, their attitudes and behavior, see "Low Rates, High Rates, Wrong Rates, Right Rates" (Chapter 27) and "'Protect the Consumer'— From What?" (Chapter 28).

network communications). Effective commissions therefore use state-of-the-art practices in customer communication and customer education. They understand customers' souls.

**Market structure:** Market structure determines who buys and sells what products and services. It addresses whether to have monopoly or competition, as well as which monopolists and which competitors. Market structure affects cost, innovation, responsiveness, accountability, even who has political muscle. Yet the status quo market structure is more often accepted or assumed than questioned and tested. Effective commissions continuously assess whether the current market structure is producing the best possible performance. (To do so, they must have identified the performance they wish to produce. See the paragraph above on "best utility practices.") Effective commissions track economies of scale and scope, entry barriers, pricing behaviors, pace of innovation, and customer satisfaction to see if the market is producing the best possible mix of products and services.

**Legislative relations:** Successful utility regulation depends on productive relations between commissions and legislatures, because policy flows from both forums. Commission–legislature overlaps are unavoidable; the question is whether those overlaps lubricate or irritate.[100] Does the commission have productive relations with its legislature? Does the commission take regular actions, backed by expert staff, to create and maintain those relations, both institutionally and personally? Does the legislature regularly consult the commission before taking action? Does the commission regularly assess its legal authority, seeking revisions as necessary?

**Skill sets, recruitment, and succession:** While many commissioners leave their posts each year, most staff professionals stay for a career. That stability is a positive force—if accompanied by professional growth. Does the commission continuously recalibrate its staff's skill sets to the new issue demands, recruiting new talent when those demands outpace current skills? Does it plan succession in the key leadership roles?

## Two Quantifiable Metrics

While most quantitative metrics don't connect well with commission success, here are two that do.

**Reading time:** Do commissioners and staff spend at least half their time studying objective materials, rather than reading parties' private pleas? Doing so places objectivity at the center.

---

[100] See "It's April—Do You Know Where Your Legislatures Are?" (Chapter 34) and "More on Legislative–Regulatory Relations: Layers, Protections, and Cost-Effectiveness." (Chapter 35).

**Meeting time:** It is unavoidable, and desirable, that decisionmakers meet with interested parties and study their materials. But of that time, is at least half spent with people who make things work—fuel buyers; plant designers, builders and operators; land buyers—the doers rather than the talkers?

# 55

# Commission Positioning I: Five Actions for Influence

> Too often we... enjoy the comfort of opinion without the discomfort of thought.
>
> John F. Kennedy

**Today's trends point** every which way. In local telecommunications services, legislatures press to diminish government regulation, even as they draw government into broadband investment. Smart grid opens the possibility of consumer empowerment and diverse service providers, even as nuclear power proponents look to lock in customers to a single utility supplier (ensuring the fixed dollar flow needed to make nuclear bankable). Some states are reevaluating their commitments to retail competition in gas, while others are reopening their prior rejection of retail competition in electricity (California 2000 now a memory sufficiently distant that facts and merits can replace "Enron" as grounds for decision). And the prospect of renewable energy sources, both local and geographically scattered, has national policymakers looking at multistate transmission planning.

This swirl of forces causes commissions to ask, "How do we position ourselves?" Some define positioning defensively, as in "How do we avoid having our commission downsized, merged with other agencies, or repealed?" Others define it actively, as in "How do we channel these trends toward the public interest?" Some define it both ways. Under any of these approaches, "positioning" has at least five components. (Thanks to my former colleagues at National Regulatory Research Institute for helping to identify these questions.)

## Focus on Utility Performance

Regardless of trends or pressures, effective regulators establish expectations: What products and services, at what quality levels, at what price ranges, does the public need? Answering that question leads to another: What market structures will most likely produce the required performance? The answers will vary with the products and services. Comparing the options requires facts—on seller cost structure, entry barriers, economies of scope and scale, and customer readiness to shop rationally. By gathering those facts, the positioning commission gets ahead of the markets so it can guide the markets. An excellent example is Maine, whose legislature directed the commission to assess the costs and benefits of appointing a "smart grid coordinator" to address market structure questions.[101]

To address performance and market structure, commissions need new skill sets. Evaluating economies of scale, reducing entry barriers, and measuring competitiveness are different from setting revenue requirements and designing rates. A positioned commission acquires these skills through internal education and new staff acquisitions. It values, through salaries and recognition, the credentials necessary to lead these efforts.

## Engage Other Jurisdictions

Privacy, economic development, climate change, exploding pipes, water shortages: These multi-jurisdictional challenges affect commissions, along with sister bodies in legislatures and executive branches both federal and state.

Statutes create legal boundaries. Those boundaries confine commissions' decisional powers but need not impede their insights. The positioned commission therefore thinks across jurisdictions—identifying extra-jurisdictional effects and intra-jurisdictional gaps, seeking to create the cross-fertilized policies that solve multi-disciplinary problems. To avoid extra-jurisdictional action because "it's not my department" is to preside rather than lead, to forget that "Commissions Are Not Courts; Regulators Are Not Judges." (See Chapter 11.)

## Communicate Complexity Objectively

Confusion and anxiety breed simplistic solutions. In Mark Twain's *Huckleberry Finn*, the Duke and Dauphin did this with Huck and Jim and countless Missourians: They found the fearful and sold them snake oil. The tool is language. Even

---

[101] See Me. Rev. Stat. tit. 35-A §§ 3143(1)(B), (5) (noting that "the commission may authorize no more than one smart grid coordinator within each transmission and distribution utility service territory"). The Maine Commission in 2010 opened a proceeding entitled *Investigation into Need for Smart Grid Coordinator and Smart Grid Coordinator Standards*, Docket Number 2010-267. As of spring 2013, the Commission had suspended the proceeding, in order to conduct a pilot program in which a contractor is hosting a competitive bidding process to select "non-transmission alternatives" (to transmission) in a defined subregion within the state.

a simple term like "increase" is easily abused. Renewable energy's opponents say it will "increase" your rates. Sure it will—but compared to what? Compared to status quo prices, yes, but status quo prices are not future prices. Considering likely price paths, those steepened by carbon pricing, oil and gas shortages, environmental retrofits, and global commodity inflation, will renewable energy "increase" your prices? Maybe not.

In regulation, we risk our own oversimplifications. A pipeline regulator insisted to his parliament that his commission tolerated "zero fatalities." Is this truthful? If we intended no highway deaths, we'd set speed limits at 20 mph. We don't. If we intended no pipeline explosion deaths, we'd bury the pipes 100 yards deep and encase them in concrete. We don't.

Regulation's credibility comes from its objectivity. With other actors so tempted to cut communication corners, the positioned regulator should aim for the straightaway. The trust gained will outweigh the discomfort caused.

## Expand Time Horizons

A rate case focuses on the foreseeable—five years at most. Regulators now need to think and see farther out. For a utility merger, an investment in broadband, or a multistate transmission facility, the time horizon is more like 40 years. A nuclear power plant? Try 100,000 years. (See *Into Eternity*, a documentary on ONKALO, Finland's permanent waste repository.)

In contrast to companies tied to quarterly earnings and annual reports, regulators now must deal with the less foreseeable and the non-foreseeable. As economist David Boonin has pointed out, regulators now must deal not only with plans but also with scenarios. Commission positioning, therefore, means creating internal thought-cultures that expand to the relevant time horizons.

## Recalibrate Procedures

Today's issue-swirl calls for new procedures, recalibrated to the need to lead. Here are two examples.

**Active procedures:** Processing a rate case is reactive; establishing performance expectations is active. Processing a merger proposal is reactive; establishing market structure standards is active. (These are poles on a spectrum. Any procedure mixes reacting and acting, listening and deciding. What counts are the relative emphases.) The more that industry participants aim for advantage, the more that commissions must act rather than react, by channeling those aims toward the public interest.

**Decisional off-ramps:** Greater uncertainty means greater risk—the risk of an uneconomic result. There is value, therefore, in options that are change-friendly. Energy efficiency programs can expand or contract, but a half-built power plant cannot be returned to the vendor for refund. Related to off-ramps is the segmented decision. Say a commission, looking to hedge against climate change costs, chooses nuclear. But what size nuclear—one large plant for $12 billion, or six much smaller ones totaling $18 million, each entering service as load grows? The smaller versions cost more per kW but pose less risk because a change in facts involves less sunk cost. What we lose in scale economies we gain in risk reduction. (Credit goes to Thomas Stanton for stimulating this thought.) The positioning commission creates procedures to make these comparisons, at the time of investment and continuously thereafter.

## Conclusion

Pressing for performance, talking across jurisdictions, embracing complexity, expanding time horizons, and recalibrating procedures: These are five ways to position your commission.

# 56

# Commission Positioning II: Can "Vision" Avoid "Too Big To Fail"?

> Vision is not enough. It must be combined with venture. It is not enough to stare up the steps, we must step up the stairs.
>
> Vaclav Havel

> Vision without execution is hallucination.
>
> Thomas Edison

**Uncertainty is everywhere:** economic growth, industry structure, utilities' business strategies, technology's effects, commissions' budgets, and especially political tolerance for regulation. Uncertainty has regulators asking, "How do we position our commissions?" The question recognizes that others—utilities, new entrants, large customers—are positioning themselves. The commission that fails to position itself risks becoming passenger rather than pilot.

## Start with "Vision"

This book's opening essays identified the key attributes of effective regulators, including purposefulness, education, independence, and decisiveness. A prerequisite for purposefulness is vision. (Thanks to a sharp southeastern regulator for that insight.) Vision is not an abstraction, an inspiration, or an emotion; vision is a mental picture of what things should look like and how things should work, within one's regulated industries and within one's regulating agencies.

Vision is a set of preferences informed by experience, observation, and logic. A regulator's vision depicts five things: (a) standards for utility performance; (b) the industry structures most likely to produce that performance (i.e., Alfred Kahn's "best possible mix of inevitably imperfect regulation and inevitably imperfect competition"); (c) the specific regulatory inducements—and only those inducements—necessary to produce that performance; (d) the personnel and practices within the commission necessary to design and apply those inducements; and, finally, (e) utilities consistently meeting the regulator's high standards.

Vision has less tangible elements, too. We know that private political tensions can block public interest progress. (See the essays "Politics: The Public and Private Versions" (Chapter 18) and "Politics: How Do Regulators Respond?" (Chapter 19).) To confront these political obstacles, effective regulators envision an internal utility culture that mirrors the commission's standards, a culture that treats the commission as an ally for excellence, then works to induce the utility to build that culture. The regulator also pictures commission–legislative relations that produce joint decisionmaking, rather than legislative overrides sought by those dissatisfied with commission outcomes. (See "It's April—Do You Know Where Your Legislatures Are?" (Chapter 34) and "More on Legislative–Regulatory Relations: Layers, Protections and Cost-Effectiveness" (Chapter 35).)

## Questions about Positioning

With a vision in place, the positioning commission asks, about each regulated industry, six questions: (a) What are the likely trends in products, services, providers, technology, and customer needs? (b) Which trends should we encourage and discourage? (c) Where will private behavior conflict with the public interest? (d) What regulatory efforts are necessary to align that private behavior with the public interest? (e) Within the commission, what skill sets are necessary to support those efforts—to set standards and judge performance—and what education and recruitment will attract, retain, and build those skill sets? (f) What investigations and proceedings will get the facts and insights necessary to answer all these questions?

## Positioning Steps

As the answers arrive, a commission can start positioning. First, a reminder of what we are trying to accomplish.

Regulation's purpose is performance. Regulation establishes standards and assigns consequences. Standards need to be proposed, imposed, absorbed, and exceeded: proposed by independent experts, imposed by the regulator, absorbed into the utility's culture, and exceeded by the utility's leaders and employees. The key is to find, for each performance area, the industry's best-performing utility, then replicate its practices here. Performance reviews should be continuous, not only conducted post-failure. Continuous review creates a culture of urgency inside the utility, felt and reflected by all utility employees, from executives to managers to line workers (and back again: As the West Virginia Commission's investigation of layoffs revealed, sometimes the workers set standards for the executives), to satisfy the standards established by regulation.[102] So when a CEO assures citizens that the company will improve its performance while his hearing room lawyers are busy badgering witnesses who critique that performance, that is urgency uncommunicated.

Commission positioning then means building an infrastructure capable of creating vision, setting and enforcing standards, and conducting self-critique. The ingredients are:

- **Staff skills:** Diverse skill sets must match the diverse standards that measure performance.

- **Staff pay:** The pay scale must be sufficient to attract to the commission the professional equals of the utility managers whose performance the staff must judge.

- **Staff quantity:** Baseload staff sufficient in quantity will allow the commission both to react and to pro-act, and also to access top consultants for the unusual demands.

- **Leadership:** Commission leaders should be expert in regulation, undistracted by other career goals, politically secure enough to assign consequences, all exemplifying the purposefulness, education, decisiveness and independence of effective regulators.

- **Legal authority:** The boundaries of the regulator's authority must match the terrain covered by the utility's activities. The authority must include the power to assign consequences for all adverse effects of those activities.

- **Accountability:** The commission must be accountable, legally and politically, to all those with responsibility for, or affected by, the commission's decisions: the legislature, the consumers, the utility, the financial community and the courts.

- **Cost responsibility:** There are two types. Expenditure responsibility focuses on cost-effectiveness: Over the long run, are customers receiving value for their money? Causation responsibility is pay-as-you-go: Each cohort—

---

[102] *West Virginia-American Water Co.*, Case No. 11-0740-W-GI, 2011 W. Va. PUC LEXIS 1351, at *7-8 (W. Va. Pub. Serv. Comm'n June 9, 2011); *West Virginia-American Water Co.*, Case No. 10-0920-W-42T, at 64 (W. Va. Pub. Serv. Comm'n Apr. 18, 2011); *West Virginia-American Water Co.*, Case No. 11-0740-W-C, 289 P.U.R.4th 507, 2011 W. Va. PUC LEXIS 1258, at *3-4 (W. Va. Pub. Serv. Comm'n May 31, 2011).

temporal and geographic—pays for the costs it causes. Exceptions should be minor, transparently justified, and temporary.

## Essential to Positioning: Having Alternatives

Positioning requires alternatives, because reality never fits plans. Consider regulation's dependence on the utility incumbent. Regulation's credibility depends on its ability to assign consequences for poor performance. But if the poor performer is poor financially—or will be made poor by the consequences—regulation loses its clout. In the early 1990s, a midwestern commission found its utility a billion dollars imprudent. Rather than see the utility fail, the commission allowed the imprudent dollars in rates—labeling them "stabilization rates." I recall asking the commission's utility director, "How could you allow imprudent dollars in rates?" His response: "Sometimes you have to put aside your principles and do what's right." In other words, he had no alternatives.

For regulated markets that are potentially competitive, ensuring alternatives means removing historic entry barriers, along with the incumbent's unearned advantages, while preventing the incumbent from creating new entry barriers. But where economies of scale require a monopoly, alternatives are absent. How then can commissions preserve their power to assign consequences? The logical answer is to avoid "too big to fail" situations—to avoid approving a utility investment so large that an imprudence penalty would kill the company. Our near future will bring proposed investments in nuclear, smart grid, coal plant repowering, pipeline replacement, and long-term renewables purchases. When examining those offerings, keeping "too big to fail" avoidance in mind is commission positioning.

# 57

# Commission "Branding": Can It Improve Utility Performance?

> William Wrigley of Wrigley's Chewing Gum Fame was once asked by a fellow-passenger on a commuter train why his firm continued to advertise when it already had almost totally captured the chewing gum market. Wrigley's answer was to observe that the train on which they were riding at the time was moving along very well, hence, "Why don't we just take off the engine?"
>
> Norman R. Augustine, *Augustine's Laws*

**Branding connotes oversimplification** and slickness, manufacturing loyalty by manipulating emotions. The product "I Can't Believe It's Not Butter!" brands as "Zero Calories!" a spray-shot having five calories, only because below that level the FDA allows ads to assert, falsely, zero calories.

But branding can have a positive purpose. Commissions can use it to increase understanding, appreciation and respect, producing the political deference they need for hard decisionmaking. Given the surfeit of manipulative messages that does permeate politics, a principled effort to brand can distinguish a commission both substantively and ethically.

There is also a defensive purpose. Eric Filipink's paper, *Serving the "Public Interest"—Traditional vs. Expansive Utility Regulation*,[103] describes how commissions' statutory roles are expanding. Old world (setting reasonable rates) has

---

[103] National Regulatory Research Institute No. 10-02.

become new world (establishing market structures, promoting energy efficiency, increasing renewable energy, empowering consumers, protecting the environment, financing broadband, stimulating economic development). With these new roles come new pressures. What James Madison called "factions"[104] we now call "stakeholders." Shopping for outcomes, they seek to cast their commission in the roles they want played. Consider transmission lines. Opponents see the commission as land protector; proponents stress the commissions' duty to "open up markets." Whoever loses then denounces the commission for shirking its duty—the duty as defined by that faction. The commission can defend by branding.

## Branding Begins with Self-Definition

Branding begins by defining oneself, by differentiating coherently. Coherence is a challenge. A commission's responsibilities arrive piecemeal, each year's legislature shoe-horning new ideas into the commission's 1930s-era statute. To sum up these disparate duties in a single "brand" is not easy. Consider a composite branding statement drawn from several websites: "The Commission regulates the state's electric, gas, telecommunications and water industries in the public interest." This sentence is a start, but its words raise several questions.

"**Regulate.**" The term "regulate" has suffered from mixed use and overuse. Any five commissioners would likely define it in five different ways. To "regulate" is to influence an actor's behavior, to produce performance that promotes the public interest. That means setting standards, enforcing them, and getting results. A commission regulates effectively not when it issues a stated number of orders, but when the utility's performance satisfies the public interest. Branding, therefore, should focus less on the ideology-laden term "regulate" and more on the public interest goal of performance.

"**Industry.**" To say one regulates an "industry" is legally inaccurate. A commission does not regulate an industry; it regulates only specified actions of specified actors within that industry. With any of these four "industries" there are actors who affect the industry's performance but who lie outside the commission's jurisdiction: the equipment makers, the money lenders, the entities that train and license the skilled craftspeople. The commission's goal might be to improve performance of an entire industry. Its orders might affect industry structure (competition or monopoly, vertical integration or disaggregated ownership, bundled or unbundled services). But its authority is limited to specified actors and actions.

---

[104] *Federalist Papers,* No. 10, *The Utility of the Union As a Safeguard Against Domestic Faction and Insurrection.* ("By a faction, I understand a number of citizens, whether amounting to a majority or a minority of the whole, who are united and actuated by some common impulse of passion, or of interest, adversed to the rights of other citizens, or to the permanent and aggregate interests of the community.")

"Public interest." Each regulated actor defines it differently, usually in terms of that actor's pecuniary well-being. A commission needs its own definition. The essay in Chapter 1, "Purposeful," defines "public interest" as a composite of economic efficiency (achieving the best feasible benefit-cost ratio), sympathetic gradualism (moderating efficiency's short-term pain, so that the public accepts the need for long-term gain), and political accountability (adjusting the angle and pace of change—without caving in—to ensure that acceptance).

So, the three main elements of this composite commission self-description—"regulate," "industries," and "public interest"—all deserve more precision. To brand is to differentiate. A commission cannot differentiate using shopworn terms. Eliminate confusion and ambiguity first; then branding can portray purpose.

## Branding Creates Accountability for Performance

The Ontario Energy Board Act (1998) includes this Board objective:

> To promote economic efficiency and cost effectiveness in the generation, transmission, distribution, sale and demand management of electricity and to facilitate the maintenance of a financially viable electricity industry.

The focus is performance. The key word pairs—"economic efficiency," "cost effectiveness" and "financially viable"—are all about results. Applied conscientiously, they lead to expectations and standards, and from there to measurements and judgments. The Board had made itself accountable.

But what about the term "promote"? The word implies, accurately, that the Board is not responsible for achieving economic efficiency, cost effectiveness, and financial viability; that's the job of the utility. But if a regulator's job is merely to "promote," for what is it actually accountable? Bridging this gap between promoting and producing, between defining standards and extracting performance, between words and results, is what defines success.

## From Branding to Mission Statement

Larry Landis, an Indiana commissioner and former advertising executive, asserts that "as a part of a commission's branding process, it needs to develop a meaningful mission statement. The shorter, and the more likely it is to be assimilated, internalized, and even committed to memory, the better...AND the more it says about the 'togetherness' and focus of the organization. Organizations with long, rambling mission statements tend to be unfocused and undisciplined." He offers two favorites—one from his alma mater and the other from the Indiana Historical Society:

Wabash College educates young men to think critically, act responsibly, lead effectively, and live humanely.

Indiana's storyteller: Connecting people to the past.

When I led the National Regulatory Research Institute, I introduced this mission statement: "By creating and democratizing knowledge, we empower utility regulators to make public interest decisions of the highest possible quality." I hope these examples help.

# 58

# Pharmacies and Regulatory Conferences: Do They Have Anything in Common?

> Unskilled competitors do not stick to the points in dispute but "end up exchanging random insults, insulted and insulting, so that bystanders are disgusted with themselves for having listened to such poor contenders."
>
> Socrates, discussing public debates, in *Gorgias* (quoted in Garry Wills, *Certain Trumpets: The Nature of Leadership* at p.165 (1994))

**B**ehind the main checkout counter, my local chain store pharmacy displays a dozen brands of cigarettes. Two feet away, the adjoining shelf offers products that fight nicotine addiction.

Setting aside the question why a store devoted to health sells products that kill (imagine a driver's ed school selling speed trap detectors, a dentist selling sugary donuts, a financial advisor selling lottery tickets), one wonders if the irony is intentional. Is the store's strategy to cause a cognitive conflict so intense that it draws attention and stimulates sales? Or to overcome the cigarette purchaser's hesitation by advertising exit ramps? Or is this simply the senselessness that occurs when a single-minded goal—store profit maximization—crowds out other values?

If the store's sole mission is profit, the practice makes sense. If its mission is to help its customers' health, the practice makes no sense. It all depends on the purpose.

## Regulatory Conferences: Are Our Purposes Clear?

Regulatory conferences should address the imbalances in our business. Regulators tell me that statutory deadlines force them to allocate their time disproportionately to interest group submissions rather than objective studies. This disproportionality undermines their decisions. Regulatory conferences should seek to even things out.

Consider your last-attended conference. Were the panels weighted toward advocacy or education? Were the speakers spokespersons or professionals? Who had the lion's share of floor time: ax-grinders and position-pitchers, or educators and problem-solvers? Was the purpose of regulation at the center or at the margin?

"We have to air all sides," we're told. All sides of what? We should master all sides of the issue—the data, the conflicting purposes, the uncertainties, the likelihood of inadvertent outcomes. Mastery demands objectivity. Advocates do not "air all sides." They downplay negatives and showcase positives. It is a battle of exaggerations. That's how the smoke-filled room gets its smoke. To "air all sides," the regulator has to air the room out and fill it with facts.

The point is not to ban interest groups from conference presentations, or to censor their messages. Regulatory isolation breeds regulatory ignorance. But we can create a culture that grants floor time to experts who honor the regulatory obligation—the obligation to make the best decisions regardless of ox-goring. There is nothing wrong with efforts to persuade, if they are fact-based, if they minimize adjectives and adverbs, appeal to intellect rather than emotion, and help regulators make good decisions. Speakers can have their "narratives," but their genre should be nonfiction. There can be legitimate differences over what is "objective." But even airing those differences will raise consciousness about presentational quality.

## Recommendations

At regulatory conferences, there is competition for limited air time. Leverage this competition by replacing political wheel-squeakers with objective educators. We need to find the right people, give them guidance, and then enforce. Specifically:

1. Ask "Who knows the most about this issue?" not "Who has a stake in the matter?"

2. Ask "On whom can we rely to speak straight?" not "Who's famous?"

3. Skip the vice presidents for regulatory affairs and find the managers who make things work—the ones who buy the gas, do the hedging, run the plants—people who can describe for the commissioners the practical

challenges that need regulatory clarity. Make them the stars. We regulate utilities to induce performance excellence. So invite those who perform, who embody excellence. So what if they aren't famous? They should be.

4. If you must have a mix of objectivity and advocacy, slot the objective speaker first, give her the most time, then have the advocates respond. This approach orients the panel toward "serving regulators' needs" rather than "affording air time to all sides." It makes objectivity central rather than marginal.

5. Instruct speakers: Your role is to educate and empower, not advertise your company or its goals.

6. Give each speaker 30 to 45 minutes (questions included). A 15-minute slot makes oversimplification unavoidable. If longer slots mean fewer interests heard, we've doubled the benefit.

7. If a speaker pitches products, oversimplifies, or exaggerates, don't re-invite him. A few muscular decisions like that, and conference culture will improve rapidly. What we might lose in attendees we will gain in credibility.

# PART EIGHT
## Conclusions

---

These two final essays pair aspiration with thanksgiving. The aspiration is that our varied communities—political actors, regulatory practitioners, companies, investors, consumers and citizens—accept regulation's great mission as a public good, something to nurture, protect and preserve. That mission, as discussed throughout these essays, is to produce performance, to align private behavior with the public interest. Regulation is not hostile to profit when profit is earned responsibly. Regulation is not hostile to consumers when they consume efficiently. If all our communities can accept these points, much of what regulation needs to succeed—statutes, political support and resources—can be available.

The final essay on thanksgiving recognizes the many blessings that regulation does enjoy, such as ownership diversity, professional consumer advocates, craft workers, democratic governments and their taxpayers, and the many examples of regulators whose attributes and actions make them leaders.

# 59

# Essential to Effectiveness: Community Acceptance of Regulation's Mission

[E]asy labels do not always supply ready answers....

*Broadway Music, Inc. v. CBS*, 441 U.S. 1, 8 (1979)

These essays have addressed the attributes and actions of effective regulators, and the obstacles they face. Essential to improvement is acceptance, by and throughout the regulatory and political communities, of regulation's mission.

Currently, acceptance is incomplete and episodic. Regulation's many participants bring different ideas about regulatory purpose, performance standards, and the consequences of falling short. This absence of commonality undermines effectiveness. I'll first remind us of the effective regulator's attributes and actions, then introduce the challenges that inhibit community-wide acceptance of regulation's mission.

## The Effective Regulator: Attributes and Actions

The effective regulator has nine attributes: She is purposeful, educated, decisive, independent, disciplined, synthesizing, creative, respectful and ethical.[105] Recognizing that commissions are not courts and regulators are not judges,[106] she not only presides; she leads. Her commission's relationship with the legislature is one that allocates duties according to comparative advantage—legislators making the big tradeoffs, commissioners making the technical judgments, both reworking their jurisdictional boundaries together as facts change. Because she understands,

---

[105] See Part One.
[106] See Chapter 11.

per Alfred Kahn, that the "central, continuing responsibility of legislatures and regulatory commissions" is "finding the best possible mix of inevitably imperfect regulation and inevitably imperfect competition,"[107] she rejects rhetorical bipolarity in favor of conversational clarity based on facts and logic.[108]

She accepts the pressures of public interest politics—the need to make tradeoffs among meritorious but conflicting goals; but avoids the distortions of private interest politics—the pressures from narrow forces seeking benefits for themselves.[109] And she accepts settlements as public-spirited only when the agreement arises not from short-term baby-splitting, not from one-party dominance masked as compromise, but from idea-sharing by experts.[110]

## Essential to Effective Regulation: Community Consensus on Regulation's Purposes, Standards, and Consequences

In any line of work—political, policy or business—leadership exists when there is acceptance of the leader's mission by those whom the leader seeks to lead.[111] In regulation, leadership remains elusive. Regulation's many participants do not share a common view of (a) the purpose of regulation and regulators, (b) standards for utility performance, or (c) the consequences of noncompliance. The views vary with the viewer. The electorally oriented legislator wants prices lowered before the next election. The utility shareholder wants share value maintained until he sells his stock. The industrial customer wants reliable service priced to meet global competition; the residential customer wants protection from monopoly abuse. The environmentalist wants emissions reduced; the union member wants jobs protected.

Even within a commission, there are differences in mission. Ask five commissioners, get five answers. "We process submitted cases within the statutory deadline, determining each outcome based on facts presented." "We are members of the governor's economic development team, helping to attract and maintain business investment." "We diversify the state's fuel use to reduce price volatility." "We keep the utility healthy so it can serve reliably." "We hold utilities to state-of-the-art performance standards." Then there are the differences over performance standards (excellence, optimality, average performance, lowest feasible cost, do no harm) and how to enforce them (fines, franchise revocation, cost disallowance, rate-of-return penalty, "if you do that again we'll clobber you").

---

[107] Alfred Kahn, *The Economics of Regulation: Principles and Institutions* at Vol. I at p. xxxvii, Vol. II at p. 114 (1970, 1988).

[108] See Chapter 24.

[109] See Chapter 19.

[110] See Chapter 48.

[111] See Garry Wills, *Certain Trumpets: The Nature of Leadership* (2007).

There is general agreement over the following purpose of regulation: to align private behavior with the public interest. Applied to utilities, this purpose requires regulators to define standards of performance, create financial inducements (both positive and negative) to produce that performance, and impose consequences for subpar performance. Applied to consumers, the duty is to implement pricing and programs that produce consumption behavior consistent with society's long-term interests.

Where consensus evaporates is over the "if, when, and how." Regulatory intervention covers mandates, prohibitions, encouragements, discouragements, and non-involvements. Any participant's sweet spot on this spectrum should depend on facts (Would private behavior, unregulated, undermine a societal goal? If so, what intervention will most likely achieve that goal at reasonable cost?) But one's spot also depends on one's view of the societal goal. If one favors immediate economic development over long-term environmental protection, then one might prefer immediate plant construction over customer conservation investments. Differences over societal goals prevent consensus over the commission's roles. If legislatures specify large goals more often, then less often must commissions be the forum for determining the big tradeoffs.[112]

## Differences over Regulation's Scope and Longevity

Absent a common view of regulation's purposes, each interest assesses regulation's worth self-interestedly. If protecting you obstructs me, I want regulation weakened. If obstructing you protects me, I want regulation strengthened. These oppositional, context-varying approaches make regulation's political support unstable. Absent a community-wide commitment to a core purpose, those aggrieved by a commission's current action lobby to shrink its jurisdiction. In contrast, those committed to regulation's purpose accept the commission's jurisdiction: They make their cases and take their lumps.

The instability in regulation's political support appears less explicitly, but more pervasively—and dangerously—in state legislatures' hesitance to fund regulatory staff at the size, salary and expertise levels commensurate with their billion-dollar responsibilities and comparable to the regulated entities whose performance they are to assess. This canyon in the regulatory landscape is so deep, so longstanding, yet so infrequently acknowledged that it will require far more public attention before it is fixed.[113]

---

[112] See Chapter 33, "Legislatures and Commissions: How Well Do They Work Together?"

[113] See Chapters 50 and 51, "Regulatory Resources I: Why Do Differentials Exist?" and "Regulatory Resources II: Do the Differentials Make a Difference?"

## Recommendations

A regulator's effectiveness requires not only personal attributes and practices, but community acceptance of regulation's mission. Regulators, therefore, should:

1. Develop, and articulate publicly, a clear statement of that mission.

2. Work to persuade participants that regulation's mission is larger than any policy difference; an issue grievance is not grounds to diminish the institution.

3. Remind participants that almost everyone occupies both ends of the protection–obstruction spectrum. Those who bemoan regulation's "burdens" should remember that government intervention provides (a) for traditional utilities, protection from competition; and (b) for new competitors, removal of bottlenecks that historically precluded competition.

# 60

# A Regulatory Thanksgiving

> Knowledge will forever govern ignorance; and a
> people who mean to be their own governors must arm
> themselves with the power which knowledge gives.
>
> James Madison

Each **November, families** give thanks for what enriches their personal lives. For those of us in utility regulation, there also are many thanks to give. Here are ten examples.

**Ownership diversity:** We have utilities owned by investors, by consumers, and by federal, state, county, city, and town governments. In their scatterplot of failures and successes, no data point is static. This gives the lie to worn-out rhetoric about "public vs. private," and induces humility in those who are certain of solutions (like some of Montgomery County, Maryland's outage sufferers, who want public ownership of the investor-owned Potomac Electric Power Company; and *Newsday*, the paper of record for Hurricane Sandy-tortured Long Island, which wants investor ownership of the government-owned Long Island Power Authority). Let the comparisons continue.

**Professional consumer advocacy:** Egregiously absent from most nations' regulatory systems, our brand of tax-funded and rate-funded consumer advocacy ensures alternative views presented by professional practitioners. Exemplified by such icons as the recently retired Sonny Popowsky, former New Hampshire Commissioner Nancy Brockway, the low-income advocate Roger Colton, and the binomened West Virginian Billy Jack Gregg, our system persists while underfunded, tolerated but only minimally supported by tax-frightened politicians. It is a system in which captive ratepayers pay for shareholder advocacy while legislative budget-cutters lower the level of consumer advocacy. The result is hearing rooms where $500/hour private lawyers battle $50/hour government lawyers, and utility witnesses outnumber consumer witnesses 4 to 1. To bridge that distance even halfway would better balance utility-heavy hearing records with expertise aimed at values broader than "return on equity" and "competitive positioning"; values like consumer education, consumer choice, and calibrating utility compensation to utility performance.

**Engineers, craft workers and line workers:** Most of us sit at computers and stand at lecterns, filing pleadings, writing briefs, giving testimony, cross-examining witnesses, drafting statutes and promulgating rules, all arguing endlessly about market structure, rate structure, corporate relationships, interest rates and hurdle rates. Others, thankfully, are designing and building our infrastructure, and fixing it when storms bring it down. Utility workers and their unions deserve our thanks, but they also need our support—the funding that will prepare our community colleges and universities to replenish workers' ranks as the current cohort retires.

**Unbundling:** Unbundling means "making available for sale separately." This three-decade effort has tested, and at times disproved, the century-old assumption that the only efficient utility is a vertically integrated monopoly. Unbundling has given us new entrants in electric generation (large and small, conventional and renewable, remote and local, bulk and distributed); retail energy sales and metering; long distance, local, wireline and cellular telephony; demand management purchased and sold locally and regionally. Unbundling may even give us competition in transmission service, if FERC bolsters its landmark Order 1000 with financial consequences for foot-draggers—those transmission owners hoping to leverage their "rights of first refusal" to protect their incumbencies. Unbundling will continue to succeed if seen as experimental rather than ideological, if assessed based on facts rather than imposed based on faith.

**Federal government and its taxpayers:** Our national infrastructure needs a national supporter. Federal agencies support the research into pollution control, broadband speed, water treatment and transmission technology—research that utilities and their states underfund individually, for fear of increasing their rates relative to their neighbors'. Federal agencies also pour money into storm-damaged service territories that local regulators and ratepayers have protected insufficiently, and identify our vulnerabilities to sabotage, terrorists and weather. But these federal faucets cannot flow forever; state commissions and their utilities will need to spend more from their own spigots to reduce the many risks of environmental damage, price volatility, service shortages and disruptions.

**State governments:** They deserve our thanks for creating and sustaining a regulatory infrastructure; an infrastructure that, while under-staffed, under-paid, under-resourced, under-respected, and under-supported by the political sectors, has the near-impossible job of tempering the market power of incumbents, of extracting competitive performance from companies whose government-protected status was neither gained nor retained through competitive merit. As with consumer advocacy, if we could couple this recognition with revenue, the return would be worth it.

**The Canadian regulators:** Their annual conference planning team taps major actors for funds: not to advertise their market presence but to subsidize the conference presence of advocates for the under-represented. Delightfully, those advocates do not repay this beneficence with reticence.

**The Nigerian Electricity Regulatory Commission:** Its staff in 2010 held an educational conference for judges who hear appeals, teaching them the engineering, economics and law of regulation. When the conference closed, I heard judges saying, "With all this complexity, perhaps we should defer more."

**The Federal Energy Regulatory Commission:** It has sprung itself and state regulators loose from the long-time, zero-sum disputes over electricity jurisdiction, in two ways. First, FERC has ordered transmission providers to consider "public policy requirements" when planning regionally, its Order 1000. With their utilities thus directed, states can lead regional decisionmaking: by establishing their own state plans, and then directing their transmission-owning utilities to mesh those plans into least-cost, best-fit regional plans. Second, FERC has ordered regional transmission organizations to accommodate demand response bids from sources in states that permit them (and compensate those bids the same as generation bids). This innovation allows each state full control over its demand-side market structure—from traditional monopoly to may-the-best-deal-win competition. FERC's solution gives states clout they have not had—the clout to discipline their utilities' generation and purchase decisions by comparing them to regional demand response prices.

**Hawaii, Oregon, Maine, and Vermont:** They escaped the competition vs. monopoly dichotomy by using both market structures. Observing a natural monopoly in energy efficiency services, they used competition to select the provider, through a process that valued skill and guts rather than political connections or incumbency. They then based the continuing right to serve not on inertia and indifference, but on performance, according to state-of-the-art criteria. This is a formula for economic efficiency and customer service we could stand to use for utilities who received tenure a century ago, for reasons no one remembers.

\* \* \*

No doubt readers can add to this list. The more our successes are highlighted, the more they can be replicated. But by whom? We often think of our infrastructure industries in terms of physical infrastructure: poles, wires, rights-of-way, reservoirs, towers, pipes and power plants. The foundation of that physical infrastructure, however, is people: legislators who determine powers, rights and responsibilities; regulators who establish and enforce standards; line workers, operators, and executives who make things work; consumers and taxpayers who pay for it all; and most importantly the citizenry, whose votes and vigilance preserve the democratic process that keeps us accountable.

# About the Author

Scott Hempling has taught public utility law and policy to a generation of regulators and practitioners. As an attorney, he has assisted clients from all industry sectors—regulators, utilities, consumer organizations, independent competitors and environmental organizations. As an expert witness, he has testified numerous times before state commissions and before committees of the United States Congress and the legislatures of Arkansas, California, Maryland, Minnesota, Nevada, North Carolina, South Carolina, Vermont, and Virginia. As a teacher and seminar presenter, he has appeared throughout the United States and in Canada, Central America, Germany, India, Italy, Jamaica, Mexico and Nigeria.

His articles have appeared in *The Electricity Journal*, *Public Utilities Fortnightly*, *ElectricityPolicy.com* and other professional publications, covering such topics as mergers and acquisitions, the introduction of competition into formerly monopolistic markets, corporate restructuring, ratemaking, utility investments in nonutility businesses, transmission planning, renewable energy and state–federal jurisdictional issues. From 2006 to 2011, he was the Executive Director of the National Regulatory Research Institute.

Hempling is an adjunct professor at the Georgetown University Law Center, where he teaches courses on public utility law and regulatory litigation. The first volume of his legal treatise, *Regulating Public Utility Performance: The Law of Market Structure, Pricing and Jurisdiction*, will be published by the American Bar Association in fall 2013. This is the first volume of a two-volume treatise, the second of which will address the law of corporate structure, mergers and acquisitions.

Hempling received a B.A. *cum laude* in (1) Economics and Political Science and (2) Music, from Yale University, where he was awarded a Continental Grain Fellowship and a Patterson research grant. He received a J.D. *magna cum laude* from Georgetown University Law Center, where he was the recipient of an *American Jurisprudence* award for Constitutional Law. More detail is available at www.scotthemplinglaw.com.